The Vineland Papers

Literary Criticism from Dalkey Archive Press

Edward Dahlberg • *Samuel Beckett's Wake and Other Uncollected Prose*

Ford Madox Ford • *The March of Literature*

Marie-Lise Gazarian Gautier • *Interviews with Latin American Writers*

Marie-Lise Gazarian Gautier • *Interviews with Spanish Writers*

Jack Green • *Fire the Bastards!*

William McPheron • *Gilbert Sorrentino: A Descriptive Bibliography*

Clifford Mead • *Thomas Pynchon: A Bibliography*

Paul Metcalf • *Where Do You Put the Horse?*

Leon Roudiez • *French Fiction Revisited*

Viktor Shklovsky • *Theory of Prose*

The Vineland Papers

Critical Takes on Pynchon's Novel

Edited by Geoffrey Green
Donald J. Greiner and Larry McCaffery

Dalkey Archive Press

The essays by Cowart, Hayles, Porush, Safer, and Slade first appeared
(in slightly different form) in *Critique: Studies in Contemporary Fiction*,
vol. 32, no. 2 (Winter 1990), pp. 67-144. Reprinted with permission
of the Helen Dwight Reid Educational Foundation. Published by
Heldref Publications, 1319 Eighteenth Street, N.W., Washington, DC
20036-1802. © 1990.

Library of Congress Cataloging-in-Publication Data

The Vineland papers : critical takes on Pynchon's novel / edited by
    Geoffrey Green, Donald J. Greiner, and Larry McCaffery.
    Includes bibliographical references.
    1. Pynchon, Thomas. Vineland. I. Green, Geoffrey, 1951-   .
II. Greiner, Donald J. III. McCaffery, Larry, 1946-   .
PS3566.Y55V563   1994   813'.54—dc20   93-27255
ISBN 1-56478-038-4 (cloth)
ISBN 1-56478-039-2 (paper)

Partially funded by grants from the National Endowment for the Arts
and the Illinois Arts Council.

Dalkey Archive Press
4241 Illinois State University
Normal, IL 61790-4241

*Printed on permanent/durable acid-free paper and bound in the United States
of America.*

Contents

Introduction

Geoffrey Green

IN the decade between 1963 and 1973, Thomas Pynchon published three books: *V.* (1963, winner of the Faulkner Prize); *The Crying of Lot 49* (1966); and *Gravity's Rainbow* (1973, denied the Pulitzer Prize despite being recommended by the Pulitzer's literary board). After an interval of eleven years, he released *Slow Learner: Early Stories* (1984), a collection of his previously published short fiction. Seventeen years after *Gravity's Rainbow*, in 1990, Pynchon published *Vineland.*

In the seventeen-year interval since Pynchon had published a novel, he became recognized as the most significant author of contemporary literature. His novels were taught consistently in colleges and universities. It was accepted generally that his novelistic vision had captured a dynamic sense of America in our time. As a result, there was an incredible sense of anticipation accompanying the announcement that a new novel by Pynchon would appear in 1990. This heightened state of awareness and receptivity existed as much as a result of Pynchon's literary reputation as it did his absolute reclusiveness. Eschewing all public appearances and interviews, Pynchon lived an utterly private life; when he published no new books, he was absent *totally* from the literary scene. This silence called out for interpretation and analysis.

Now there have been other major artistic silences in the arts. And each major silence conveys at least as much information about the nature of the artistic audience's expectations as it does about the creative state of the artist. Joseph Heller's *Something Happened* (1974) appeared a full thirteen years after his acclaimed first novel, *Catch-22* (1961). But the question with Heller was conceived along the lines of whether he was, in truth, a "one-book author": his reputation as a writer of major significance had not been fully established.

Related questions were asked still more pointedly during the full twenty years of silence between William Gaddis's *Recognitions* (1955) and *J R* (1975). Was Gaddis even alive? Further, would his second novel live up to the example of the first? William Gass's *Tunnel* has been over twenty years in the making; but he has maintained for his audience a consistent nonfictional publication presence during that interval. Perhaps the figure most reminiscent of Pynchon's situation would be J. D. Salinger, whose lengthy silence has yet to be broken and whose continued absence has taken on the condition of a deliberate retirement.

Similarly, Vladimir Horowitz, the brilliant classical pianist, opted for a deliberate semi-retirement. He did not perform from 1953 to 1965, an interval of twelve years. But his silence was not strictly maintained, for he continued to release new recordings. His audience remembered that he had previously silenced his artistic spirit earlier in his career with an announcement of retirement, only to reappear again.

But Pynchon's absence from the scene was more profound and more complete. Why had Pynchon been silent? Why seventeen years? Had he been working all the while on the novel that was about to appear? Would the new novel be so great, so large an undertaking, that it would justify the seventeen years spent in anticipation? Could anything Pynchon wrote live up to the precedence of *Gravity's Rainbow*, which (in the absence of any novel following it) had been received as the ultimate Pynchon novel and the exemplary postmodernist text? Could Pynchon still write? Would the Pynchon we encountered in *Vineland* be recognizable as the Pynchon who had been so admired and individualistic in his earlier novels?

Or else, had Pynchon been experiencing some nightmare of literary drought? Had he been unable to write for seventeen years out of some major life crisis? Would *Vineland* be so weak and ill-formed as to challenge our accepted notions of Pynchon as a major author and creative talent? Would our received sense of Pynchon be threatened by this new appearance from the living, breathing, functioning Pynchon?

Vineland's publication stimulated many questions and concerns. Pynchon had been viewed as *the* writer best able to document the influences of technology and artificial intelligence on the contemporary ethos. His use of psychological themes—most notably, paranoia and the contrary drives toward love and death—demonstrated a profound sensitivity to the mental processes of our postcontemporary world. He was inherently interdisciplinary: incorporating references to literature, mythology, physics, astronomy, painting, music, mathematics, movies, popular culture, history, politics, anthropology, and social theory, reading Pynchon was not unlike gazing at the image of our own concerns and desires in a mirror. His comprehensive and highly textured approach to writing was acclaimed as achieving a truly contemporary literature—a worthy heir to the classic works of modernist writing published earlier in the century. The new novel announced that Pynchon was back in earnest, but there were numerous and puzzling considerations.

Where Pynchon's previous emphasis had been on the historical foundations of our twentieth-century world, *Vineland* situated itself obsessively in the countercultural realm of sixties popular culture. For many readers, Pynchon's single-minded emphasis on contemporary and sixties popular culture constituted a change from what might be termed a high literary style. Previously, when Pynchon had addressed paranoid visions of political activity, the locale had been either generally or historically defined: readers were able to approach Pynchon's vision as a fictional one—even as the fiction emphasized themes that epitomized our own deepest fears and dreams. But *Vineland* was set in 1984, in Reagan's America: in a time and place familiar to readers and with material about which most readers had particular political views. In his introduction to *Slow Learner*, Pynchon had confessed: "somewhere I had come up with the notion that one's personal life had nothing to do with fiction, when the truth, as everyone knows, is nearly the direct opposite." Could this be seen as expressing a difference between the creative philosophy operating in *Vineland* and the previous creative perspective in effect in all of Pynchon's other work? Certainly, Pynchon was admitting that the nature and state of his private, concealed life was of crucial significance in determining the face of the new novel. If Pynchon's personal life has everything to do with *Vineland*, does this make him more exemplary of our collective identity or more eccentric and idiosyncratic?

The question turns on how much an artist reveals of personal identity in the process of representing a fictional vision. Does the decision to focus, say, on the sixties indicate that Pynchon is nostalgic still for that momentous era in our past? Or does it demonstrate merely his desire to document the themes and drama of that historical epoch? Does Pynchon's dynamic and poignant evocation of countercultural life-styles indicate an embrace of those life-styles as well? Does Pynchon's emphasis on television and popular culture signify an anti-intellectual or anti-literary inclination on his part?

Certainly, *Vineland* marked a turning for Pynchon to some new regions of concern—the family, for instance: his paranoid feelers are now focused on the deceptiveness of appearances in relation to childhood itself. DL remembers childhood as "a swamp full of intrigue, where, below, invisible sleek things without names kept brushing past, barely felt sliding across her skin, everybody pretending the surface was all there was" ([Boston: Little, Brown, 1990] 125). Yet another focus of his interest—the nature of memory—connects him to his teacher at Cornell University, Vladimir Nabokov: "and only about the time he was pinning the new diaper on [Zoyd] remember[ed] that he should have paid more attention, cared more for these small and at times even devotional routines he'd been taking for granted, now, with the posse in the parlor, too late, grown so suddenly precious. . ." (296). Was Pynchon, with *Vineland*, charting a new landscape for American fiction—focusing on our own recent past and searching for "secret integrations" (to recall the title of an early Pynchon story) that structure the deep reality of our lives? Or was he turning away from what marked the strongest and finest qualities of his earlier work in order to embrace a mass-culture audience attuned to images of TV and Ninja reality?

With many of these inquiries in mind, the editors of *Critique: Studies in Contemporary Fiction* assembled a special issue (Winter 1990) devoted to critical takes on *Vineland*. The idea was to examine in some depth and detail many of the suggestive and exciting realms of Pynchon's new novel. How does it affect or change our sense of Pynchon's earlier work? What does it tell us about the vision of our most significant contemporary writer? We gathered the most perceptive critical writers on Pynchon and invited them to investigate a zone of the novel that interested them. These are not your typical book reviews: we wanted to probe the implications of the novel from as many angles as possible.

The response to the special issue was so enthusiastic that we decided to expand the concept to book length. We commissioned more essays that would present perspectives that had not previously been encountered regarding Pynchon and his novel. How do we assess Pynchon's representation of women in *Vineland*? Since his fiction has been concerned with obsessive seeking for its own sake—an antiquest for information that provides no answer—how should we assess Pynchon's politics in this novel: are the political ideas expressed in the novel his? are they ours? or are they merely a parodied representation of political viewpoints? This volume is the first collection of critical responses to Pynchon and his novel; as such, it is the first major reappraisal of Pynchon—our most compelling and intriguing contemporary voice—in light of his new work.

The Vineland Papers

Attenuated Postmodernism: *Pynchon's* Vineland

David Cowart

T HOMAS Pynchon, creator of the most significant body of fiction in contemporary America, may have spent some of the last twenty years discovering the limits of the postmodernist aesthetic. *Vineland,* his long-awaited fourth novel, appeared seventeen years after the publication in 1973 of the monumental *Gravity's Rainbow,* widely recognized now as the most important American novel published since World War II. One naturally asks whether this author's art has developed or stagnated over those seventeen years. The bad news: Pynchon has made no effort to surpass *Gravity's Rainbow.* The good news: he has not stood still as a maker of fiction. In *Vineland,* which may represent a turning point for Pynchon, the author keeps his hand in, modifying some of his old tricks and trying out new ones. In a consideration of this novel's traditional and contemporary features, one encounters an evolutionary text, an experiment in literary hybridization. Conceding that the postures of literary exhaustion may themselves be exhausted, the author combines modernist concerns and postmodernist techniques with some of the features of two kinds of realism: social and magic. The following essay, while scrutinizing the vestiges of a style of aesthetic that Pynchon seems to be outgrowing, will glance at the Abish-like question *How postmodern is it?* in the course of gauging the traditional elements and fresh invention that compose this hybrid. The argument here, introduced in a brief comparison of Pynchon's career with that of Joyce, will focus on technique and the treatment given history and culture (including myth). The author of *Vineland* views these topics through a postmodern lens: they appear foreshortened, flattened, all surface. Yet the novel's title and its mythic extension of contemporary history hint at a broader view. Though Pynchon tends to deconstruct the myths he invokes, they complicate the rendering of an otherwise comprehensively ahistorical contemporaneity. Through a combination of this eccentric mythography with a moral earnestness expressed as a penchant for political didacticism, Pynchon produces, in *Vineland*, a fiction devoted less to indeterminate postmodernist "play" than to totalizing modernist "purpose."[1]

On the face of it, Pynchon's is the definitive postmodern career. In book after book, he has seemed to be Harold Bloom's "strong poet," creatively misreading his modernist forebears. Indeed, a comparison of his work with that of Joyce, a literary father to generate considerable anxiety, reveals some interesting parallels. With the exception of the late sport *Slow Learner*, Pynchon's 1984 collection of early stories, the fiction-publishing careers of these two writers match up, volume for volume. Joyce's first book-length fiction appeared in 1914, his fourth and last twenty-five years later, in 1939. Pynchon's first novel and his fourth span a nearly identical period: the twenty-six years from 1963 to 1989. In the space of exactly a quarter of a century, each of these writers has given his age its gold standard in fiction, the one defining modernism in the novel, the other postmodernism. Yet the two careers move toward an instructive divergence.

The early volumes of Joyce appeared within two years of each other; those of Pynchon, within three. Joyce's first book, *Dubliners* (1914), is a meticulously structured set of linked fictions that anatomize a culture. Pynchon's *V.* (1963), a highly episodic and fragmented novel that at least one early reviewer (Meixner) took to be a congeries of cobbled together pieces of collegiate creative writing courses, is also meticulously structured, also a cultural anatomy. *Dubliners* moves toward a final vision of snowy paralysis, *V.* toward the triumph of the inanimate. *V.* was followed in 1966 by *The Crying of Lot 49*, in which the failure of American promise gradually manifests itself to a protagonist, Oedipa Maas, whose age (twenty-eight in 1964, the novel's present), education (Cornell), and places of travel and residence (Mexico and California) seem to make her a female Thomas Pynchon. A kind of oblique spiritual autobiography or conversion narrative, *Lot 49* is Pynchon's portrait of the artist in youth and, as such, corresponds to Joyce's autobiographical novel, *A Portrait of the Artist as a Young Man* (1916).

The seven-year period between *Lot 49* (1966) and *Gravity's Rainbow* (1973) corresponds to the six-year period between *Portrait* (1916) and *Ulysses* (1922). *Gravity's Rainbow* and *Ulysses* are quests, "encyclopedic" fictions that, epic in scope, catalog whole cultures with broad attention to the literary and historical past. Each is, in its own way, a strange amalgam of family romance and Telemachiad: Stephen Dedalus discovers a father in Leopold Bloom, Tyrone Slothrop in the evil scientist Dr. Lazslo Jamf. Stephen, of course, is Joyce's autobiographical character, and perhaps one recognizes a further element of autobiography in the Pynchon novel too, inasmuch as it concerns a person who, like the author, simply fades from sight after embarking on a quest that makes him the "Zone's newest celebrity" (377) and brings him face to face with the possibility that Western culture "might be in love, in sexual love" (738), with its own death.

As the years went by after *Gravity's Rainbow*, one wondered whether its successor would, unimaginably, sustain the Joycean parallel. What complex, Viconian meditation, its hour come round at last, slouched toward Little, Brown to be born? In what idiom would it be written— would it be dense with Herero and Maltese portmanteau words? Pynchon's fourth novel was announced for early in 1990, but it was actually in the bookstores in late December of 1989. In terms of the paradigm, both dates are significant. The earlier is the fiftieth anniversary of the publication, in 1939, of *Finnegans Wake*, which appeared seventeen years after Joyce's previous novel, *Ulysses*. The year 1990, of course, marks the same seventeen-year period since the publication of Pynchon's last novel, *Gravity's Rainbow*.

But the parallel falters: *Vineland* is not the postmodern *Finnegans Wake*. At most one can say that Vineland County, California, is as mythic a landscape as "Howth Castle and Environs" and the River Liffey. One can note, too, that Leif Ericson, who gave America its first name and Pynchon his title, is among the innumerable strands in the weave of the *Wake:* "lief eurekason and his undishcovery of americle" (326). But these are frail and exiguous crossties for continuing the parallel rails laid thus far. The breakdown in the parallels suggests that the fate reserved for Pynchon's aesthetic differs radically from that reserved for Joyce's. Modernism, it seems, was fated to end with a bang, postmodernism with a whimper.

Though *Finnegans Wake* announced a new aesthetic in its structure—that of a giant Möbius strip—and in its parodic features (it burlesques the medieval dream vision), it is, first and last, the supreme modernist text. Like its modernist predecessors, it exploits myth, probes consciousness and its mysterious subsurface, and outrages aesthetic sensibility in a prose and structure of consummate "difficulty" (to use Eliot's unpretentious word). The parody, like that of *Ulysses*, is reconstructive rather than deconstructive. If like other modernist works it holds a mirror up to cultural fragmentation (it was published on the eve of the century's climacteric, World War II), it composes the fragments artistically, for the program of modernism, however iconoclastic, was always some kind of cultural reclamation.

But postmodernism has no such pretensions. It was always a hold-ing action, a "literature of exhaustion," self-canceling in its most basic premises. Parody and replication in postmodern literature exist to underscore the death of the author and to allow an extra season or two to exhausted forms. In Jean-François Lyotard's formulation, post-modern literature "puts forward the unpresentable in presentation itself" (81). A literature largely about itself and its own strategies of re-presentation, it perennially enacts the universal semiotic law: there is no "transcendental signified" behind the arbitrary signifiers—pres-ence is infinitely deferred. The postmodern aesthetic, like significa-tion itself, is a house of cards, and it seems naturally to exhaust itself at a faster rate than other literary movements. Thus the literary apo-theosis toward which modernism moves (in a number of texts) is not available to postmodernism, and thus *Vineland* corresponds not to *Finnegans Wake* but to the new literary start Joyce did not live to undertake.

Vineland does not seem to be "self-reflexive" in the approved contem-porary manner—a manner that, in all three of his previous novels, Pynchon has shown he can execute brilliantly. But it features at least a few of the quarterings of a postmodern pedigree. It relies heavily on parody, for example, and it favors historical surface to historical depth. It also resists the hierarchization of culture. This refusal to differentiate high culture from low, like the attention to surfaces, is a prominent feature of postmodernist aesthetics. The denial of author-ity, in all its senses, means the deconstructing of high culture's pre-tensions to that authority. Thus Pynchon can imagine Pee-wee Herman starring in *The Robert Musil Story* (370). Thus, too, in the multiple parody in *Vineland*—of Ninja fictions, television soap operas, espionage novels, and detective thrillers—Pynchon tends to minimize the "critical distance" that, according to parody theorist Linda Hutcheon, commonly accompanies the specific type of "repetition" that is parodic (6).

Where he does not parody popular culture, he catalogs it. What is remarkable is that, in contrast to his previous practice, he catalogs little else. He systematically denies himself the usual resources of allusion in its full range. In fact, he limits himself to one compound literary allusion and a couple of musical allusions. Only the literary reference—to an Emerson quotation in William James—is presented seriously. Both musical allusions, on the other hand, are comically undercut. When Prairie starts to learn about her mother from Darryl Louise Chastain, she appropriately hears music from *Tosca*, for the tale she will hear concerns the suffering of her Tosca-like mother and the Scarpia-like Brock Vond. But the music is played by a pseudo-Italian band at a Mafia wedding. Similarly, in the novel's elegiac conclusion, an entire Thanatoid village awakens to the strains of Bach's "Wachet Auf," evidently with the chorale's powerfully suggestive opening line intended to come to mind: "Wachet auf, ruft uns die Stimme." The music materializes as a "piping, chiming music, synchronized, coming out of wristwatches, timers, and personal computers, engraved long ago, as if for this moment, on sound chips dumped once in an obscure skirmish of the silicon market wars [. . .] as part of a settlement with the ever-questionable trading company of Tokkata & Fuji" (324-25).

Normally this author peppers his fictions with references that establish historical depth as well as cultural breadth, and readers have marveled at his ability to evoke, in *V.*, turn-of-the-century Alexandria, Florence, or South-West Africa, not to mention, in *Gravity's Rainbow*, the places and feel of much of Europe in 1944 and 1945. These evocations of place and time have generally involved a considerable body of cultural allusion, both high and low. Even in *Lot 49*, where the California setting is not particularly congenial to evocations of high art, one finds painting, literature, music, and film to be important features of the fictional landscape. But through a kind of *askesis* (to "misread" a term of Bloom's), Pynchon here dispenses with the high-culture allusion almost entirely.

Meanwhile the density of reference to the ephemera of popular culture is almost numbing. Pynchon refers often to movies, as in *Gravity's Rainbow*, but here he neglects historic films and art cinema in favor of *Gidget*, *Dumbo*, *20,000 Years in Sing Sing*, *The Hunchback of Notre Dame*, *Godzilla*, *King of the Monsters*, *Friday the 13th*, *Return of the Jedi*, and *Ghostbusters*. *Psycho* and *2001: A Space Odyssey* are the most substantial films mentioned. The author helpfully supplies dates for these films, parodying scholarly practice, and he invents a number of droll film biographies, including *The Frank Gorshin Story*, with Pat Sajak, and *Young Kissinger*, with Woody Allen. Even more insistently jejune are the allusions to the titles, characters, stars, and music of such television programs as *Star Trek*, *The Brady Bunch*, *Gilligan's Island*, *Jeopardy*, *Wheel of Fortune*, *I Love Lucy*, *Green Acres*, *Smurfs*, *CHiPs*, *Superman*, and *The Bionic Woman*. This depressing litany—the intellectual horizon of the American mass mind—subsumes less obvious manifestations of popular taste as well: mall culture, "roasts," video and computer games, new wave hairstyles, breakfast cereals, even " 'sensitivity' greeting cards" (38). Pynchon's intent here is not entirely satiric, for no doubt he is genuinely fond of much popular culture. In the introduction to *Slow Learner*, he declares that "rock 'n' roll will never die" (23), and the sentiment is shared by the founders of the People's Republic of Rock and Roll, who name their new state "after the one constant they knew they could count on never to die" (209). Perhaps, too, Pynchon wishes to eschew cultural elitism and demonstrate solidity with the masses. But the virtual absence of historical depth in this body of allusion makes a devastating statement about the shortness of the American cultural memory. This, ultimately, is the point of his constant allusion to the signs and texts of popular culture. Pynchon denies himself much of the cultural and historical dimension of the previous novels and commits himself to imagining the relentlessly ahistorical consciousness of contemporary American society. The implicit judgment of this shallowness, finally, reveals a moral dimension—always in fact an element in Pynchon's work—that distances this author from the moral neutrality or nihilism sometimes alleged to be the postmodern norm.

Unlike the world he describes, Pynchon himself has an acute sense of history that also leavens his brand of postmodernism. His historical consciousness reveals itself in the guise of that universal history called myth. If the myths invoked in *Vineland* coexist uneasily at the edge of a mutually deconstructive exclusivity, they nevertheless provide the story's action with a temporal depth: they render it "historical" in spite of itself. Thus Terrence Rafferty does not err when he observes that "American history plays itself out" in the bed of Brock Vond and Frenesi Gates (109). The play of myth, then, circumvents the nominally ahistorical vision in *Vineland*.

One can sometimes differentiate modernists from postmodernists in their treatment of myth—where modernists exploit myth as universal, instinctual truth, their successors either deconstruct myth as an unreliable "metanarrative" (the breakdown of metanarratives, says Lyotard, is the ground for "the postmodern condition" [xxiv, 34-35, 37]) or examine it as a language that, like all language, speaks its speakers rather than the other way around. Pynchon, as Kathryn Hume demonstrates in *Pynchon's Mythography*, has never divorced himself entirely from the modernist position on myth; and in *Vineland* he has it both ways—privileging at least one myth, deconstructing at least two others. The Faust myth, for example, seems to function in a fairly conventional manner: the federal prosecutor is Mephistopheles; filmmaking Frenesi is Faust. Yet the myth and the mythical identities prove unstable. The Faust here is also an Eve in the American Eden who betrays her Adam, the hapless Weed Atman. The Mephisto figure, Brock Vond, is also the serpent who tempts them to a fall and a primal murder. These two myths, however, are not at odds, for Faust's passion merely updates that of Adam and Eve. The stories contain the same elements: a diabolical tempter and human souls reaching for forbidden knowledge. But Pynchon complicates matters by introducing, through Sister Rochelle, a *mise en abyme:* a subversive, feminist version of the Eden myth with Frenesi and DL as the primal Eve and Lilith in an Eden in which "the first man [. . .] was the serpent" (166). This revision of the story seems a minor detail in the novel, and perhaps one at first disregards or discounts it in the desire for a totalizing version of a cherished American literary myth. But its seeming insignificance reveals the deconstructive point: it is one of the aporias around which at least one weave of meaning begins to unravel.

Feminism, by its very nature, is deconstructive—it locates the aporias in the "phallogocentric" discourse of patriarchy. In *Vineland,* the familiar myth undergoes a twofold feminist deconstruction: the patriarchal version of the myth is undercut once by Sister Rochelle's version—and again by the mythic action as Pynchon shapes it. For the mythic individual who makes the moral choice (traditionally an Adam in American fictions: Hawkeye, Huckleberry Finn, Isaac McCaslin) is the American Eve, Frenesi Gates. *Vineland,* then, is a surprisingly "writerly" text: it invites its reader to grapple with closure-resistant, open, multivalent myths that self-de(con)struct under the instruments of analysis.

Yet *Vineland* retains a myth that its author celebrates rather than deconstructs. Pynchon's setting is a representation of the American land; and he refuses to surrender the myth of American promise, which he seems to construe in terms of some continuing, provisional validity of a leftist political alternative to contemporaneous conservatism. The novel's title announces the mythic ground. It evokes more than the California setting and reputation for viniculture. The author situates the imaginary town that gives the novel its name up near the California border with Oregon, and he expects the reader to make the nominal connection with a town on the other side of the continent. The latitude of the real Vineland—Vineland, New Jersey—pretty much coincides with that of the imagined California "Vineland the Good" (322), haven for Zoyd Wheeler and other displaced persons. This implied spanning of the continent at the latitude of its greatest breadth jibes with the novel's symbolic detail to suggest that Pynchon's setting is really the whole vast tract that the Vikings discovered and named Vineland at the end of the first millennium. Thus the title of Pynchon's fourth novel, published at the end of the second millennium, reminds his American readers that their land has been known to history now for exactly a thousand years.

The novel contains other miniaturized symbols of America. A central example is the People's Republic of Rock and Roll, symbolically the counterculture America of the sixties, delirious with freedom, under surveillance, doomed, the Richard Nixon monolith at oceanside casting its shadow, an obvious symbol of repression to come. Perhaps, too, Zoyd Wheeler's house, of which he has been forcibly dispossessed by unconscionable federal power, is another such symbol. At the end, he is flirting with the idea of putting it to the torch— which America's dispossessed may yet do to the house they are unable fully to enter. As in *Lot 49*, Pynchon contemplates the paradoxes of dispossession and preterition in the land of promise. "How had it ever happened here," wonders Oedipa Maas in that earlier novel, "with the chances once so good for diversity?" (181).

Vineland, then, is a meditation on the American social reality, a return to the ground Pynchon seems to think he did not cover adequately in *Lot 49* (he remarks in the introduction to *Slow Learner* that he thinks his second novel merely a long story, not technically accomplished). Though *Vineland* is not *Lot 49* redivivus, one notes points of contact—most obviously the California setting—between the two. In the earlier novel the heroine, Oedipa Maas, meets a member of the Paranoids, an aspiring rock group, and offers to give her DJ husband, Mucho, a tape to plug. Now the reader learns that Mucho, "after a divorce remarkable even in that more innocent time for its geniality" (309), has become a successful recording industry executive (like *V.*'s Rooney Winsome)—and that he has shepherded Miles, Dean, Serge, and Leonard to success.

But where is Oedipa in the new novel? Oedipa realizes at the end of *Lot 49* that the only way she can go on being relevant to her country is "as an alien, unfurrowed, assumed full circle into some paranoia" (182). The heroine of the new novel, Frenesi Gates, is a version of that new, desperate Oedipa—estranged from a man with a Dutch surname and living a furtive, underground existence. Oedipa seems a less flawed person than Frenesi, but both characters are symbols of the American conscience—radicalized in the sixties, co-opted in the eighties. The two novels also explore the significance of drug use. In *Lot 49*, Oedipa does not perceive Mucho's involvement with LSD as positive, but it does link him to the marginalized Americans she will come to embrace. In the later novel, the reader learns that Mucho proceeded to addict himself to cocaine before giving up drugs altogether. Mucho's addiction and the horrors, however comic, of the "Room of the Bottled Specimens" (310) are among the book's few concessions that there might be a downside to drug use. But Mucho becomes an entrepreneur as he goes straight—and his entrepreneurism makes him suspect in Pynchon's economy. Here one glimpses the equation that partially accounts for Pynchon's somewhat disturbing refusal to depict drugs in a negative light: taking drugs (as opposed, perhaps, to dealing them) remains a powerful metaphor for the idea of an alternative to the rapacious capitalism and consumerism that afflict American society.

One sees a more meaningful contrast between these books in their handling of history. Oddly, it is the book with ostensibly the more shallow historical draft—*Vineland*, with its foreshortened historical sense—that reveals its author as truly concerned about the way the present evolves out of the past. In *Lot 49*, several hundred years of history are the means to make Oedipa's quest interesting and complicated, but this past is only superficially imagined as accounting for her American present (Oedipa's historical research serves the epistemological theme—the infinite reticulation of "paranoid" interconnectedness—rather than the sociological one that links her story to Frenesi's). In *Vineland*, by contrast, Pynchon again examines the American present, but with specific reference to a recent—and radically different—past. This equipoise between sixties and eighties keeps *Vineland* from being the simpleminded exercise in nostalgia some have taken it for. Far from the sour grapes of some bitter ex-hippie, it is a treatise on the direction history has taken, without our having given it much thought. Moreover, his own implicit political orientation notwithstanding, Pynchon exposes the millenarian canker in the flower children as rigorously as he diagnoses the reactionary carcinoma of the next generation. *Lot 49*, set in 1964, is a story of consciousness being raised—an allegory of sixties America repudiating conformity, racism, and militarism. It looks backward to the Eisenhower fifties and forward to the Summer of Love. *Vineland*, set a generation later in the portentous year of 1984, looks backward to that summer—and forward to some Republican version of the thousand-year Reich. It reveals how the nation has allowed an earlier passion for justice to go dead, to be co-opted by a conservative backlash and an attendant dissipation of liberal energy.

In a single generation—from the mid-sixties to the mid-eighties—America veered from a liberal to a conservative bias, from the New Frontier and the Great Society to "Reaganomics," from hordes of student demonstrators to whole undergraduate populations majoring in business, from Yippies to yuppies. In *Vineland* Pynchon examines these societal extremes and the historical currents they ride or embody. Interestingly contemporaneous with David Lodge's *Nice Work*, a refitting of the nineteenth-century "condition-of-England" novel, *Vineland* would seem in its hybridization also to undertake such an old-fashioned assessment. It is a condition-of-America novel. That condition, as a result of the Reagan revolution and, before that, the "Nixonian Repression" (71) or "Nixonian Reaction" (239), is imagined as darkening, a "prefascist twilight" (371), if not the actual night. "Nixon had machinery for mass detention all in place and set to go," says a Pynchon character. "Reagan's got it for when he invades Nicaragua" (264). The "Reagan program" is to "dismantle the New Deal, reverse the effects of World War II, restore fascism at home and around the world" (265).

Pynchon makes his political sympathies plain enough. But the polemics have little to do with the novel's art, which one sees in the indirection and economy that deliver this and other Pynchon works from the realm of propaganda and didacticism. This author's art—an art far superior, it seems to me, to that of such novelists on the left as early Dos Passos or Steinbeck or Vonnegut—commands the aesthetic interest of readers who may find the politics somewhat overwrought. Pynchon contrives, by diving into the wreck of mythic metanarrative, to imbue with extraordinary historical resonance a story that ostensibly depicts the vitiation of the historical sense. He remains the only contemporary writer whose grasp of history's mythic dimensions merits comparison with that of Joyce—and he may yet present us with a fiction on the scale of that writer's last book. One doubts that he spent the seventeen years after *Gravity's Rainbow* on *Vineland* alone. Who knows what post-postmodern extravaganza may follow in its wake?

NOTE

[1]These terms are among those proposed by Ihab Hassan in his tabular differentiation of modernism and postmodernism (91-92). I am indebted to Spiros Papleacos for bringing this book to my attention.

WORKS CITED

Hassan, Ihab. *The Postmodern Turn: Essays in Postmodern Theory and Culture.* Columbus: Ohio State University Press, 1987.
Hume, Kathryn. *Pynchon's Mythography.* Carbondale: Southern Illinois University Press, 1987.
Hutcheon, Linda. *A Theory of Parody: The Teachings of Twentieth-Century Art Forms.* New York: Methuen, 1985.
Joyce, James. *Finnegans Wake.* New York: Viking, 1939.
Lyotard, Jean-François. *The Postmodern Condition: A Report on Knowledge.* Trans. Geoff Bennington and Brian Massumi. Minneapolis: University of Minnesota Press, 1984.
Meixner, John A. "The All-Purpose Quest." *Kenyon Review* 25 (Autumn 1963): 729-35.
Pynchon, Thomas. *The Crying of Lot 49.* Philadelphia: Lippincott, 1966.
———. *Gravity's Rainbow.* New York: Viking, 1973.
———. *Slow Learner.* Boston: Little, Brown, 1984.
———. *Vineland.* Boston: Little, Brown, 1990.
Rafferty, Terrence. "Long Lost." *New Yorker,* February 19, 1990, 108-12.

"Who Was Saved?": Families, Snitches, and Recuperation in Pynchon's Vineland

N. Katherine Hayles

I MAGINE that Thomas Pynchon has been kidnapped and that his captors censor everything he writes. He determines to communicate with the outside world through coded writing that appears innocuously sentimental but has an ironic undertow. He finds, however, that the surface of such writing is far from passive. Forming his thoughts even as his thoughts form it, the sentimentality begins to interpenetrate with the ironic vision until the two are inseparable. No longer able to distinguish between them even to himself, he decides to use them as the basis for his next novel. The novel is *Vineland.*

This fantasy is more than a metaphor, for in a sense there is a group holding Pynchon hostage that he is both trying to communicate with and to elude. It comprises the generations grown up after the sixties, for whom the Vietnam war is as devoid of affect as is World War I or the Spanish-American conflict. The problem Pynchon sets himself is how to communicate in terms they will understand, while still recognizing the complexities of a past that for him (as for many of us) is still very much alive. The multilayered codes that result center on salvation and recuperation. When Hector Zuñiga asks Zoyd Wheeler "Who was saved?",[1] he uses the question as a touchstone to measure how profoundly the American revolution of the sixties failed. Already scripted by the dream of apocalypse that ends *Gravity's Rainbow*, the question reverberates throughout *Vineland*. Whereas in *Gravity's Rainbow* the concern with salvation took on theological, political, and economic overtones, in *Vineland* the strongest resonances center on the family.

The family as it is constituted in *Vineland* is both literal and metaphoric. The framing narrative is the teenage Prairie's search for her absent mother, Frenesi Gates, supposedly gone underground because of her involvement in a radical film collective. Turning inward toward a familial context itself constitutes part of the answer to Hector's question. Obvious to everyone is the failure of the sixties to solve the problems the radical movement shouted to the nation—poverty, racism, American economic and military imperialism. Poor people were not saved, nor people of color, nor the people of Vietnam, Cambodia, and other Third World countries. The only candidates left, apparently, are those who fought for the revolution. If they saved no one else, did their struggle and vision save themselves? The question points toward the metaphoric meaning of the family, the generation gap that separates Pynchon from readers who wonder what all the fuss in the sixties was about. Running parallel to Prairie's quest is another search, that of the narrator for his generation-gapped readers. The vector of Prairie's journey points from the present into the past, whereas the narrator's concern moves from the past into the present.

Along these vectors, two antagonistic force fields interact to organize the novel's responses to the double searches. Running in one direction are networks of family and friends that connect generations and overcome isolation. These I call the kinship system. The kinship system yields representations with which even young readers can identify, encoding emotions and events that have not changed substantially over the generations. Running in a contrary direction are networks of government agents that seek to gain information, incarcerate dissidents, and control the population—the snitch system. The snitch system, implying a skepticism about the government typical of the sixties, is likely to gain ready assent from ex-hippies but may strike younger readers as bizarre.[2]

The two systems, articulated through action and plot, are also connected by central metaphors that mediate between them. These metaphoric connections imply that the two systems may be collaborative as well as opposed, the attitudes and preconceptions associated with one serving to make possible and structure the other. Their entanglement echoes Slothrop's dark dream in *Gravity's Rainbow*, when he realizes that "They" may be only another version of us.[3] Reaching out to a generation that never knew the sixties, *Vineland* also gives voice to the bewilderment that the generation formed by the sixties felt upon finding itself in the Reagan eighties, with Tubal culture apparently flourishing in every household and greed the bottom line on every contract. How did we get from there to here, and how can we communicate with those who do not understand what "there" was?

Answers to these questions are not so much stated as intimated through metaphoric and narrative connections. One of the tropes connecting the snitch and kinship systems is the metaphor of virginity. When Hector badgers Zoyd to give him information the government will find useful, the narrator informs us that "so far—technically—Zoyd had hung on to his virginity" (12). "Your child's well-beín against your own virginity as a snitch," Hector later bargains with him (295). "Why this thing about popping my cherry, Hector, can't you see I have a kid to look after now," Zoyd says (303). To show how the metaphor overlays one set of associations onto another, I want to consider its implications as they have been worked out in feminist theory.[4] Losing one's virginity signifies inscription into a system of representations that structure relations, interpret responses, delineate options. The expression paradoxically constructs refusing to do something as a presence, while making sexual activity an absence or loss. Seeming to impart value to virginity, it also defines power relations between gendered partners that reveal how vulnerable women are in a patriarchal society. The male is the seducer; he wins if he can pop the cherry. The female is the seduced; symmetry requires that she wins if she can keep her virginity intact. In fact her virginity is useful only as a bargaining chip, for if she hangs on to it for too long it becomes useless, a sign of a spinster that no one desires. Virginity is thus valuable only as long as it is imperiled. Let the pressure diminish, and it loses its currency. Like money and information, it needs to circulate within a system of exchanges to exercise its value. Unlike them, it is a coin that can stand only one transaction before disappearing. Properly speaking, it signals an *initiation* into the exchange of money and information that follow.

Consider how these implications work to structure the snitch system when the kinship system is mapped onto it through the trope of virginity. Hector, pressuring Zoyd to turn informant, assumes the male role of seducer. Zoyd occupies the female role of seduced, a position reinforced by his responsibility for the child ("I have a kid to look after now"). Information has meaning only if it circulates, moving through the system in a series of exchanges that involve money, incarcerations, promotions, power—and not coincidentally, children. Traffic between the two systems flows in both directions: the snitch system helps to organize the kinship system, even as the kinship system provides the presuppositions and gender relations that determine its structure. The two effects are not, however, necessarily equal. The threat that the snitch system poses to the kinship system can lead to solidarity rather than betrayal, a possibility realized most clearly in Zoyd's relation with Prairie.

Zoyd enters the novel's kinship networks primarily through his tie to Prairie. Apparently having no family of his own, he is slowly incorporated into Frenesi's family, to which she herself remains peripheral. Whereas his female role makes him liable to seduction in the snitch system, his maternal position in the kinship system opens him to connection. After Frenesi deserts him and Prairie, he decides to join forces with Sasha, Frenesi's mother. Despite the long-standing enmity between them, they realize that in a custody battle the judge would find little to choose between Zoyd's doper life-style and Sasha's communist past.[5] Rather than risk losing the child to a government agency—having her circulate among the snitch rather than the kinship system—they share responsibility and, increasingly, affection. Frenesi comes from a proud line of left-wing activists. As Zoyd accepts this family as his own, the kinship system creates a context where the sixties become part of an ongoing struggle that included the Wobblies of the twenties and thirties and communist sympathizers who suffered under the McCarthyism of the fifties. The connections imply that the radicals of the sixties, with the arrogance typical of youth, may have made the movement seem more anomalous than it really was. When Zoyd makes common cause with Sasha, symbolic alliances are established that go beyond the private sphere of the family.

The nexus where the two systems come together most intricately is in Frenesi's relationship with Brock Vond, the high-level government agent who plots to incarcerate dissidents in a "re-education" camp designed to coerce them into becoming snitches. Frenesi's left-wing heritage makes her separation from her parents unusually complex. For most young people involved in the radical movements of the sixties, being politically active served the dual purpose of embracing a cause and enraging their parents. For Frenesi, radical activity and parental approval go hand-in-hand. The outrageous act from their point of view is to cooperate in fascist plots, not to engage in radical politics. Frenesi's fascination with Brock Vond, otherwise inexplicable, makes sense in this context.

As in *Gravity's Rainbow*, the forbidden exercises its spell through sexual obsession. The liaison, as dangerous politically for Brock as for Frenesi, nevertheless is constituted through an asymmetrical power relation. Brock is the seducer; Frenesi the seduced. The seduction is enacted by Brock's persuading Frenesi to turn informant (209-10). "To seduce" here returns to its etymological meaning "to separate" (from the Latin *seducere*), for Frenesi's seduction marks her slippage from the kinship to the snitch system. She is alienated by it both from her parents and from the allegiances of 24fps, the radical film collective she helped organize. Attempting to reestablish connection with a history she has lost, Frenesi tries to reenter the kinship system by leaving Brock, marrying Zoyd, and giving birth to Prairie. Not one to idealize motherhood, Pynchon scripts a plot that has Frenesi falling into a postpartum depression so severe that she can scarcely function.[6] Resenting the resources she feels the child strips from her, she imagines that the baby "went along on its own program, robbing her of milk and sleep, acknowledging her only as a host" (286). At night she fantasizes that Brock is leaning over her bed, whispering, "This is just how they want you, an animal, a bitch with swollen udders lying in the dirt, blank-faced, surrendered, reduced to this meat, these smells" (287).

Supported by her family, Frenesi gradually emerges from the depression. But she remains unable to internalize the maternal role or to connect with her own mother. Yearning to reciprocate Sasha's affection, she feels that of "all her turnings, this turn against Sasha her once-connected self would remain a puzzle she would never quite solve, a mystery beyond any analysis she could bring to it" (292). Her relation to Prairie is similarly distanced. She imagines that the "baby was perfect cover, it made her something else, a mom, that was all, just another mom in the nation of moms, and all she'd ever have to do to be safe was stay inside that particular fate" (292). Although she believes that "Prairie could be her guaranteed salvation," motherhood remains a role she could play, not an aspect of herself expressed. Because the role is so convincing yet false, Frenesi sees "*pretending* to be Prairie's mom" as "the worst lie, the basest betrayal" (292, italics added). The judgment makes it virtually certain that she will return to the snitch system. Indeed, it reveals that she never really left it.

At the center of the snitch system is Brock Vond. As such, he is deeply antagonistic to the kinship system. As far as we know he does not say to Frenesi that motherhood makes her into meat, but the sentiment is consistent with his values. He continually tries to appropriate the signs of the kinship system and reinscribe them within the snitch system, changing their significance and altering their value. His "genius," the narrator says, "was to have seen in the activities of the sixties left not threats to order but unacknowledged desire for it" (269). Where most of the country saw rebellion, "Brock saw the

deep—if he'd allowed himself to feel it, the sometimes touching—
need only to stay children forever, safe inside some extended national Family" (269). At the PREP (Political Re-Education Program)
camp he masterminds, he sees the dissidents-about-to-turn-infor-
mants as so many errant children, the "men who had grown feminine, women who had become small children, flurries of long naked
limbs, little girls naked under boyfriends' fringe jackets, [. . .] the
sort of mild herd creatures who belonged, who'd feel, let's face it,
much more comfortable, behind fences. Children longing for discipline" (269).

Significantly, the narrator describes Frenesi's inscription into the
snitch system in terms of children returning to their parents. The
echo of Brock's beliefs shows how thoroughly she has been co-opted.

[As] the Nixonian Reaction continued to penetrate and compromise further
what may only in some fading memories ever have been a people's miracle,
an army of loving friends, as betrayal became routine, government procedures for it so simple and greased that no one, Frenesi was finding out, no
matter how honorable their lives so far, could be considered safely above it,
[. . .] leaving the merciless spores of paranoia wherever [government money]
flowed, fungoid reminders of its passage. These people had known their children after all, perfectly. (239)

Within the kinship system, likeness of face and form is evidence of
lineage, visible sign of the relationships that bond families together.
On several occasions Prairie scrutinizes her image in the mirror, trying to see in it her mother's likeness. Brock encodes the lineaments
of face and form into the snitch system by being a "devotee of the
thinking of pioneer criminologist Cesare Lombroso," who believed
that certain physiognomies revealed debased mentalities and criminal tendencies (272). Scanning the "children" in the PREP camp,
Brock registers "stigmata," seeing them as "a parade of receding fore-
heads, theromorphic ears, and alarmingly sloped Frankfurt Horizon-
tals" (272). When he confronts Zoyd in a jail cell, he sees only the
cranium of a criminal, in contrast to Prairie who learns to see in her
father's face, as in her mother's, a resemblance to her own.

If the snitch system is the extension and locus of Brock's power,
the kinship system is his greatest antagonist and fear. He intuits that
if he were to slip within it, he would become powerless, wrenched
from the role of seducer to seduced. He has a recurrent nightmare in
which "he was forced to procreate with women who approached
never from floor or ground level but from steep overhead angles,
[. . .] each time it was done, a terrible sadness, violation . . . some-

thing taken away. He understood, in some way impossible to face, that each child he thus produced, each birth, would be only another death for him" (276-77). His fear is not unfounded. Because the systems are articulated together, it is always possible to slip from one to another, as Frenesi does when she turns her back on her family and starts a new life, not as Prairie has been led to believe in the radical underground, but in the demimonde of the snitch system. In this semiotic, Brock's fear represents hope turned inside out, for it hints that transitions in both directions are possible.

Before this possibility is realized, the text explores the entanglements implicit in Frenesi's transition from kin to snitch. She works as a government operative in an "infinite series of increasingly squalid minor sting operations of steadily diminishing scope and return, against targets so powerless compared to those who were setting them up that some other motive, less luminous than that of the national interest, must have been at work" (72). Though we get only glimpses of what those motives might be, we know that for Brock they include the desire to appropriate into the snitch system as much of the kinship system as he can, thus aggrandizing his power and weakening what he most fears. His success can be measured by how family life is constituted within the snitch system. After she abandons her family, Frenesi hooks up with Flash, another informant whom she met at the re-education camp. Their relationship is based on the mutual toleration of lies—lies that they tell the victims they help to entrap; lies that they tell each other about fantasized or realized infidelities; lies that the monthly stipend checks and cheap transient apartments constitute security. The one bright spot is their child Justin, a precocious preteen who keeps his parents informed by watching MacNeil-Lehrer.

The two ingredients essential to the snitch operation are money and the computer, dollars and information. Both are coded in alphanumeric characters, ultimately in ones and zeros. The possibility that human action, perhaps even the human soul, can be reduced to the ones and zeros that in *The Crying of Lot 49* loom in the sky over Oedipa reappears in *Vineland*. In a complex play of narrative framing, metaphor, and image, this reductive coding is set in tension with the photographic image. Somewhere in their intersection, the narrative implies, lies the key to understanding why the revolution failed.

The credo of 24fps (frames per second) was based on the belief that through the medium of the human face the photographic image would reveal lies for what they were.

They particularly believed in the ability of close-ups to reveal and devastate. When power corrupts, it keeps a log of its progress, written into that most sensitive memory device, the human face. Who could withstand the light? What viewer could believe in the war, the system, the countless lies about American freedom, looking into these mug shots of the bought and sold? Hearing the synchronized voices repeat the same formulas, evasive, affectless, cut off from whatever they had once been by promises of what they would never get to collect on? (195)

Their philosophy reflects and inverts Brock's belief in criminal physiognomy. Directed at government officials rather than dissidents, the camera exposes their secret crimes by interrogating their faces. The credo implies a basic faith in the American public. The public supports a bad war only because it has been misinformed. In thus constituting a good public separate from a bad government, the credo reveals a naïveté that Brock is not slow to exploit. This is where money comes in. If enough of the public can be put on the government payroll, they will be co-opted into the system that the credo assumes they will resist.

The credo is naive also in its belief that the image can speak for itself, without mediation, and that it will speak truly, without distortion. Brock is a master not so much at getting people to believe in him, as poisoning their belief in what matters to them most. Having seduced Frenesi into taking money from him, he proceeds to poison her faith in Weed Atman, the charismatic mathematician who haphazardly became the leader of the rebellion at College of the Surf, restyled by the revolutionaries as the People's Republic of Rock and Roll, PR³. Brock tells her that what is already true of her—she has slipped into becoming his informant—is also true of Weed. It is not altogether clear whether the charge is true, but the evidence seems to indicate that it is not.[7] Very likely Weed's cooperation extends no further than appearing at mysterious sessions with the dentist that Brock planned as "reality" treatments (240). Brock is adept at insinuating that, because small breaches in propriety have occurred, integrity of any kind is a chimera. At crucial points in the narrative Brock lies in just this way, attempting to undermine what someone holds most dear.

The question of Weed's innocence is important, because it bears on whether the camera can lie. After Frenesi plants the rumor that Weed is a snitch, in an act of consummate bad faith she persuades him to tell his side of the story to the camera while she films it. The collective's weapon is now aimed at itself, like a wounded shark that

eats its own innards. On some level Frenesi understands that the act
of shooting is already a betrayal, for she tells Brock, "Once we have
him on film, whether he lies or whether he confesses, he's done for,
it doesn't matter" (240). Realizing the collective is falling apart,
Frenesi feels her consciousness split in two, as though she were both
acting the role of herself and watching the image of herself acting.
The feeling she has later about only pretending to be Prairie's mom
has its origins here.

Beginning the night she and Rex had publicly hung the snitch jacket on
Weed, Frenesi understood that she had taken at least one irreversible step to
the side of her life, and that now, as if on some unfamiliar drug, she was walking around next to herself, haunting herself, attending a movie of it all. [. . .]
No problem anymore with talk of "taking out" Weed Atman, as he'd gone
turning into a character in a movie, one who as a bonus happened to fuck
like a porno star . . . but even sex was mediated for her now—she did not enter in. (237)

Tortured and schizophrenic as the collective has become, Brock is
not content with its turning the camera as metaphorical weapon on
itself. He wants a real shooting. He thinks of metaphors as unreal and
therefore ineffectual. He does not understand that the gun, too, is a
metaphor, a point that does not escape Frenesi.

Men had it so simple. When it wasn't about Sticking It In, it was about Having
The Gun, a variation that allowed them to Stick It In from a distance. The details of how and when, day by working day, made up their real world. Bleak,
to be sure, but a lot more simplified, and who couldn't use some simplification, what brought seekers into deserts, fishermen to streams, men to war, a
seductive promise. She would have hated to admit how much of this came
down to Brock's penis, straightforwardly erect, just to pick a random example. (241)

In this reading seduction and aggression are two sides of the same
coin. Men compete directly by killing each other and indirectly by
seducing each other's women. The woman is a mere counter in a
game men play, a receptacle that allows them to achieve a coupling
they are forbidden to have directly.
    The metaphor of the gun as a homo/phobic/erotic coupling is
translated into actuality when Brock tells Frenesi that he wants to do
more than destroy Weed's credibility; he wants to possess his spirit.
He might have said, perhaps in a coded way did say, the same of
Frenesi. He reminds her that when they last had sex he told her not
to wash "because I knew you'd be seeing [Weed] that night, knew
he'd go down on you—didn't he? ate your pussy, hm? of course I

know, because he told me. You were coming in his face and he was tasting me all the time" (214). He tells her that she is merely "the medium Weed and I use to communicate, that's all, this set of holes, pleasantly framed, this little femme scampering back and forth with scented messages tucked in her little secret places" (214). The coding of Frenesi into the snitch system is nearly complete. She exists not as a person with choice, free will, consciousness, but as a message sent back and forth between two male rivals and/or vicarious lovers. It is a small step from here to her full co-optation into the snitch system, complete with monthly stipend check and computer code.

The logic of seduction/aggression requires that Brock get Frenesi to take the gun into the collective, where it will be delivered to Rex, the tool Brock will use to Stick It In to Weed at a distance. "It's only a prop" (240), Brock tells Frenesi, but she notes that it is loaded. Rex, believing Weed has betrayed them, works himself into a frenzy with Frenesi's help. He watches her coaxing Weed to talk into the camera: " 'This will be your best chance, your most sympathetic forum, all you have to do is tell how it happened, how you think it *could* have happened, no one is judging you, Weed, the camera's only a machine . . .,' and so forth, movie sincerity" (244). Finally Rex can stand it no longer and screams, "Tell this asshole we know everything" (245). The result is the consummation for which Brock has yearned—the possession of Weed's spirit.

What she would then have to bear with her all her life, what she would only succeed in denying or disguising for brief insomniac minutes here and there, was not only the look on his face [. . .] but the way that what he was slowly understanding spread to his body, a long, stunned cringe, a loss of spirit that could almost be seen on the film, even after all the years between then and the screen in Ditzah's house in the Valley . . . some silvery effluent, vacating his image, the real moment of his passing. (245-46)

Even after years have passed, Frenesi does not fully realize that Weed's spirit was killed not by others knowing of his betrayal, but by his knowledge of their betrayal. In a sense the act of filming itself stole his soul, for turning the camera on him in bad faith destroyed him more surely than the gunshot that followed. The collective's assumptions about the camera as weapon, then, proved untrue. The unmediated image did not tell its own story, and the camera's eye did not necessarily tell the truth.

These plot developments reflect the interpenetration of the kinship and snitch systems on another level. They confirm that purity of action and image is an impossibility. After Weed's shooting, it appears that the revolutionary potential of the image has been shattered and the coercive power of the computer established, for Frenesi goes from this final confrontation to Brock's "re-education" camp. DL Chastain, "lady asskicker" in charge of security for 24fps, takes it upon herself to rescue Frenesi from the armed camp. Although DL succeeds in extracting her compatriot, Frenesi's spiritual imprisonment is not so easily remedied. Throughout a two-day marathon session with Frenesi in Mexico, DL probes for answers to why the disaster erupted. "Who'd we save?" Frenesi asks (259), echoing Hector's originating question and confirming that she can no longer believe in the efficacy of radical politics. After that, DL tells Prairie a generation later, "It was all just sad human shittiness" (261).

In the "now" of the narrative, Prairie has grown to young womanhood in northern California and lives with Zoyd in one of the few pockets of counterculture terrain America still has to offer. But the marijuana growers, zany towing service, and mystical pizza joint that make up the local culture are a far cry from the revolutionary fervor of the sixties. Prairie, watching the birth of PR³ on the film archives of 24fps, senses "[e]ven through the crude old color and distorted sound" how different it was then, feeling "the liberation in the place that night, the faith that anything was possible, that nothing could stand in the way of such joyous certainty" (210). From this vantage the present can only be measured as a long, painful fall into ineffectuality and government "cooperation." It is typified by the bargain Zoyd struck with Brock years before to make sure that Prairie was kept away from Frenesi. As a sign of his continuing fealty to this arrangement, Zoyd agreed to stage an annual crazy stunt, receiving in exchange a monthly stipend check. The choice to crash through a plate-glass window was originally his. Over the years the media have become accustomed to filming the event, however, and when Zoyd tries to vary the routine by sawing up a bar with a chain saw, he finds that he must crash through a window nevertheless, this time (unknown to him) with the glass replaced by stuntman's crystallized sugar. The message is clear. The only craziness happening now is that approved, or rather *demanded*, by the authorized codes in the computer and the "inexhaustible taxpayer millions" of the snitch system, with the media and private enterprise as collaborators.

So much has been given up. What are the chances for recuperation? In contemporary discourse the phrase "to recuperate" has a double edge. On the one hand it is used in critical theory in the condemnatory sense of recovering, often obliquely or underhandedly, traditional values whose falsity has been demonstrated by deconstructive analyses. On the other hand it also retains some of its older meaning of recovery, especially from illness. Both senses are applicable to *Vineland*. Compared with *Gravity's Rainbow*, *Vineland* can be seen as a recuperation in a negative sense. Gone are the sweeping scale, daring narrative techniques, hallucinatory imagery, implicit deconstruction of essentialist subjectivity, and dense texture that frustrated attempts at totalization. *Vineland* looks pallid by comparison. But there are also chances for recovery in *Vineland*. Precisely because it operates on a diminished scale, the problems seem more solvable, more as if they had a human face in contrast to the inhuman, looming presences that haunt *Gravity's Rainbow*.

The movement toward recuperation is signaled by Prairie's yearning to find the mother who exists for her only as a legend. The quest takes this teenager "back to and through an America of the olden days she'd mostly never seen" (198). The flashbacks are themselves attempts to connect generations, to build or rebuild alliances across fatigued memories, broken promises, ruptured networks. Prairie gets her first solid information about her mother from the computer banks at the retreat of the Sisterhood of Kunoichi Attentives, the quasi-religious, quasi-martial-arts order with which DL is associated. Prairie finds that the computer screen can, in addition to alphanumeric characters, also yield images. More than the data, these images evoke for her the person her mother may have been.

She lingers over a shot of DL and Frenesi together, fantasizing about what they might have said. After she shuts off the computer and goes to bed, the narrator imagines that within the data bank, DL and Frenesi continue their conversation.

Back down in the computer library, in storage, quiescent ones and zeros scattered among millions of others, the two women, yet in some definable space, continued on their way across the low-lit campus, persisting, recoverable, friends by the time of this photo for nearly a year, woven together in an intricacy of backs covered, promises made and renegotiated, annoyances put up with, shortcuts worn in, ESP beyond the doubts of either. (115)

The movement from the data grid back to a humanly imagined reality is achieved, significantly, through the mediation of a photograph. It marks the transition within the narrative to the flashbacks that tell the story of DL and Frenesi's friendship, the early days of 24fps, the heady intoxication of PR^3, and the final betrayals. Even as the narrative's content draws the revolutionary potential of the image into question, its structure asserts the power of the image to reconnect this history to a new generation looking for answers to some of the same questions.

That the image is rendered by a computer makes clear that the image cannot speak for itself, nor can the camera eye reveal an impartial truth. The lesson that all images are mediated and all camera angles encoded with presuppositions was devastating in the context of Weed's shooting. As Prairie watches the old films it becomes recuperative, opening a passage between Prairie and her mother when the young woman realizes that the eye selecting the camera shots is the one she most yearns to behold.[8]

Prairie floated, ghostly light of head, as if Frenesi were dead but in a special way, a minimum-security arrangement, where limited visits, mediated by projector and screen, were possible. As if somehow, next reel or the one after, the girl would find a way, some way, to speak to her. . . . (199)

The idea that one could be dead but in a "minimum-security" way is the basis for the Thanatoids, a cult that has accepted their death as the only reality worth noticing. Weed Atman, apparently only wounded by the gunshot, shows up years later as a Thanatoid convert. His conversion makes clear the ambivalence of the novel's recuperative movement. Memories can be recovered and images reconstituted, but the spirit of the time, like Weed's spirit, is irrecoverable.

The recuperative movement reaches its zenith at the annual family reunion "meant to honor the bond between Eula Becker and Jess Traverse [Sasha's parents], that lay beneath, defined, and made sense of them all" (369). The highlight is the communal meal at which Jess reads a passage from Emerson, quoted in William James's *The Varieties of Religious Experience:*

"Secret retributions are always restoring the level, when disturbed, of the divine justice. It is impossible to tilt the beam. All the tyrants and proprietors and monopolists of the world in vain set their shoulders to heave the bar. Settles forever more the ponderous equator to its line, and man and mote, and star and sun, must range to it, or be pulverized by the recoil." (369)

The passage implies that the kinship system will finally be vindicated by "divine justice," a possibility the plot endorses when its two major strands intersect, but with ironic qualifications. Prairie finally meets the mother for whom she has been searching. At the same time Brock Vond is preparing to make a "surgical strike" (377) that would wipe out the clan—or more precisely, gather them together in the reconstituted form he envisions. The double climax reveals both the potential for recuperation and the limitations of a recovery in which good and evil intermingle, for the purity of the past was always already interpenetrated with what it fought against.

The limitations are clear in Prairie's encounter with her mother. She perceives this figure come to life from image and camera as "a woman about forty, [. . .] heavier than Prairie expected, sun damage in her face here and there, hair much shorter and to the cognizant eye drastically in need of styling mousse" (367). Throughout the encounter Sasha babbles about Tubal trivia to cover the embarrassing silence that threatens to engulf them, for Prairie and Frenesi discover they have little to say to one another. What, indeed, could they say? Lifetimes lived apart do not suddenly conjoin because of genetic replication. Amidst this celebration of family unity, there is also a recognition that families cohere because of shared experiences and mutual commitments. Where these are lacking, kinship bonds are no more than accidents of birth. Moreover, families often do not cohere. In DL's abusive family physical terror reigned; with Prairie's friend Ché, the incest that can mark or destroy children was a staple of family dynamics. These instances notwithstanding, in this novel dedicated to his mother and father Pynchon uses the family to represent the best chances for connection and bonding.

The second climax occurs when Prairie, overdosed on family unity, leaves the group to be by herself in the woods. In a parody of a deus ex machina, Brock Vond swoops down on her dangling from a helicopter line. He intends to incarcerate her in a re-education camp, but first he goes after her spirit, telling her that he is her father, not Zoyd. " 'But you can't be my father,' " Prairie ripostes, " 'my blood is type A. Yours is Preparation H' " (376). The insult comes together with Reagan budget slashes to cut Brock off in mid-line. As word comes through that the PREP program has been axed, he is winched back into the copter over his vociferous protests. Sometimes the good guys do win, not because of the infallibility of Emersonian justice, but because of the ironic patterns of fate or Pynchonesque whimsy.

Other voices murmur through the text too, nonwhite, nonhuman —Yurok Indians, dolphins, and the mythical *woge*, river spirits who were "creatures like humans but smaller, who had been living here when the first humans came" (186). These voices represent presences who have withdrawn from active participation in the world and watch from the sidelines to see whether the dominant culture can survive. If it can, Pynchon seems to say, it will not be by achieving the purity and innocence that seemed, for a brief time in the sixties, capable of transfiguring America. Tubal culture and the greed that the snitch system signifies did not spring from nowhere. The seeds were already present in the very movements that opposed them. If salvation comes, it will arrive by cherishing the small everyday acts of kindness that flourish in networks of kinship and friendship.

The conclusion is so recuperative in the negative sense that one may wonder whether the author of *Gravity's Rainbow* has not vanished into the mists of time, like the sixties themselves. Yet amidst the retractions that *Vineland* embodies, insights glimmer that make it in some respects the wiser book, although not the more accomplished. Chief among these is the realization that apparently totalized structures have fissures that can be exploited for progressive purposes.[9] A case in point is Hector Zuñiga. Cast in the opening pages as the novel's heavy and Zoyd's archenemy, Hector falls victim to a Tubal detox squad and becomes a fugitive himself. By the novel's end he has changed sufficiently so that he saves Frenesi, Flash, and Justin from Brock Vond's net and makes it possible for them to attend the family reunion. Granted, his motives are scarcely altruistic. He hopes to cast Frenesi in an unctuous movie based on her radical days in 24fps, the message of which will be the evil of drugs.

The incident expresses precisely the complexity of action in a recuperative era. At a time when the nation seems more conservative and capitalistic than ever, what is saved is not the vision that the sixties represented but a few moments of grace. One of the most resonant arrives the day of Zoyd and Frenesi's wedding, when the gods seemed to smile and the world responded. Zoyd particularly remembers a moment when he and Frenesi had sat together under a tree. Feeling blessed, he asks, "Frenesi, do you think that love can save anybody? You do, don't you?" (39). Although she remains silent and the narrator remarks that "he hadn't learned yet what a stupid question it was" (39), Zoyd is determined to capture something of the moment. "He thought, At least try to remember this, try to keep it someplace secure, just her face now in this light, OK, her eyes quiet like this, her mouth poised to open. . ." (39). The memory of the image, like the images in the computer, is not unmediated or untouched by time. Nevertheless, in whatever fashion and through whatever medium, it has managed to be saved, rendered again to a generation that never knew the intensity and hope of the sixties directly. In *Vineland* this is enough, must be enough, because it is all there is.

NOTES

[1]Thomas Pynchon, *Vineland* (Boston: Little, Brown, 1990). All quotations are from this edition. Ellipses that have been added to quotations appear in brackets; otherwise they are present in the original. [This practice has been followed for all essays in this book. —EDS.]

[2]It is a staple of Pynchon criticism to recognize his concern with systems; see Siegel, for example. The snitch system in *Vineland* has an extensive parallel in Don DeLillo's *Libra*, where it represents the underside of the idealism of the sixties. It may not be too strong to say that *Libra* is an intertext for *Vineland*, alluded to throughout but never mentioned directly.

[3]In Slothrop's dream in *Gravity's Rainbow*, he looks up Jamf in a dictionary and finds "I" (287).

[4]On virginity as a cult, see Warner (68-80), Theriot, and Muriel Dimen, "Power, Sexuality and Intimacy," in Jagger and Bordo (34-51).

[5]Raymond M. Olderman, in "The New Consciousness and the Old System" (Clerc, 199-228), writes about the nonlinear, connection-seeking consciousness typical of marginal groups he calls "freaks," in contrast to the rigid, linear, system-bound thinking of "straights." Zoyd Wheeler and Brock Vond continue these patterns in *Vineland*. In this context the alliance between Sasha and Zoyd is a system-breaking connection as well as a familial bond.

[6]On this aspect of Pynchon's fiction see Marjorie Kaufman, "Brünnhilde and the Chemists: Women in *Gravity's Rainbow*," in Levine and Leverenz (197-228).

[7]Brock tells Frenesi that Weed is the "key log, pull him and you break the structure" (216). Weed occupies this role, Brock (or perhaps the narrator) says, because he is the only one "innocent enough" to enjoy everyone's "unqualified trust" (216). If Weed were already corrupted, Brock would not need the elaborate plot with Frenesi to plant rumors about him.

[8]Frenesi's intensely blue eyes are mentioned so often that they become an identifying feature. The feature is, of course, useful in creating her character; but beyond this, it also forges an implicit connection between the radical credo and the inescapability of viewpoint.

[9]The Counterforce attempts a similar recuperation in *Gravity's Rainbow* but is doomed to fail. Resistance in *Vineland* is less dramatic but more sustainable—and also more successful.

WORKS CITED

Clerc, Charles, ed. *Approaches to Gravity's Rainbow*. Columbus: Ohio State University Press, 1983.

Jagger, Alison M., and Susan R. Bordo, eds. *Gender/Body/Knowledge: Feminist Reconstructions of Being and Knowing*. New Brunswick: Rutgers University Press, 1989.

Levine, George, and David Leverenz, eds. *Mindful Pleasures: Essays on Thomas Pynchon*. Boston: Little, Brown, 1976.

Pynchon, Thomas. *Gravity's Rainbow*. New York: Viking, 1973.

———. *Vineland*. Boston: Little, Brown, 1990.

Siegel, Mark R. *Pynchon: Creative Paranoia in Gravity's Rainbow*. Port Washington, NY: Kennikat Press, 1978.

Theriot, Nancy. *The Biosocial Construction of Femininity: Mothers and Daughters in Nineteenth-Century America*. New York: Greenwood Press, 1988.

Warner, Marina. *Alone of All Her Sex: The Myth and Cult of the Virgin Mary*. New York: Knopf, 1978.

"Purring into Transcendence": Pynchon's Puncutron Machine

David Porush

O NE of the problems that Pynchon poses for his academic camp followers is that so many of his sentences make good titles for papers. Indeed, whole dissertations can be (and have been) built out of his neatly turned phrases and bons mots. *Vineland* doesn't disappoint. I'm sure some New Historicist will put another nail in the coffin of poststructuralism by taking Pynchon's tease a little too seriously: "the indispensable *Italian Wedding Fake Book*, by Deleuze & Guattari."[1] Someone eventually will fall prey to the allure of his great one-liner: "this geist that could've been polter along with zeit" (208). It's only a matter of time before we see a paper on Pynchon's (or Frenesi's) theology of "the hacker we call God" (91). Someone ought to write a short monograph about Pynchon's view in *Vineland* of motherhood as redemptive (sort of, some of the time, if you aren't Frenesi) and entitle it "a nation of moms" (292). I imagine a no-longer-naive graduate student finding a way out of Pynchon's black box to complete a retrospective dissertation on Pynchon's complete oeuvre by naming it "Watch the paranoia, please!", which is found in one of the most paranoia-inducing moments of *Vineland* (160). And there's bound to be a great dissertation about the deep sleep of our best writers during the Reagan-Bush years, the link between leftist politics and postmodern rhetoric called "Lingering in the Prefascist Twilight: . . ." (371)— that's if we'll be allowed to publish anything at all by that time—". . . Orwell's *1984* Prophesy Fulfilled."

As you can see from my title, this article has already succumbed— twice—to the allure of Pynchon's phrasings. The main title is taken from a relatively minor moment (if any moment in Pynchon's infra- intertextual texts can be said to be minor) that illustrates my central thesis: Pynchon's machinery of narrative excites and entices us by sending us "purring" (like well-tuned machines or self-satisfied cats) "into transcendence." Yet, as I hope to show, these almost ritual ges-

31

tures at transcendence are reserved only for that part of *Vineland's* narrative that concerns the "sixties"—which here represent not only hope, but a view of realpolitik that Pynchon seems unwilling to discard or abandon. By contrast, transcendence is absent from *Vineland* when the narrative turns to farcical and depressing portraits of the periods when American power politics controlled and afflicted the lives of its characters. In brief, Pynchon uses this tactic—of constructing his prose so that it purrs into transcendence—to romanticize the sixties, a period we can take to mean roughly the years 1962 to 1972, which neatly defines the period when Pynchon was most fertile.

My subtitle alludes to the second part of my thesis: Pynchon slyly and self-referentially alludes to his own transcendental narrative tactics in a maneuver we have learned is typical of Pynchon: using a technological metaphor for his own technique, in this case the "Puncutron Machine."[2]

The numerous collisions of the transcendent with the mundane in *Vineland*, whether through direct allusion to the transcendental or through metaphorical machinery, further signify (or model) a more macrocosmic posture that Pynchon seems committed to: that the only hope for redemption from pedestrian, but ubiquitous, evil is to allow epistemological and ontological commitments to collapse into the transcendental—to suspend the quest for certainty (as Prairie learns to do) and to give up simply surviving and immersing (as Zoyd is forced to do) in favor of recognizing deeper and unutterable truths. This revelation does not come all at once, and neither Prairie nor Zoyd particularly embraces the transcendental by tale's end. But it does come piecemeal and can be demonstrated by a careful analysis of the text. We can even discern—in the retrospective light shed by *Vineland* when we read it in this way—this existential, and perhaps mystical, position evolving through Pynchon's previous works.

Vineland's Magic Middle

The two allusions in the title and subtitle of this article collide in a scene in *Vineland* when Takeshi, Japanese agent and schlemiel, victim of other people's plots, cannot quite accept that DL, the consummate Ninjette, has indeed laid on him the Ninja Death Touch. Since her girlhood, DL has trained in the Eastern martial arts, apprenticing herself finally to Inoshiro Sensei, who teaches her the Death Touch among other mystical procedures. After fleeing the wrath of Mafia don Ralph Wayvone because of her refusal to assassinate Brock Vond —the Darth Vader of *Vineland*—she is kidnapped, taken to Tokyo, and auctioned into white slavery by the Yakuza. This all turns out to be engineered by Wayvone, who also is the highest bidder. Placed in a notorious Tokyo whorehouse, Haru No Depaato, and seeing no other recourse, DL prepares to put the Death Touch on Brock Vond after all.

Unfortunately, Brock Vond has gotten wind of the plot and he, in turn, kidnaps Takeshi, Vond's Oriental double (a fact we are supposed to accept at face value, so to speak). Takeshi is put into DL's embrace in Brock's stead, but she is too out of focus to detect the switch. In the act of intercourse she puts the evil touch on Takeshi, which is destined to work its black magic on his bladder for a year and a day until he dies or some cure can be found. In a fit of remorse, DL persuades Takeshi to take refuge among the Sisterhood of Kunoichi Attentives, an order of Eastern mystical nun-Ninjettes who run "a sort of Esalen Institute for lady asskickers" (107) where DL had completed her training. The Sisters try to heal Takeshi and correct DL's error by an application of spiritual and mechanical technologies: they bond DL to him as a sort of karmic bodyguard and at the same time use on him the "Puncutron Machine," a mysterious therapeutic technology designed to correct the imbalance in a subject's karma.

Like many other Pynchon characters who find themselves caught in the toils of plots that go beyond their ken or capacity for accepting incontrovertible data, Takeshi finds himself entering that peculiar state of paranoid rapture that seizes many Pynchon characters:

Most of the time he couldn't believe she'd really Done It to him, because even this long way down the line he still had trouble believing in his own death. If she'd killed him, why stick around? If she hadn't, why put him, a complete stranger, through all this? It was driving him toward what, in fairly close to it now, he could detect as some state of literally mindless joy. There was no way he knew of to experience such joy and at the same time keep his mind. He wasn't sure this might not be her real mission—to make of his life a koan, or unsolvable Zen puzzle, that would send him purring into transcendence. (180)

This passage is revealing, for it describes Pynchon's own play with the reader throughout his works—his penchant for posing paradoxes and unsolvable puzzles. To many of us literary critics, immersed in a rationalizing profession that is itself the expression of a rationalizing culture, these Pynchonesque koans tend to launch us on flights of scholarly and interpretative acrobatics that have served most to expose the limitations of the very rationality on which we depended. Clues in *Vineland* hint that Pynchon's purpose all along was to send us "purring into transcendence."

The passage above becomes emblematic of a series of other passages that surround it. Indeed, in virtually every scene from the time when DL enters the Kunoichi retreat with Prairie, who is officially beginning her search for her mother (109), to the time that the narrative returns to the "present" of 1984 (294) the reader is treated to a long, complex, and varied system of gestures at transcendent or magical realms. It is helpful to review just a very few of these simply to make the point.

When Prairie first meets Sister Rochelle, Head Ninjette of the Kunoichi Attentives, she discovers that the Sister Superior has learned how to make herself invisible ("she could impersonate [the room] in its full transparency and emptiness" [111]). Sister Rochelle ("Rocky"?) tells Prairie that during her stay among the Attentives "knowledge won't come down all at once in any big transcendental moment" but, as their name suggests, will come by paying attention, "out at the margins, using the millimeters and little tenths of a second, you understand, a scuffling and scraping for everything we get" (112)—a message that might as well be a warning to the hungry reader about the structure of Pynchon's method in constructing the book we are reading. Then, Prairie accesses the Attentives' computer and its elaborate data bank, "a girl in a haunted mansion, led room to room, sheet to sheet, by the peripheral whiteness, the earnest whisper, of her mother's ghost" (114).

Prairie's search through the data base of the past launches the narrative back in time to the sixties: DL's training in the martial arts leads her to "discover that all souls, human and otherwise, were different disguises of the same greater being—God at play" (121). DL receives "another message from beyond, no doubt. She saw a pattern" (124). And so on throughout these middle pages the stories of the sixties unfold: Takeshi and DL's Death Touch, Brock Vond and Frenesi, Frenesi and DL and the 24fps film crew, the revolution at PR³ and its sabotage by Vond and Frenesi, the murder of Weed Atman, Takeshi and DL's encounters with the Thanatoid. . . . Each story is tinged by its own hint of the mystical and of levels or worlds beyond and outside the realm of perception, worlds of secret motives and irrational operations and death beyond life and karma and ESP (a lot of ESP). In Vineland, "something waited, over a time horizon that not even future participants could describe" (222). Van Meter's children learn to meet at the edge of a South American jungle; "Van Meter had been searching all his life for transcendent chances exactly like this one" (223). Godzilla's footprint obliterates Chipco's seaside laboratory. Thanatoids demonstrate the facticity of life after death. Pynchon hints at Ninja magic, feline and plant knowledge, astrological interventions in human affairs, "worms of song" sung by the not-yet-dead from the future to the present; the universally "easy suspicion of another order of things" (202); and plenty of stuff lifted out of the *Tibetan Book of the Dead*. Takeshi explains to Thanatoid Ortho Bob, a Viet "grunt" killed in the war, why revenge for him may not come swiftly:

In traditional karmic adjustment, he went on, sometimes it had taken centuries. Death was the driving pulse—everything had moved as slowly as the cycles of birth and death, but this proved to be too slow for enough people to begin, eventually, to provide a market niche. There arose a system of deferment, of borrowing against karmic futures. Death, in Modern Karmic Adjustment, got removed from the process. (174-75)

In brief, then, *Vineland* comprises three comic acts: act 1 (to page 109) portrays Zoyd Wheeler, his daughter Prairie, and her mother (his former wife) Frenesi Gates with her new family (husband Flash and son Justin) in 1984 and how their lives have been mutually and tragicomically haunted, thoroughly repressed and victimized, and kept separated and unhappy by Brock Vond and the forces of official evil for which he is the agent. With only one notable exception (Frenesi's rumination on the hacker God), all the gestures at transcendence in these first hundred pages concern the sixties. Act 3 takes up this story again in 1984 (page 295). It follows the Wheelers—Zoyd, Frenesi, and their daughter—who are ultimately reunited around a crisis provoked by Brock Vond (who is threatening to destroy Zoyd's home and kidnap Prairie). In act 3, finally, all three are liberated from Brock through the intervention of the Thanatoids, ghosts who haunt the hills around the little northern California coast town of Vineland, in the context of the larger Becker–Traverse family reunion. Thus, despite its dark overtones, the whole is a neat comedy, tinged by nostalgia, or worse, a depressing sense of irretrievable innocence, lost opportunity, and impending fascism.

Act 2, what I like to think of as *Vineland's* "magic middle," concerns the Revolution. The nostalgia of act 3 is not only the mutual longing of Zoyd, Frenesi, and Prairie for a reunion, but is a desire for a return to the transcendent origins to which Pynchon has been pointing throughout act 2.

There are hints of the magical outside these pages. Zoyd hands Prairie an "amulet" (Takeshi's business card) as she is about to leave home to seek her mother. A near-suicidal Zoyd, just separated from Frenesi, signs on to Kahuna Airlines because he discovers it is a " 'gig of death'. . . . The list of passengers who arrived was not always identical to the list of those who'd departed. Something was happening, in between, up there" (61) and Zoyd hopes perhaps he will fall prey to the same phenomenon. So in search of a Kahuna connection, he acts not unlike Oedipa Maas of *The Crying of Lot 49*: "He bounced slowly from one Honolulu bar to another, allowing himself to trust to the hidden structures of night in a city, to a gift he sometimes thought he had for drifting, if not into intersections of high drama and significant fortune, at least away, most of the time, from danger. At some point he found himself back in the toilet of the Cosmic Pineapple, a then-notorious acid-rock club" (61). Similarly, in the first third of the novel, Frenesi has an elaborate reverie about whether human deaths registered on a computer eventually spell out God's intention, making God a sort of ultimate hacker.

But Pynchon's narrative swiftly returns to the 1984 realities of Frenesi's unfortunate domestic arrangement with Flash and their son, Justin. This section (pp. 64 ff.) serves to bracket the terms that will define Pynchon's history of our times: Frenesi is haunted by her desultory and regrettable past: "the past was on her case forever, the zombie at her back, the enemy no one wanted to see, a mouth wide and dark as the grave" (71). With this somber introduction, Pynchon now gives us some of the terms of his argument—disguised as Frenesi's story, which he might have well have entitled, "When the Sixties Were Over" (71). In brief his argument is *the Nixonian Repression put an end to the magic. By contrast with periods of repression, the sixties were crazed but magical, doomed but hopeful.* The years 1972 through 1984[3] are devoid of hope and even the possibility of transcendence. Frenesi as much as anybody was agent provocateur of that Repression, a willing tool, a masochistic victim of Brock Vond's plan to end the People's Republic of Rock and Roll (PR³). The account of her own ancestry—"third generation Red"—serves to illustrate not only that the struggle between the forces of Good (left-wing labor: Wobbly, resistant, self-sacrificing, hardy, rugged, coalminers and lumberers, anti-scab) and Evil ("Hitler, Roosevelt, Kennedy, Nixon, Hoover, Mafia, CIA, Reagan, Kissinger" [372] and one other unnameable) was almost a half-century old but that the deepest of hereditary commitments to Truth and Justice could be subverted to help usher in the Repression Years. Frenesi's grandmother and grandfather, Eula Becker and Jess Traverse, were old-style Wobblies. Sasha, their daughter and Frenesi's mother, suckled on left-wing strikes and the cause of labor, gets caught way on the wrong side—in the wrong labor union —of the Hollywood crackdown of the fifties, led by Joe McCarthy and Ronald Reagan, then-president of the Screen Guild. Nevertheless, Frenesi helps effect the fall of PR[5].

So on the one side of the sixties lay the thirties and fifties, which were mere rehearsals for these Republican years of evil. On our side of the sixties lies the dreadful pedestrianism and political hopelessness that mark the seventies and eighties—"the Repression went on, growing wider, deeper, and less visible" (72). Zoyd is sentenced to acting out hilarious but humiliating acts of madness every year so that he can both secure his government paycheck and signal to Brock Vond, always watching, that he has remained separated from Frenesi. Meanwhile, Frenesi and her new husband Flash, a minor government sleaze agent, are together caught in a spiral of increasingly "squalid minor sting operations of steadily diminishing scope and return."

On the other hand, Pynchon sings a popular line: *In between were the sixties, which still held, however naively, to the possibility of redemption.*

Another notable exception to the confinement of transcendence to the magic middle comes in the final scene of the book. Brock Vond appears as a creaking deus ex machina about to descend from the skies—on a cable held by a helicopter—with malevolent intent onto the sleeping Prairie. But, through Pynchon's own machinations, he is called back just before consummating his evil plan; Pynchon decides to coordinate that very second with a Reagan rollback for Department of Justice maverick operations that cuts off funds for Brock and his party. Then, the Thanatoids intervene, kidnap him, and take him to the underworld.

These three loosely defined acts correspond to two rather distinct narrative techniques: one is the narrative of the remotely plausible; the other is the narrative of the completely implausible, or what we might think of as narratives of the inevitable and the ineffable.

The inevitable narratives deal mostly with the rise and fall of the student rebellion: Frenesi's double-agency and its attendant sexual enslavements and betrayals that circumscribe the lives of her lovers, Brock Vond and Weed Atman; the politics of the sixties, seventies, and eighties; the harassment of Zoyd by Hector the DEA agent; and the little family comedy that gives the book its fundamental structure:

the Wheelers—Zoyd, Prairie, and Frenesi—find their way back into each other's orbits against all odds but in definite accordance with the forces of destiny, kismet, and Pynchonesque inevitability. These plots resolve into the theme of how the evil power-death-tech-government-official-reality politics of our age, represented by Brock Vond and enabled by the Big Brotherish computer, poisons our personal lives, our psychic health, and our family life, no matter how we try to insulate ourselves from it and remain hidden and small. In short, politics and the world of 1984.

The ineffable narratives include all the aforementioned references to the thoroughly implausible but longed-after world of magic, a world of living spirits and intuitions fulfilled, but also a world of dark revelation lurking just beyond our senses, of secret and inexplicable acts. Interestingly, this magic middle also concerns the fertile years of 1962 to 1972, the years that bracket Pynchon's writing of *V.* (1963), *The Crying of Lot 49* (1966), and *Gravity's Rainbow* (1973), the essential Pynchon. If we take this correlation as more than mere coincidence, then we might conclude that the happy and transcendent ending of *Vineland* in 1984 has some subtle autobiographical significance: perhaps something happened that year to permit Pynchon to write again, to shake off, somehow, the demons of the Nixonian Repression and, in the dead middle of the Reagan years, to rediscover "the magic." Just as Reagan unwittingly calls his dog Vond off the backs of the Wheelers and the Gates, so perhaps something—whether belonging to official reality or Pynchon's own imagination, one can only guess—lifted for Pynchon. If this is at all true, then the transcendental references in *Vineland* also signify something essential about Pynchon's imaginative sources and his freedom to invent.

But this speculation about the deeper, more spiritual autobiographical hints in *Vineland* can only remain a poor critic's tantalizing reverie, given how little we know about the circumstances of Pynchon's life and how easy it is to overinterpret his texts.

Pynchon's Transcendent Machines

Vineland continues the romance with communication technology and machines that Pynchon began in his earliest stories. Pynchon seems to favor machines as metaphors for his own authorial acts and the condition of his searcher-heroes. In "Entropy," for instance, Pynchon uses the hypothetical machine offered by James Clerk Maxwell to illustrate the second law of thermodynamics to portray the author, through self-reflexive tactics, as an incarnation of Maxwell's Demon. In *V.*, Mondaugen monitors 'sferics on his radio and picks up a code that Weissmann interprets as containing a reference to Wittgenstein's famous proposition from the *Tractatus Logico-Philisophicus*, "Die Welt is Alles was der Falles ist" (The world is all that is the case). However, this novelistic contrivance is so acute that we know Mondaugen has somehow tuned into the voice of the Being who has authored the text he inhabits.

In *The Crying of Lot 49*, Oedipa Maas wonders if she shouldn't strive to become what Randy Driblette, the stage director, had been: "the dark machine in the centre of the planetarium, [striving] to bring the estate into pulsing stelliferous Meaning, all in a soaring dome around her."[4] In *Gravity's Rainbow*, the metaphor is the V2 rocket itself whose parabolic flight brackets the entire novel—or more precisely, the *Schwarzgerät* in its nosecone, the mysterious black box guidance system—which comes to mean everything, including Desire, the searches of his characters, and not least, Pynchon's own mysterious authorial imagination.

In *Vineland*, the intensity of this romance with the cybernetic machine has been muted. But because Pynchon has trained us so well, it seems writ large nonetheless. The two significant technologies in *Vineland* are the computer and the Puncutron Machine, and both add incontrovertible proof that Pynchon, somewhat paradoxically, sees technology and technique—including his own technique as author and the technologies of narration—to be potential means to transcendence.

For instance, take the contrast between analog and digital, one of those clean and simple dialectics that lie beneath much of Pynchon's complexities. Here it applies to the good and the bad, to the sixties and the ensuing Nixon repression, respectively. The metonymy for the analog is Mucho Maas's stereo system, which stands for what it delivers, rock and roll, which in turn stands for the Revolution. Ushered into Mucho Maas's posh town house, Zoyd, baby Prairie in arms, on the lam from his failed marriage, finds "here was period rock and roll, over audio equipment that likewise expressed, that long-ago year, the highest state of the analog arts all too soon to be eclipsed by digital technology" (308). The sixties were rock and roll, analog, full of love and magic; at worst, reality was 24fps, twenty-four frames per second, faster than the eye's own sixteen and thus, for all intents and purposes, effectively analog. 24fps is the name of the rolling docudrama film crew commune that represents the best of the sixties, the one perfect instant where sorority, transcendence, a righteous cause and art collaborate. By contrast, the years to come were unmusical and digitized; they led to Brock Vond's burning of the 24fps archives in Ditzah's home.

Metonymy for the digital is the ubiquitous computer. Pynchon's code words are the "zeros and ones" to which he alludes throughout this text, having carried them over from that magnificent—and oft-analyzed—image in *The Crying of Lot 49* for Oedipa Maas's paranoid situation: Oedipa feels herself to be walking "among matrices of a great digital computer, the zeroes and ones twinned above. [. . .] Behind the hieroglyphic streets there would either be a transcendent meaning, or only the earth."[5] In the Pynchon mythography, the whole nexus of conceits—communication systems, codes of hidden meaning, technologizing of the Word, the reduction of options, the alliance between tech and Death, *especially* the alliance between tech and Death—all resolve into the image of flashing electronic gateways, meant to imitate the shining paths (neurons) of the human brain. That remarkably prophetic metaphor in Pynchon's vision from his 1966 novel is rewritten with a vengeance in *Vineland* in a passage that deserves as much attention. After her husband's desperately needed paycheck has been stopped by the computer, Frenesi meditates on the extent to which her own life has been expunged by the computer:

If patterns of ones and zeros were "like" patterns of human lives and deaths, if everything about an individual could be represented in a computer record by long strings of ones and zeros, then what kind of creature would be represented by a long string of lives and deaths? It would have to be up one level at least—an angel, a minor god, something in a UFO. It would take eight human lives and deaths just to form one character in this being's name—its complete dossier might take up a considerable piece of the history of the world. We are digits in God's computer, she not so much thought as hummed to herself to a sort of standard gospel tune, And the only thing we're good for, to be dead or to be living, is the only thing He sees. What we cry, what we contend for, in our world of toil and blood, it all lies beneath the notice of the hacker we call God. (90-91)

In fulfillment of her reverie—or in answer to her dark prayer— Pynchon sends Frenesi her angel of redemption, her own daughter, not quite as remote and unregistering as her God but nowhere as deep into the ones and zeros as she is. Prairie—descendent of all of Pynchon's anti-heroic searchers—plays the computer keyboard, searching for her mother.

She already knew about how literal computers could be—even spaces between characters mattered. She had wondered if ghosts were only literal in the same way. Could a ghost think for herself, or was she responsive totally to the needs of the still-living, needs like keystrokes entered into her world, lines of sorrow, loss, justice denied? . . . But to be of any use, to be "real," a ghost would have to be more than only that kind of elaborate pretending. . . . (114)

Prairie powers down the computer, having found a picture of her mother and DL that was "sharpened up pixel by pixel into deathlessness." To seal this conceit of the merging of the super- and sublunary worlds through the computer, Pynchon shifts our focus to the DL and Frenesi of that picture, "back down in the computer library, in storage, quiescent ones and zeros scattered among millions of others" (115). Pynchon then uses this crossing among terms of a metaphor to cross over to the story of their, and the nation's, sixties experiences.

In keeping with the hilarity and comedy of his story, however, the best technological image for Pynchon's thematics is the Puncutron Machine, designed to "get that chi back flowing the right way" (163). The language in which Pynchon registers Takeshi's first impression of it might easily be a gloss on the complex plot of *Vineland* and the relationship with the text that Pynchon intends for the reader.

It was clear that electricity in unknown amounts was meant to be routed from one of its glittering parts to another until it arrived at any or all of a number of decorative-looking terminals, "or actually," purred the Ninjette Puncutron Technician who would be using it on Takeshi, "as we like to call them, electrodes." And what, or rather who, was supposed to complete the circuit? *"Oh, no,"* Takeshi demurred, "I think not!" (164)

(Pynchon often makes us feel as if we are caught in a servo-mechanical loop of interpretation with the text.) Subsequently, Takeshi wonders if the elaborate Puncutron sessions and everything they imply weren't just another plot to get him to purr into transcendence (op. cit.). In other words, if we take the analogy seriously, the machinery of Pynchon's plot aids the reader in crossing between worlds, just as the Puncutron aids the reader's avatar, Takeshi, in striking a karmic balance.

In his story "In the Penal Colony," Franz Kafka describes an elaborate torture device meant to inflict on the subject a religious cognizance of his own crimes, as if the message were signaled from another world. This "sentencing machine" uses sharp needles and the victim's own blood to inscribe, in an extremely ornate, elaborate (and therefore even more excruciating) script, the victim's "sentence" on his skin. Indeed, the sentence itself is written only on a narrow band across the torso; the rest of the body is tortured by curlicues and flourishes and embellishments, we are told. Kafka, in a rare moment of authorial intrusion, invites us to "look beyond the harrow" to where the true significance of the machine, as it inscribes the law on the body of its victim, lies. For Kafka, this Sentence Machine also enables a dark transcendence.

By contrast with this grim fable of a writing machine, and finally, as relief for our curiosity, on nearly the last page of the novel, we get a glimpse of the workings of the Puncutron Machine itself as it operates on Takeshi. It seems clearly Pynchon's answer to Kafka: "the Head Ninjette had managed to corner him while he was on the Puncutron Machine, all hooked up with no escape, and while an inkjet printer moved along the meridians of his naked skin, laying down trigger-point labels in different colors, adding reference numbers and Chinese ideograms, [. . .] a Senior Ninjette Puncutech stood by with an ivory fescue, noting and commenting" (382). Here the machine is a means to a happier transcendence, as the text of Takeshi's body gets punctuated with a chart of his chi nodes in preparation for acupuncture. However, Sister Rochelle, "as so often in the past, now socked Takeshi with another one of her allegories, this time about Hell."

In her elaborate allegory, Earth is a Third World country, not unlike Vietnam, that is first fought over by two superpowers, Heaven and Hell, then exploited as a tourist stop by the winners from Hell, and finally abandoned, leaving the inhabitants forlorn and strangely guilty "at not having been good enough for them, the folks who lived in Hell. So, over time, Hell became a storied place of sin and penitence, and we forgot that its original promise was never punishment but reunion, with the true, long-forgotten metropolis of Earth Unredeemed" (383).

Pynchon uses the machinery of his narrative—Takeshi endures Sister Rochelle's sermon while undergoing therapy on the machine that leads to transcendent manipulations—to deliver his own version. Somehow, machinery and metaphor collaborate to transcend, though whether in service of darkness or light remains in doubt.

The Collaboration between Epistemology and Ontology

One of the beauties of Pynchon's novels is that they are so rich, so filled with interreferential metaphors, that the ground of the literal threatens to dissolve in favor of the system of interlocking meaning implied in those metaphors. Any significant phrase might resonate through the whole book or act like a palimpsest on which other readings might be written. This creation of the feeling that "everything is connected" and that everything might refer both outside the text and to another part of the text creates a kind of "infra-intertextuality" that lies at the heart of the Pynchon technique, hallmark of his singular genius. Nor is this tactic a mere mechanical application; rather, it is the place where Pynchon's style meets his message, the place where epistemology meets ontology: the transcendence.

In *Vineland*, Pynchon has not only *not* lost his touch, but he has brought into sharper focus his system, or let us say, the posture, disposition, fundamental commitment as artist, behavioral mode, style that we have watched evolve through his previous fictions. By showing us how the lives of his characters are oppressed by systems of motives that lie beyond their influence, *Vineland's* plots seem fundamentally committed to making us *understand* how ontology, our at times inexpressible immersions in life, is influenced by and founded on our epistemologies, our systems of understanding. At the same time, Pynchon's style itself—with its long aptotic and periodic sentences that suspend sure knowledge in favor of immersion—seems bent on making us *experience* how our epistemologies are already fated and determined by our ontologies, by how we are immersed in our lives. Finally and at the same time, the machinery of his narrative is devoted to convincing us that a transcendental realm lies beyond both epistemology and ontology as they dissolve into each other, a transcendental realm that Pynchon occasionally salutes, and at which he asks us to laugh. So the Thanatoids and ESP and strange coincidences and Godzilla's footprint are the source of much of the joy and outright laughter *Vineland* gives (along with the hilarious rock verses and Pynchon's robust, acrobatic, and joyful sentences themselves).

Such a collaboration is oxymoronic, like the idea of transcendental machine, but Pynchon has always favored such self-contradictory metaphors: he even named his magnum opus using one to signify the collaboration between the calculus of a rocket's trajectory and God's promise to redeem the earth. Indeed, as William Plater noted in his fine study of Pynchon's work, even Pynchon's use of metaphor itself implies a yearning for transcendence, for it "permits the poet a mode of existence that is a self-conscious delusion, almost like the paranoid's structure, without the obligations to believe it."[6]

Pynchon uses code for the oxymoronic collaboration between ontology and epistemology that leads to the dissolution of boundaries and transcendence: he calls it "crossing between worlds." One need only count the number of occasions in *Vineland* when one character experiences another world as a form of transcendence to get the message. We have already considered some of these: Frenesi imagines the Big Brother computer controlling her destiny as a hacker God. Prairie yearns to use the computer to cross over to her mother's ghostly world of the past. The Thanatoids eventually take Brock over to their side just as he is about to commit his most heinous act at the family reunion. Some we haven't yet discussed: Van Meter visits the Thanatoid hotel with his Fender guitar. Weed Atman finds that upon every mysterious visit to his dentist he was "back across a borderline, invisible but felt at its crossing, between worlds" (228). Prairie opens the refrigerator of the Sisters and imagines that the food isn't dead but sleeping, and the chill "sent her back out into the less clearly haunted world" (189). The *woge*—spirits in the tale of the Yurocks— withdraw to another world, leaving the forests up above Humboldt haunted but always threatening to come back and teach humans how to live in the world if they fuck up too badly (186). The kidnappings from the Kahuna Airlines. The worm songs Frenesi hears from the future, transmitted by the shade of Weed Atman. And finally, Sister Rochelle lays the big daddy of these "tales of crossing over" on Takeshi as he lies helpless in the grips of the Puncutron Machine.

In *Horizons of Assent*, Alan Wilde argues convincingly that postmodernism (especially as illustrated by Donald Barthelme's work) is distinguished from modernism in that it has abandoned the modernist epistemological posture, the quest for certainties or the creation of fictional realms in which certainties are possible, in favor of an ironic, skeptical, ontological one, the "acceptance of a world that is, willy-nilly, a given of experience."[7] Even Pynchon's work itself hints at acceding to a philosophy in which the epistemological questions are answered by Wittgenstein's dictum—"The world is all that is the case" —or more simply replaced by the slogan of ontology in *V.:* "Keep cool but care."

I have argued elsewhere that postmodernism inherently uses the epistemological potency of the literary act itself to resist impotence caused by systems of information bearing down on us.[8] However,

Vineland convinces me that, if neither Wilde's view nor mine is incorrect, then at least they describe a movement in postmodern fiction that has been transcended or surpassed, or whose terms have since changed. A new view of postmodernism is suggested, or perhaps even a new sort of fiction in which the ontological and epistemological resolve into each other (and seem equally speechless) in the face of facts and plots both historical and supernatural. The happier characters here—Prairie, Zoyd, Sasha, Jess and Eula, DL, and Takeshi—learn to roll with history's punches and shrug their shoulders at the ineffable, while, finally, affirming as Pynchon quotes Jess Becker quoting James quoting Emerson, that "Secret retributions are always restoring the level, when disturbed, of the divine justice" (369). Again, we can only speculate that for Pynchon, writing is a form of transcendence that permits him to remake the world and cross over to other ones: a variety of religious experience.

NOTES

¹Thomas Pynchon, *Vineland* (Boston: Little, Brown, 1990), 97; hereafter cited parenthetically.

²"Puncutron" even bears phonemic similarities to his name, as well as hiding puns about the diacritical aspects of writing itself.

³Although it does not quite suit his comic structure, Pynchon cannot resist hinting that the terrors go on. Pynchon implies in the last pages of his book that George Bush's CIA-cocaine connection continues the legacy through today.

⁴*The Crying of Lot 49* (Philadelphia: Lippincott, 1966), 82.

⁵*The Crying of Lot 49*, 181.

⁶William Plater, *The Grim Phoenix: Reconstructing Thomas Pynchon* (Bloomington: Indiana University Press, 1978), 228.

⁷Alan Wilde, *Horizons of Assent: Modernism, Postmodernism, and the Ironic Imagination* (Baltimore: Johns Hopkins University Press, 1981), 173.

⁸David Porush, "Fiction as Dissipative Structure: Prigogine's Postmodern Roadshow," in *Chaos and Order*, ed. N. Katherine Hayles (Chicago: University of Chicago Press, 1992), 54-84.

Pynchon's World and Its Legendary Past: Humor and the Absurd in a Twentieth-Century Vineland

Elaine B. Safer

THOMAS Pynchon's *Vineland*, like *Gravity's Rainbow* (1973), *The Crying of Lot 49* (1966), and *V.* (1963), directs attention, with sharp-edged humor, to people's quest for meaning and fulfillment in the twentieth century, a time when many have become upset by the repeated failure of their dreams and aspirations. This continued yearning and frustration helps set up an absurd perspective, absurd by Camus's definition, which focuses on a "divorce between the mind that desires and the world that disappoints, [the] nostalgia for unity, this fragmented universe and the contradiction that binds them together."[1]

In Pynchon's earlier novels, the main characters, and the reader as well, search for life's meaning and for hope. Slothrop (in *Gravity's Rainbow*), Oedipa Maas (in *The Crying of Lot 49*), and Stencil (in *V.*) quest for some form of order (no matter what kind) and fulfillment in the face of absurdity.[2] *Vineland*, likewise, uses humor of the absurd to develop several frustrated quests. Of primary concern are the quests of Prairie and her father Zoyd Wheeler, the schlemiel figure who is somewhat like Slothrop in *Gravity's Rainbow*. Zoyd is continually disappointed in his attempts to be reunited with his former wife Frenesi. Prairie, their daughter, spends much of her time futilely trying to feel closer to her mother by piecing together secrets from Frenesi's past.

In addition to the frustrated quest of the protagonists, *Vineland* focuses on the extravagantly ludicrous and often destructive behavior of most of the other characters in modern Californian society. Pynchon invites us to consider how the TV-oriented culture of his twentieth-century Vineland—with its interest in Zen, the martial arts, and the New Age movement—has replaced the dreams that helped found this nation: dreams of those who rushed for gold in the 1850s in northern California; of pilgrims in the seventeenth century, for

46

whom America represented a "city upon a hill"; and of the Vikings, in the eleventh century, who followed their leader Leif the Lucky in his exploration of a pristine land that they called "Vinland the Good."[3]

For Pynchon's characters in northern California's Vineland of the 1960s, 1970s, and 1980s, the New Age movement and some quasi-Buddhist practices represent the new American life-style. In addition, for these people, TV programs like *Star Trek*, *Hawaii Five-O*, and *The Bionic Woman*, and TV characters such as Captain Kirk, Steve McGarrett, and Jaime Sommers substitute for active, living heroes. The novel, which begins in 1984, suggests connections with George Orwell's vision of a world whose people are directed by a television screen, but in Pynchon's world the viewing is voluntary. Pynchon grimly makes fun of society's addiction to TV by describing chronic watchers, whom he calls Thanatoids, and by naming his addiction center the Tubaldetox institution. The spiritual and traditional goals of modern Californians are thus lampooned in this comedy of a cartoon world.

Like John Barth, William Gaddis, and other comic writers, Pynchon uses specific methods to tempt and then frustrate the reader, thus creating the black humor of the absurd: (1) he develops traditional themes and myths in a highly allusive manner and then uses such patterns from the past to create "a half-farcical, half-passionate spirit"[4] in his contemporary comic novel; (2) he presents fascinating and fantastic episodes—like those in a tall tale—and then shifts the focus to similar situations in the present era that are real and terrifying; (3) he moves swiftly between a high and a low style and between farce and horror.

Most of the scenes in *Vineland* have a humorous quality even though the novel has a serious undercurrent. Humorous episodes use such devices as slapstick, incongruity, verbal play, and puns. Slapstick humor usually involves the antics of Zoyd Wheeler, a figure who resides "between the comedy of errors and a comedy of terrors," one who seeks fun, is usually without money, and threatens no one because he is so low on the "scale of competition."[5]

Slapstick humor is evident in the first major episode in which Zoyd, dressed in drag, enters the Log Jam bar in Del Norte, planning to enact his annual bizarre stunt in order to collect his mental-disability check from the government. His garb is a party dress of multicolors that he believes "would look good on television" (4). Much of the humor in this opening scene is based on incongruities, particularly the image of Zoyd wearing a large-size woman's dress from a

discount store and carrying a small lady's chain saw that is orna-
mented with mother-of-pearl and rhinestones, a saw advertised as
"tough enough for timber [. . .] but petite enough for a purse" (6).
The room is filled with tough-looking loggers, who are perched on
designer barstools, chatting about George Lucas's third *Star Wars*
film, *Return of the Jedi* (1983), as soothing New Age music is audible in
the background. Comic irony is developed by means of the contrast
between the powerful, heavy-set, rough-looking California loggers on
the one hand, and on the other, their yuppie life-style signified by
"three-figure-price-tag jeans" and their trendy New Age consciousness
with its borrowings from Far Eastern religion and philosophy boiled
down to accommodate an easy and comfortable life in the United
States.

The tone becomes more serious when the narrator indicates that
underneath a calm exterior is the smoldering violence of these "dangerous men" with "coarsened attitudes" (5), big men who are thinking about lunging at the intruder, Zoyd. Humor and pain continually
collide in these passages. When Zoyd finally yanks at the silk cord
that starts the chain saw's action, Buster, the bartender, cautions: "no
channel's gonna send no crew this far out of town, why are you not
down in Eureka or Arcata someplace? [. . .] If you would've come
around last month, you 'n' 'at little saw, could've helped us gut the
place" (6-7). Bewildered by this strange New Age scene, Zoyd hedges:
"Sorry, Buster, guess I did come to the wrong bar, I sure can't saw any
of this stuff, not with the money you must've put in" (7). Then the
humor takes on a more caustic tone as the lumberjacks and their
New Age attitudes are satirized: Buster informs Zoyd, "since George
Lucas and all his crew came and went there's been a real change of
consciousness" (7).

The sharp-edged tone then shifts to a farcical one that once again
relaxes the reader as Zoyd quickly drives to the Cucumber Lounge
where the local TV station is ready to film his annual leap through a
window, a "publicly crazy" (3) stunt that allows Wheeler to get his
government stipend (and also keeps the government agents, Hector
and Brock Vond, informed of his whereabouts). Here, too, incongruities add to the humor. Zoyd braces himself to run "empty-minded at
the window" only to find that there is hardly any impact: "it all felt
and sounded different, no spring or resonance, no volume, only a
sort of fine, dulled splintering" (11-12). The window, Zoyd finally
realizes, is made of candy, not glass. "He was no media innocent,"
explains the narrator ironically, "he read *TV Guide* and had just re-

membered an article about stunt windows made of clear sheet candy, which would break but not cut. That's why this one had felt so funny" (12).

Myths and Decline

References to the "change of consciousness" caused by the influence of the nearby Skywalker Ranch of George Lucas and his third *Star Wars* film, *Return of the Jedi*, indicate that Pynchon, like Lucas, is dealing with ancient themes and motifs in modern dress, what Joseph Campbell has termed "a valid mythological perspective." Such references also indicate that Campbell's comment on Lucas's achievement applies most strikingly to Pynchon's success in *Vineland:* the ability to "put the newest and most powerful spin" on the time-honored story of the hero.[6]

Pynchon achieves the dark humor of the absurd by evoking nostalgia for the American dream and turning it into a nightmare. The myths associated with a new Garden of Eden decline to urban legends that connect man to the machine and this world to hell instead of heaven; the pastoral scenes of the New World and the frontier are converted by modern American entrepreneurs (like Donald Trump) into shopping malls; the desire for freedom and peace (which caused many of the New Age movement to seek Nirvana or "absorption into the supreme spirit"[7]) is transformed by New Age enthusiasts into a pattern of insular existences and materialistic and technological interests; the quest for family unity—the "little commonwealth"[8] so important in the history of England and America—is treated casually, especially by characters like Frenesi, who leaves husband and daughter. These subjects are treated with comic absurdity throughout.

Suggesting the pastoral world of years gone by, Pynchon's Vineland is still geographically a "Harbor of Refuge" as it was in the 1850s "to Vessels that may have suffered on their way North from the strong headwinds." It looks out on the bay (probably Humboldt Bay) with the city of Vineland curving "the length of the harbor's shoreline" (316).[9] Even in later years, as one drives toward it, one comes "at last up a long forest-lined grade [. . . and as] the trees fold away [. . .] dizzily into view," one sees Vineland, with its pale bridges, salmon boats, and beautiful shoreline (317). The narrator muses over Vineland: "Someday this would be all part of a Eureka–Crescent City–Vineland megalopolis, but for now the primary sea coast, forest, riverbanks and bay were still not much different from what early visitors in Spanish and Russian ships had seen" (317). Such thoughts recall the celebrated reveries of Nick Caraway at the close of *The Great Gatsby:* "And as the moon rose higher the inessential houses began to melt away until gradually I became aware of the old island here that flowered once for Dutch sailors' eyes—a fresh, green breast of the new world."[10] Pynchon's passage has been described as ringing "a dirgelike note of corroboration. Out there at the New World's newest New World—the coast of California—one catches an echo of hopes mislaid, a continent betrayed."[11] The novel's title also recalls the discovery of America by Leif the Lucky and his fellow Vikings. For these Norsemen exiled from their homeland, Vinland represented an opportunity for a new life in a land with rich woods, white sandy beaches, grapes and vines, and a good climate.[12] What was done with this opportunity in northern California is treated with grim humor throughout.[13]

Urban Legends and the Tube

The urban myths and legends of northern California serve as a basis for humor in *Vineland,* in much the same way as such tales are at the center of *Gravity's Rainbow, The Crying of Lot 49,* and *V.* Much of the novel's comic absurdity arises, as it does in the other novels, from the confrontation between contemporary legends and mythology and their traditional counterparts in history. In *V.,* the narrator shows the comic deflation of the Puritan dream in twentieth-century society by using such terms as "Matilda Winthrop's" bar (321) to create a black humor joke on how far the Street of the twentieth century has fallen from the Garden of John Winthrop.[14] *V.* also has several "sewer legends," including one about alligators that grow and reproduce and later are hunted by a sewer patrol. Preoccupation with streets and the sewers below comically indicates the decline of our culture. The folklorist Jan Brunvand points out that "only themes that the folk find appealing will be absorbed into their lore. In other words, 'Alligators in the Sewers' fits right in with [. . .] a general fascination with what is 'down there' in the sewers."[15]

Vineland, like *V.,* has many legends that pose ironic counterparts to the American dream and thus suggest its loss. The novel's jacket cover alerts the reader to destruction of the natural terrain (the willful burning of the beautiful forests). It, like the book as a whole, points to the purposeful wiping out of the country's natural resources (most often by government decree) and the absence of imaginative and creative development that is the American heritage.[16]

During the rush to California in the 1840s and 1850s, promotional literature contained many tall tales and legends. Extravagant descriptions appeared in newspaper accounts of gold growing "to the roots of the grass [that] is pulled up and the gold shaken off, as gardeners pull up the vines to shake off young potatoes." There also were tales of strawberries the size of pumpkins, which were served "cut into slices, like pineapples."[17] Still other tall tales arose about California's healthful and mild climate and its "horses that retain their vigor past thirty years."[18] A California paper is said to have reported: "The climate out here is so healthy, we had to shoot a man before we could start our burying ground."[19]

Vineland's legends are not about a land of natural fruitfulness but rather of death and decline. According to one legend, America, like the earth as a whole, is an extension of hell. Sister Rochelle, the "Senior Attentive, or mother superior" (108) of the Sisterhood of Kunoichi Attentives, explains to Darryl Louise (DL) and Takeshi that the battle between hell and heaven was won by the inhabitants of hell, not the heavenly angels. And, when the creatures from the lower realm left to explore earth, they found that what they encountered was another hell:

The visitors began to realize that Earth was just like home, same traffic conditions, unpleasant food, deteriorating environment, and so forth. Why leave home only to find a second-rate version of what they were trying to escape? So the tourist business began to dwindle, and then the Empire was calling back first its administrators and soon even its troops, as if drawing inward, closer to its own chthonian fires. After a while, the tunnel entrances began to grow over, blur, and disappear behind poison oak and berry bushes, get covered by landslides, silted up in floods, till only a few lone individuals— children, neighborhood idiots—now and then would stumble on one. [. . .] And then all the gateways to Hell were finally lost to sight, surviving only in local tales handed down the generations, sad recitals that asked why the visitors never came anymore, and if they would again. [. . .] So, over time, Hell became a storied place of sin and penitence, and we forgot that its original promise was never punishment but reunion, with the true, long-forgotten metropolis of Earth Unredeemed. (382-83)

A corollary to the conception of our world's being no different from hell is the vision of our life as being similar to that of the Thanatoids whose existence is "like death, only different" (170), that is "not living but persisting" (173). We are "in wand'ring mazes lost."[20] This is, however, not because we are damned and thus have lost the possibility of redemption. We are this way, to a great extent, because life has been "trivialized" and thus deadened.

The Thanatoids believe that "the soul newly in transition often doesn't like to admit—indeed will deny quite vehemently—that it's really dead [. . .] it finds *no difference between the weirdness of life and the weirdness of death*" (218; italics added). Takeshi attributes this leveling to television's "picking away at the topic [death] with doctor shows, war shows, cop shows, murder shows [. . . thus having] trivialized the Big D itself" (218). Such "televisual reality," as Christopher Walker explains, works to "form the pantheon of our modern *spirit* world."[21] That the television screen directs people's vision is an Orwellian horror, intensified, as I mentioned previously, because viewing is done by choice.

In *Gravity's Rainbow*, people roam the streets in bombed-out London like lost souls, defenseless and homeless. The opening scene of the novel describes the streets filled with stench and smoke. Ravaged by war, London is a darkened habitat, fit "to accommodate the rush of souls" (4). In *Vineland*, the wandering souls—the Thanatoids—are treated more comically because their hell is self-imposed.

The range of humor relating to the Thanatoids progresses from the comedy of farce to the edge of black humor. At the farcical tip, we laugh at these creatures and enjoy the jokes about them: "What do you call a Thanatoid with 'Sir' in front of his name? Knight of the Living Dead! [. . .] What does a Thanatoid do on Halloween? Puts a fruit bowl on his head, two straws up his nose, and goes as a Zombie!" (219). The tall tale about the Thanatoids is that they spend almost all of their waking hours "with an eye on the Tube" (171). All else, even food, is insignificant. During times when nothing is on TV, they wander aimlessly through the streets like ghosts. Ortho Bob predicts: "There'll never be a Thanatoid sitcom [. . .] 'cause all they could show'd be scenes of Thanatoids watchin' the Tube!" (171). Enslaved to the Tube, more machine than human, these characters are a manifestation of Henri Bergson's point that "something mechanical encrusted on the living" evokes laughter.[22] At first we laugh at the Thanatoids and their bizarre situation, but our laughter falters when we begin to appreciate that we are really looking at a microcosm of our own twentieth-century society and thus share the dilemma of the characters at whom we have been laughing. Thanatoids, with their addiction to the Tube, epitomize a loss of humanity to the machine. This preoccupation seems to have eradicated the line between death and life, just as the line between earth and hell has been eradicated in Sister Rochelle's legend about the planet earth. The tall tale affects us because it plays on our fears. These zombies, the living dead, are described as an "insomniac population" (173). Their obsession is shared by most members of Vineland's society, ranging from Frenesi, the government informer, to her lover Brock Vond, the federal prosecutor, and to Hector, agent for the Drug Enforcement Agency (DEA). Hector's own addiction to the Tube even causes him to place a TV in his car: "In the back seat, on loud and bright, was a portable Tube, which Hector had angled the rearview mirror at so he could see, for the highway was a lonely place, and a man needed company" (335).

For Thanatoids, as for others sharing the addiction, the Tube is all powerful, as the following "house hymn" at the Tubaldetox institution points out:

THE TUBE

Oh . . . the . . . Tube!
It's poi-soning your brain!
Oh, yes. . . .
It's driv-ing you, insane!
It's shoot-ing rays, at you,
Over ev'ry-thing ya do,
It sees you in your bedroom,
And—on th' toi-let too!
          Yoo Hoo! The
Tube. . . .
It knows, your ev'ry thought,
Hey, Boob, you thought you would-
T'n get caught—
While you were sittin' there, starin' at "The
Brady Bunch,"
Big fat computer jus'
Had you for lunch, now Th'
Tube—
It's plugged right in, to you! (336-37; italics added)

Humor in the hymn ranges widely from a parody of lines from the Christmas jingle "Santa Claus Is Coming to Town" ("He knows when you are sleeping; he knows when you're awake") to the darker parody arising from echoes of the totalitarian society of *1984* where Big Brother and the Thought Police know "your ev'ry thought." For twentieth-century viewers who sit passively at the Tube, death and life merge. For them, as for the Thanatoids, there is "no difference between the weirdness of life and the weirdness of death" (218).

Pynchon moves from the black humor depiction of the deadly effects of TV on those in Tubaldetox treatment to the importance TV has for Frenesi, Zoyd's former wife. We laugh at her dependence on TV, whose rays she hopes "would act as a broom to sweep the room clear of all spirits" (83). We experience something close to Hobbes's feeling of "sudden glory" or "eminency"[23] as we contemplate this woman's foolish addiction to reruns of shows like *CHiPs*, with its two motorcycle cops, men in uniform who cause Frenesi to be so sexually stimulated that she has "a rising of blood, a premonitory dampness" (83). We laugh at the narrator's ironic downgrading of Frenesi's desire for men in uniform: policemen, athletes, "actors in movies of war through the ages, or maître d's in restaurants" (83). The narrator compounds the irony by relating that Frenesi's mother and grandmother got just as excited by men in uniform.

Frenesi, in young adulthood, moves from being a passive viewer of TV to being the unemotional, mechanical user of a camera. She becomes the mechanical eye of the camera and thus elicits our laughter as an example of Bergsonian humor, a personification of "the transformation of a person into a thing."[24] For Frenesi, "it was herself and the Scoopic" (209). The tone progresses from farce to pain as Frenesi gets so caught up in photography that she begins to put a higher value on filmmaking than on her companionship with those who used to be her friends: activists of the sixties, college students who are upset at the double whammy of the Nixon presidency and of the Reagan governorship (of California). Offsetting this point with a joke about beliefs and dreams, the narrator explains ironically that the student revolutionaries, wishing to secede from California, selected a name for their new nation after "the one constant they knew they could count on never to die, the People's Republic of Rock and Roll" (209). The tone gets more serious as a student screams, "They're breaking people's heads" (207) and the narrator reports that "what [the police] lacked in coordination" was "made up for by their eagerness at a chance to handle, however briefly, some college-age flesh" (206).[25]

Scenes get progressively darker and eventually reach what Wolfgang Kayser observes is "the comic and caricatural fringe of the grotesque."[26] At this dark tip of the humor continuum, the "ludicrous" and the "fearful" merge.[27] Frenesi, more zombie than human being,[28] is used by the government in a sting operation to trap the politically innocent Weed Atman. She films him as he is being shot, all the while thinking of herself as "attending a movie of it all," watching Weed as "a character in a movie" (237). At the death scene, "Frenesi tried to find enough cable to get one of the floods on them [. . .] her camera, her shot [. . .] shapes may have moved somewhere in the frame, black on black, like ghosts trying to return to earthly form, but Sledge was right there on them, and the sound of the shot captured by Krishna's tape. [. . .] Weed was on his face with his blood all on the cement" (246).

Frenesi, like Pynchon's earlier character V., has become a twentieth-century monster. Her movement toward the inanimate recalls V., with her glass eye, star sapphire in her navel, and her artificial feet (V. 321-22). Frenesi's tight hold on the camera, because she is absorbed in watching Weed until he is shot, recalls V.'s fascination, as a young woman in Florence in 1899, as she watches rioting: "Inviolate and calm, she watched the spasms of wounded bodies, the fair of violent death, framed and staged, it seemed, for her alone in that tiny square. From her hair the heads of the five crucified also looked on, no more expressive than she" (192-93).

Frenesi's connection to the inanimate, her machinelike actions, also connect her to a twentieth-century urban nightmare or legend, popular because it plays on people's fear of becoming victims of technology. This legendary fear of the machine is dramatically portrayed in Star Wars by means of the character Darth Vader, who, in depending on the mask in order to breathe, seems to take on the evil of the machine. Before Darth Vader's death, Luke Skywalker takes off Vader's mask and, according to Joseph Campbell, thus vitiates the "machine role that the father has played. The father was the uniform. That is power, the state role."[29]

In Vineland, as in Star Wars, there is some relief from watching the machination of such evil characters as Darth Vader or the transformed Frenesi. As Prairie watches Frenesi's film (shown to her by DL), she hears the shot, and "in its aftermath the slack whisper of the surf against this coast" (246). The slight touch of the pastoral here (as well as the connotations of the name Prairie) presents a sort of ironic respite to the callous, almost demonic actions of Frenesi. So, too, the parodic joke on motherhood relieves the tension. Before actually showing Prairie the film, DL tells her about Weed's death: "Only reason I'm tellin' you's if you put those facts together—" "They spell Mother?" [Prairie responds] (189).

From Pastoral Setting to Shopping Mall

Another example of an urban counterpart to the pastoral vision that I wish to examine is the shopping mall and its accompanying legends. Two scenes at shopping malls illustrate their meaning for Pynchon. The first is the setting for the "Great South Coast Plaza Eyeshadow Raid," which according to the narrator is still being talked about by the mall police. With extravagant description and slapstick humor, the narrator burlesques California's focus on two ostensibly unrelated pastimes—roller-skating and shopping. The episode also is a burlesque of holdups in the Wild West. Instead of men on horseback, the raiders are two dozen young girls on roller skates. Instead of the town bank, the locale is a shopping mall. The raid has no purpose other than to get the stuff that teenage girls love—eyeshadow, mascara, lipstick, and even panty hose. The heist is quickly turned over for cash to an older person, who heads away in a panel truck (327-28). Slapstick humor is evident in Prairie's rescue of her friend "Ché" (an odd name for a woman, especially because it is the name of a Cuban revolutionary—Ché Guevera). Gradually, it, like so many episodes in the novel, all turns into a TV experience. Prairie appears to be like the Bionic Woman. The narrator reports: "It felt like being bionically speeded up, like Jaime Sommers." Then, increasing the farce with exaggeration and coincidence, the narrator reports that the tune coming out of the speakers is Chuck Berry's "Maybellene" (328).

The joke about shopping malls gets darker when we recall an earlier episode with DL that taps into the fears arising from living in congested urban areas that are large enough to have shopping malls. Abduction legends focus on women being kidnapped in shopping malls and sold into white slavery. According to Brunvand, these stories are "fueled by news reports of actual crimes, of which there are, of course, many with full [. . .] media coverage."[30] With absurdist humor, Pynchon uses such horrific legends but then gives the tale an unexpected twist that evokes our laughter.

DL is kidnapped in a Pizza Hut parking lot and taken to Japan: "They took her with a matter-of-factness that made her feel like an amateur. Her little car was left alone in its space." She finally hears that a client wanted "an American blonde with advanced asskicking skills." DL's friend Lobelia tries to make her look more glamorous: "Sugar, I'm trying to help. [. . .] you'll be up there on the block, how are you gonna feel if all they sell you for's a dollar ninety-eight?" DL responds with a black humor joke: "Pretty cheap" (135). The humor develops a frenzied quality as the comic and the phantasmagorical merge. Instead of being sold into prostitution, DL is to be a Ninjette hit woman for Mafia figure Ralph Wayvone, who wants her to kill Brock Vond with the Ninja Death Touch (130-31).

In *V.* Pynchon moves swiftly between realistic details and the fantastic to develop a comic subplot out of the popular urban legend about alligators in the sewers of Manhattan. The metaphor of the Street defines the experiences of the antiheroes in relation to those of America's founding heroes and their new Eden. In *Vineland*, the relationship is set up through the metaphorical implications of the shopping mall. The mall also is where Takeshi establishes a "karmic adjustment business," the very terms of which are an ironic inversion of the meanings of karma and the philosophy of Zen Buddhism. The image of Zen being used therapeutically in a shopping mall for New Age practices clearly reflects the author's black humor tone.

From Sacred History to New Age Zen

The materialistic spin that Pynchon's characters give to Zen is a corollary to the movement from the sacred to the profane that exists in the novel as a whole. Allusions to Zen Buddhism in terms of its adoption by the New Age movement are evident in scenes ranging from the Log Jam bar, with its "New Age music that gently peeped at the edges of audibility, slowing, lulling" (6), to the Bodhi Dharma Pizza Temple, where Prairie works. The "change of consciousness" mentioned by the bartender at the Log Jam refers to the New Age movement as a whole, a movement that has expensive sessions (like Shirley MacLaine's) on meditation, reincarnation therapy, and other means by which to "feel the cleansing power of the stream of life."[31] Such therapies are parodied in many of the activities of the Ninjette Sisterhood of the Kunoichi Attentives. That these new believers selected a religion from the Orient rather than from their Western heritage adds to the humor and also becomes the link to tall tales about the martial arts and their use by the Ninjettes.

The links to Zen are parodied by the novel's casual references to its tenets and to its leaders like Bodhidharma. Zen Buddhism goes back to the teachings of Bodhidharma, who left India for China in the fifth century A.D. and spent his days meditating in monasteries. He engaged in meditation to block out the desire for attachment to things of this world and thus to effect an "extinction of individual existence and absorption into the supreme spirit."³² To earn Nirvana, Bodhidharma sat motionless for hours, progressively extinguishing all desires and passions in "the attainment of perfect beatitude" (*OED*). There are many legends about him, ranging from his concentrating for days on a wall so as to shut out all sense of things outside (leaving the mind free to move toward Nirvana) to his contemplation of the Lankavatara Sutra, the text containing the orthodox teaching of Buddhism, a dialogical sermon supposedly delivered by the Buddha himself.³³ Those who follow Bodhidharma's teachings believe that the quest for Nirvana is facilitated by meditation exercises that focus on such things as sutras, mandalas, chants, koans, and controlled breathing (where one concentrates on the rhythm of breathing). All these are given a comic deflation in *Vineland*, particularly in relation to the activities in the Bodhi Dharma Pizza Temple.

At this fast-food pizza restaurant, workers take "meditation break[s]," practice Tibetan chants (as a means to keep away government helicopters of the Campaign Against Marijuana Production [CAMP]), and gaze at a stained-glass window "made in the likeness of an eightfold Pizzic Mandala, in full sunlight a dazzling revelation in scarlet and gold" (49-51).

The Bodhi Dharma's eight-sectioned mandala is a comic inversion of the Buddhist mandala. The traditional mandala is a complicated artistic pattern with intricate symmetries used in Zen as a subject for concentration, a means to block out this world and move toward enlightenment. The eight-sectioned pizza mandala in the fast-food eatery is funny because its purpose is to call attention to the body and its needs rather than to block out such things. It functions to make customers hungry. The ironic juxtaposition of traditional Zen practices and their deflation in the present day is typical of Pynchon's comedic method throughout the novel.

Pynchon even uses the Buddhist term karma for witty purposes. Traditionally, karma has been defined as the "sum of a person's actions in one of [the] successive states of existence" that determines one's fate in the next state. On a broad scale, it is "the unvarying chain of cause and effect that governs the universe" (*OED*). Karma in Pynchon's absurdist work is used as the subject of a joke to explain the incredibly bad food served at the Sisterhood of Kunoichi Attentives, the Ninjette retreat for "devotees of the Orient" (107). Prairie, introduced to the rituals of the retreat by DL, is told of the effect of equal and opposite forces: "The karmic invariance is, is we're paying for high discipline in the Sisterhood with a zoo in the kitchen" (109).

Increasing the humor in relation to yoking together incongruities is Takeshi's use of the concept of Zen, specifically of karma, for profit in his business of "karmic adjustment" conducted at the mall. In the conference room there is a portable sign on the door reading "OPEN KARMOLOGY CLINIC, WALK RIGHT IN, NO APPT. NECESSARY" (177). Takeshi explains: "In traditional karmic adjustment [. . .] sometimes it had taken centuries. Death was the driving pulse—everything had moved as slowly as the cycles of birth and death, but this proved to be too slow for enough people to begin, eventually, to provide a market niche. [. . .] Death, in Modern Karmic Adjustment, got removed from the process" (174-75). He tells a patient, "Don't worry—if this doesn't work—we can always go for the reincarnation option!" (175). Adding to the farce is the fact that Takeshi, despite his light treatment of Zen, actually takes many of its tenets seriously: when he is upset about his relationship with DL and about his own possible death as a result of the Ninja Death Touch, he tries to focus on a koan, which the narrator defines as an "unsolvable Zen puzzle, that would send him purring into transcendence" (180).

Another salient example of the farcical mixing of the spiritual and the material is the changed emphasis of the Ninjette retreat from selecting those best suited for spiritual progress to letting in anyone who can improve the "cash flow": "I'm finding my life's true meaning as a businessperson," explains Sister Rochelle (107, 154).

Zoyd's Dream of Family

Since the beginning of civilization, romantic and heroic myths have helped mankind adapt. Myths and legends and dreams also help to explain the vision of a nation and elucidate the world of a literary work and its characters. In a similar way, dreams and aspirations are at the heart of Pynchon's *Vineland*. In Humboldt County, California (Pynchon's Vineland), where people shift from one relationship to another and get involved in what they term "reconstituted" families, Zoyd continually dreams of the nuclear family. His aspiration is to reunite with his former wife Frenesi. He clings to a pastoral vision of the day he and Frenesi were wed.

All through it, Frenesi was smiling, serene. Zoyd would be unable to forget her already notorious blue eyes, glowing under a big light straw hat. Little kids ran up, calling her name. She and Zoyd were sitting together on a bench under a fig tree, the band on a break, she was eating a cone of rainbow-patterned fruit ice whose colors miraculously didn't seep together, leaning forward to keep it off her wedding dress, which had also been her mother's and grandmother's. A tortoise cat who kept appearing from nowhere would walk directly under the dripping cone, get hit with ice-cold drops of lime, orange, or grape, meow as if surprised, squirm in the dust, roll her eyes around insanely, run off at top speed, and then after a while amble back to repeat the act. (39)

This nostalgic recollection of the wedding day (with echoes of T. S. Eliot) extends to Zoyd's joy in attending family reunions, even though he and Frenesi are divorced. Family for Zoyd means taking Prairie to the annual Traverse–Becker reunions in Vineland. For Zoyd, the reunions of his divorced wife's family acquire spiritual associations that invest all possible connections with pregnant significance. For Zoyd, the experience of participating in the reunion is overwhelmingly joyful. He feels compelled to return each year to what, for him, is a harbor of refuge, an Edenic spot: "To relax some . . . he must have chosen right for a change, that time they'd come through the slides and storms to put in here, to harbor in Vineland" (322). Zoyd understands that "this has been the place to bring [Prairie] and himself after all" (322).

Zoyd sees Prairie and Frenesi in terms of his ideal, the family unit. His serious tone, pastoral references, and romantic orientation are incongruous with the expectations of Frenesi and the rest of the Whole Sick Crew (the term is from V.). Zoyd rhapsodizes over the togetherness of family, calling the meadow in which all gather "Vineland the Good" (322).

The disparity between Zoyd's reveries of the wedding and the reunions and the crude aspects of his marital relationship in the novel as a whole is part of the continuum of black humor. Throughout, we laugh at Zoyd, blind to all signposts. We laugh at the slapstick comedy, early in the novel, describing Zoyd's rush to Honolulu, "red-eyeing in" to see Frenesi, who quickly departs, while he in his room indulges in sexual fantasies about her. We laugh at his antics while working a "Hawaiian cruise gig" for Kahuna Airlines's flight from Hawaii to California and back, a flight that is an easy target for air pirating by "faceless predators" (56-65, 383). We also laugh at Zoyd's zany behavior with relation to acquiring disability checks. Concomitantly, we appreciate that Zoyd, like Fitzgerald's Gatsby, has a dream, one that is akin not only to that of the Dutch sailors, but also to the Norsemen's pastoral vision of the New World, "Vinland the Good."[34] This sharpens the grim contrast between the practices of virtue and patterns of family near the end of the twentieth century and the dreams that existed previously—specifically the closeness of the "family society" that existed in America's past.

Zoyd's aspiration connects him to the people who founded our nation. For the colonists and their forebears in England, the family was considered "the little commonwealth." Families and the great houses that symbolized their importance are part of the American tradition.[35] The family was a way of imposing "a meaningful order upon reality."[36] The family unit was vitally important economically and socially in making decisions ranging from buying land to choosing marriage partners.[37] In the late eighteenth century, according to Daniel Smith, concern about children grew. Particularly for the well-to-do, families became the "centerpiece of . . . attention and affection as childhood was perceived as a distinct stage of life characterized by innocence, delightful 'prattling,' and the growth of an individual identity" (286).

Frenesi's abandonment of Prairie at a young age, occasionally seeing her at family reunions, is a far cry from this ideal. Frenesi leaves Zoyd for Brock Vond, engages in several other love affairs, and then marries Flash. As for hopes with regard to marriage, the narrator's comment is significant: "Marriage and Justin and the years had brought her no closer to Flash" (354). Frenesi's erratic activities form a good deal of the humor in the novel, but underlying that humor is a sense of entropic decline. The deflation of the family is a metaphor for the whole of society; our society lost great adventurers and gained passive Tube-watchers and spiritually uncommitted wanderers.

In Pynchon's absurdist novel Prairie and Zoyd finally meet with Frenesi at the annual reunion. The setting is pastoral, but we soon find out that the content turns all into an absurd quest. Prairie and Zoyd travel to the reunion with hopes for family. They attend even though Prairie is upset over the history of Frenesi, and Zoyd is depressed over Frenesi's rejection. The meetings of Zoyd and Prairie with Frenesi are fraught with black humor.

At the Traverse–Becker "wingding," Prairie finally sees her mother: "a woman about forty, who had been a girl in a movie, and behind its cameras and lights, heavier than Prairie expected, sun damage in her face." Sasha, Prairie's grandmother, is "giddy with her own daughter's return" and thus tries to "clown them through it" (367). She pinches the cheeks of Prairie, calls her "adorable," and then commands that she sing the theme from Gilligan's Island for Frenesi. The recollections Sasha brings up, like so many recollections in the novel, relate to the TV: "First time she ever noticed the Tube, remember, Frenesi? A tiny thing, less than four months old—'Gilligan's Island' was on, Prairie, and your eyes may've been a little unfocused yet, but you sat there, so serious, and watched the whole thing" (368). The contrast between Prairie's desire for something meaningful and the inane conversation turns all to farce. Prairie's appeal to her mother for help gets no response. There is a "profusion of aunts, uncles, cousins, and cousins' kids and so on," each telling a story and then "waving corncobs in the air, dribbling soda on their shirts, swaying or dancing to the music of Billy Barf and the Vomitones" (368).

In Pynchon's first novel *V.*, Hugh Godolphin quests for the Edenic land Vheissu, where he once sees splendid spider monkeys that are "iridescent" and "change color in the sunlight" (155). He searches for the land again and again until the quest finally ends in horror, at a lonely place, where he sees, "perfectly preserved, its fur still rainbow-colored [. . .] the corpse of one of their spider monkeys [. . .] a mockery of life." "If Eden was the creation of God," ponders Godolphin, "God only knows what evil created Vheissu" (189-90).

This is a fanciful tale, one that stresses the loss of an Edenic wilderness and the estrangement of man from nature. In *Vineland*, Pynchon's message is more ambiguous. One reason for the ambiguity is that the plot moves so swiftly from one scene to the next that the reader has difficulty keeping up with the eye of the camera. Another reason for the ambiguity is that Pynchon seems to encourage the reader to believe that the book ends positively.

The word *home* closes the novel; there is togetherness that includes Zoyd, Prairie, Frenesi, Sasha, and also their dog Desmond, who believes he is home; and the setting is pastoral; Prairie goes off by herself and sleeps until dawn in the meadow. Nearby are "deer and cows grazing together [. . .] sun blinding in the cobwebs on the wet grass, a redtail hawk in an updraft soaring above the ridgeline, Sunday morning about to unfold" (385).

However, the reader feels jostled by contradictory actions and by Pynchon's shifts between the serious and the comic and also between a high and a low style.[38] There is a conflict between the pastoral setting for the Traverse–Becker "wingding" and the inane TV conversations of its participants. This is accentuated by Prairie's almost embarrassing desire to connect with Frenesi in a meaningful way and their vapid, incommunicative dialogue. It also is underlined by Zoyd's eager anticipation of being with family and its deflation as he finds himself "trying to help [Frenesi's] Flash with the shock of meeting so many in-laws in one place" (371). Such crude inconsistencies are brought to bear on *fourteen-year-old* Prairie's comment on her mother: "I can see why you guys [Zoyd and Flash] married her" (375). All this adds a contradictory harsh tone.

The shifts from the serious to the comic and from a high to a low tone in *Vineland* are presented as a tour de force in the Mafia wedding scene. Here a concentration of evil is developed that is diametrically opposed to the idealistic wedding day that Zoyd remembers and whose conversations are much harsher and more violent than the incommunicative dialogues of the Traverse–Becker family reunion. The Mafia reception is one that moves between the threat of Uzi submachine guns and the prayers in the nuptial Mass. It is on an opulent estate, with a wealth of lush vegetation—fruit trees (olive, apricot, peach) and all kinds of flowers ("plantations of jasmine, spilling like bridal lace")—all in honor of the bride; but there is a great need to *protect* the bride "from such possible unlucky omens as blood on the wedding cake" (92, 97). The lavishly prepared reception for mobster Ralph Wayvone's daughter is one in which there is danger of losing an Italian flavor because, ironically enough, it relies on Billy Barf and the Vomitones, who have little knowledge of Italian songs or opera. With sardonic humor, the narrator points out the romantic family concerns of the Mafia boss Ralph Wayvone who "liked, and was genuinely attentive to, the platoons of children who always showed up at family gatherings like the one today" (92).

The primary tone at the novel's close is that of a fallen world. The novel begins with blue jays bothering the dog Desmond and ends with their demise. At the end, Desmond is in the meadow, smiling, but he has blue-jay feathers in his mouth. At the end, Brock, too, is dead and is ferried off to the underworld.[39] Before Brock dies, however, he meets Prairie and tries to lure her, asserting: "I'm your father. Not Wheeler—me. Your real Dad" (376). Oddly enough (well, not "rilly" odd), after Prairie leaves Brock, she ruminates over him, indicating that she, like her mother, finds him very seductive:

She lay in her sleeping bag, trembling, face up, with the alder and the Sitka spruce still dancing in the wind, and the stars thickening overhead. "You can come back," she whispered, waves of cold sweeping over her. [. . .] "Take me anyplace you want." [. . .] The small meadow shimmered in the starlight, and her promises grew more extravagant as she drifted into the lucid thin layer of waking dreaming. (384)

American dreams and their loss provide the background for the ironic quests of Prairie and her father Zoyd who, in his eccentric way, has more sensitivity and deep feeling than anyone else in the novel. Zoyd's nostalgia for the primordial beauty of his wedding day—a day of new beginnings—reinforces, on a personal level, the desire to celebrate the transcendental meaning inherent in the beginning of a new nation, whose unsullied beauty is evoked by the novel's title. With grim humor, the novel retells the tale of "the beginning and the end, the first and the last" (Revelation 22:13)—reinterpreted as the tale of the American dream and its loss.

ACKNOWLEDGMENT

The author wishes to thank Kevin Robert Swed for his research assistance.

NOTES

[1]Albert Camus, *The Myth of Sisyphus,* trans. Justin O'Brien (New York: Random House, 1955), 37.

[2]Page references from the following editions of Pynchon's novels will be placed parenthetically in the text: *The Crying of Lot 49* (Philadelphia: Lippincott, 1966); *Gravity's Rainbow* (New York: Viking, 1973); *V.* (1963; New York: Bantam, 1968); *Vineland* (Boston: Little, Brown, 1990). I have discussed *V.* and *Gravity's Rainbow* in *The Contemporary American Comic Epic: The Novels of Barth, Pynchon, Gaddis and Kesey* (Detroit: Wayne State University Press, 1989), 79-110.

[3]Magnus Magnusson and Hermann Pálsson, trans., *The Vineland Sagas: The Norse Discovery of America* (Middlesex, England: Penguin Books, 1987), 93. The editors cite the text of Haukshók for this phrase.

[4]See John Barth's comments on his own method: Alan Prince, "An Interview with John Barth," *Prism* [Sir George Williams University] (Spring 1968): 48.

[5]See Morris Dickstein's description of such a figure in "Black Humor and History: Fiction in the Sixties," *Partisan Review* 43.2 (1976): 188-89.

[6]Joseph Campbell, *The Power of Myth,* ed. Betty Sue Flowers (New York: Doubleday, 1988), 18, xiv.

[7]*The Compact Edition of the Oxford English Dictionary Complete Text Reproduced Micrographically* (Oxford: Oxford University Press, 1981). Subsequent references will be cited as *OED*.

[8]Robert Thompson refers to the well-known concept "a family is a little commonwealth, and a commonwealth is a great family" in *Women in Stuart England and America: A Comparative Study* (London: Routledge & Kegan Paul, 1974), 135.

[9]The connection with the first territory discovered in America and the last American frontier—northern California—is underlined by the narrator's reference to the map of Vineland, which locates the mythical city in Humboldt

County of which Eureka and Arcata are also a part. To the south is Mendo-cino; to the north is Del Norte. The territory referred to on the Vinland Map, on the other hand, has been the subject of controversy for years. The map, housed in Yale's Beineke library, was the subject of scholarly conferences, books, and articles. An examination of its ink proved the map to be a forgery. See David Woodward, "The Manuscript, Engraved, and Typographic Tradi-tions of Map Lettering," in David Woodward, ed., *Art and Cartography: Six Historical Essays* (Chicago: University of Chicago Press, 1987), 174, 238, n1. The author points out that though "this map is a twentieth-century fabrica-tion, the identification of the lettering as genuine [. . .] has still to be challenged in print." See also F. Donald Logan, *The Vikings in History* (Lon-don: Hutchinson, 1983), 105-11. For further discussion of the issue, see R. A. Skelton, Thomas E. Marston, and George D. Painter, *The Vinland Map and the Tarter Relation* (New Haven: Yale University Press, 1965); and Wilcomb E. Washburn, ed., *Proceedings of the Vinland Map Conference* (Chicago: University of Chicago Press, 1971).

[10]F. Scott Fitzgerald, *The Great Gatsby: The Authorized Text* (New York: Collier Books, 1992), 189.

[11]Brad Leithauser, "Any Place You Want," *New York Review of Books*, 15 March 1990, 7. Leithauser, however, argues that the style of *Vineland* lacks the beauty to sustain a comparison with Nick's passage. For Salman Rushdie, on the other hand, the style is exciting—"the balance between light and dark is expertly held throughout this novel," and in *Vineland* Pynchon "come[s] triumphantly home": "Still Crazy After All These Years," *New York Times Book Review*, 14 January 1990, 26. The novel has been widely reviewed and de-bated: Edward Mendelson exclaims: "To find another novel that is as tedious, as tendentious, and as exhilarating as Thomas Pynchon's *Vineland* you have to search far back [. . .] perhaps as far as *War and Peace*": "Levity's Rainbow," *New Republic* 9 & 16 July 1990, 40; John Leonard calls the novel "a *Star Wars* for the counterculture": "The Styxties," *The Nation*, 26 February 1990, 281; Frank Kermode, surprisingly, finds much of the book a "trial of the reader's education or ingenuity": *London Review of Books*, 8 February 1990, 3; Christo-pher Walker responded to Kermode by calling *Vineland* "a brilliantly crafted, deliberately centreless comedy in which Pynchon reconciles himself with his own history": "Thomas Pynchon's 'Vineland,' " letter to the editor, *London Review of Books*, 8 March 1990, 4.

[12]Magnusson and Pálsson, esp. 59-61.

[13]Frank McConnell asserts that *Vineland* is "a brilliant reexamination of what has remained . . . the only real American theme: the proposition that if, with these principles and this continent, we cannot bring about a *truly* kind and gentle community (not the wimpish, "kinder, gentler" thing)—then we are, of all men, the most to be pitied": "Fabulous, Fabulous California," *Los Angeles Times*, 31 December 1989, 7.

[14]Similarly, in *Gravity's Rainbow*, humor is developed as the narrator indi-cates that Tyrone Slothrop, an officer in the modern military, is the "last of his [Puritan] line, and how far fallen," an absurd hero who "hangs at the bot-tom of his blood's avalanche, 300 years of western swamp-Yankees" (569, 25).

[15]Jan Harold Brunvand, *The Vanishing Hitchhiker: American Urban Legends*

and Their Meanings (New York: Norton, 1981), 98. Brunvand cites V. for having "included one of the most detailed versions of the legend" (92).

[16]In Vineland, there is a deflation of the hopes of the adventurers who migrated to northern California in the nineteenth century, not only for its rich resources in lumbering, gold mining, farming, and fishing, but also for its dazzling natural beauty and the opportunities offered by its "untrodden valleys" and uncharted wilderness, what many termed its paradisical quality. See Walter Blair and Hamlin Hill, America's Humor: From Poor Richard to Doonesbury (New York: Oxford University Press, 1978), 223.

[17]Blair and Hill, 226, 224.

[18]J. S. Holliday, The World Rushed In: The California Gold Rush Experience (New York: Simon and Schuster, 1981), 20. For a fine discussion of the history of Humboldt County, see Daniel A. Cornford, Workers and Dissent in the Redwood Empire (Philadelphia: Temple University Press, 1987), 1-75. Cornford discusses the growth of Humboldt County as a microcosm for the United States as a whole.

[19]Blair and Hill, 224.

[20]John Milton, Paradise Lost 2:561.

[21]"Thomas Pynchon's 'Vineland,' " 4 (italics added).

[22]Henri Bergson, "Laughter," in Comedy, ed. Wylie Sypher (1956; Baltimore: Johns Hopkins University Press, 1980), 84.

[23]Thomas Hobbes, The Elements of Law, Natural and Politic, ed. Ferdinand Tonnies (Cambridge, Mass.: Cambridge University Press, 1928), 32.

[24]Bergson, 97.

[25]This calls to mind the violence outside the 1968 Democratic convention in Chicago, violence that was shown on TV.

[26]Wolfgang Kayser, The Grotesque in Art and Literature, trans. Ulrich Weisstein (New York: McGraw-Hill, 1966), 187-88.

[27]John Ruskin, "Grotesque Renaissance," in The Stones of Venice, The Works of John Ruskin, ed. E. T. Cook and Alexander Wedderburn (London: George Allen, 1904), 11:151.

[28]She realizes that she has taken an "irreversible step" and begins to feel that she is "walking around next to herself, haunting herself" (237).

[29]Campbell, 18. See also Dale Pollock, who says that George Lucas conceived of Vader as "more of a machine than a man; his incredible strength and armored visage made him the perfect symbol of rapacious technology. Vader had to be terrifying, but still a man—Lucas insisted that his characters remain human": Skywalking: The Life and Films of George Lucas (New York: Harmony Books, 1983), 144. I wish to point out that technology is not consistently sinister, however. In The Empire Strikes Back, Luke Skywalker loses his hand in battle and it is replaced with a mechanical wonder. This mechanical part, for Luke, is not a symptom of depravity.

[30]Jan Harold Brunvand, The Choking Doberman and Other "New" Urban Legends (New York: Norton, 1984), 80.

[31]See Otto Friedrich, "New Age Harmonies," Time, 7 December 1987, 63; see also Richard Blow, "Moronic Convergence: The Moral and Spiritual Emptiness of New Age," New Republic, 25 January 1988, 74-76, and Ted Peters, "Discerning the Spirits of the New Age," Christian Century, 32 August-7 Sep-

tember 1988, 763-66. For a fascinating exploration of the era of the sixties
and its emphasis on mystical traditions of the East, see Fritjof Capra, *Uncommon Wisdom: Conversations with Remarkable People* (New York: Simon and
Schuster, 1988).

³²*OED*. See Dwight Goddard, *A Buddhist Bible: The Favorite Scriptures of the
Zen Sect* (Thetford, Vermont: Dwight Goddard Publisher, 1932), 25-27;
Walpola Sri Rahula, "The Buddhist Attitude of Mind," in *What Buddha Taught*
(New York: Grove Press, 1959), 1-15.

³³See Daisetz Teitaro Suzuki, *Studies in the Lankavatara Sutra* (London:
George Routledge & Sons, 1930).

³⁴Magnusson and Pálsson, 93.

³⁵See Thompson, 134. For further discussion, see J. A. Leo Lemay, *Robert
Bolling Woos Anne Miller: Love and Courtship in Colonial Virginia, 1760* (Charlottesville: University of Virginia Press, 1990), 10-13, 32-34, and passim;
Daniel Blake Smith, *Inside the Great House: Planter Family Life in Eighteenth-Century Chesapeake Society* (Ithaca: Cornell University Press, 1980); Jan Lewis, *The
Pursuit of Happiness: Family and Values in Jefferson's Virginia* (Cambridge: Cambridge University Press, 1983).

³⁶Lewis, xvi.

³⁷Particularly informative is Smith, 281-99.

³⁸I agree with Edward Mendelson's praise of Pynchon: "No other American writer moves so smoothly and swiftly between the extremes of high and
low style, or accommodates so generously the shrill patois of the valley girl
and the rotundities of Emerson" (41).

³⁹The narrator reports: "Across the river Brock could see lights, layer after
layer. [. . .] 'They'll take out your bones,' Vato explained. 'The bones have to
stay on this side. The rest of you goes over. You look a lot different, and you
move funny for a while, but they say you'll adjust. Give these third-worlders a
chance, you know, they can be a lotta fun' " (379-80).

Communication, Group Theory, and Perception in Vineland

Joseph W. Slade

10:30 P.M. (13-[PBS]) "Nabokov on Kafka." A
half-hour reenactment of a lecture at Cornell
University by Vladimir Nabokov on "The Meta-
morphosis"; with Christopher Plummer. (Re-
broadcast)   —New York Times, 31 May 1990

FANS of *Gravity's Rainbow*, dazzled by a narrative given texture by the litter of Thayer's Slippery Elm Throat Loz-
enges packages and Kreml Hair Tonic bottles on Tyrone
Slothrop's wartime London desk, are less likely to be
impressed with the Froot Loops cereal, Ninja lore, and designer
bottled waters scattered throughout *Vineland*. The artifacts in the earlier novel, made resonant by the romanticism of the blitz, seem fragments of history; *Vineland'*s artifacts, however appropriate to a culture comfortable with Ronald Reagan and Shirley MacLaine, appear
slight by comparison. To such readers, *Vineland* may be too trendy,
the fictional equivalent of recent movies like *Running on Empty* (1989)
and *Flashback* (1990), which are similarly concerned with the
thwarted promise of the American sixties. Pynchon does mix in some
bits of classic popular culture, like the mythological allusions to Pluto
and Proserpine, which add weight to the adventures of Brock Vond
and Frenesi Gates in the underworld, but the references to television shows like *Gilligan's Island, Jeopardy, Star Trek,* and *The Brady
Bunch* are numerous enough to turn off academic audiences. Assuming that *Vineland* reduces to a hackneyed insistence on the homog-
enizing effects of television on culture, even newspaper reviewers dis-
miss the book's fanciful examples of media trivialization—"Woody
Allen in *Young Kissinger*" or "Pee-wee Herman in *The Robert Musil
Story*"—as cheap jokes. As always, however, fact can make Pynchon's
humor seem mild: PBS's "real" re-creation of a lecture by one of
Pynchon's own teachers—cited above—indicates that not even the
icons of high culture can escape the appetites of an information

economy. Pynchon is too aware of the writer's complicity in this economy to be more than occasionally churlish about Tubal syndromes, and *Vineland*'s own rapid recycling of recent history, though hardly in the same league as the operations of electronic media, is part of its assessment of our present.

The question for many readers nevertheless remains whether a work so grounded in popular culture can support the themes that have earned Pynchon admiration in the past. The quest for *Vineland*'s goddess lacks the pacing of earlier Pynchonian chases, perhaps because he feared that a kinetic narrative would in this case too closely resemble a television melodrama—though one could argue in a general sense that the electronic medium, with its oddball rhythms and improbable juxtapositions, has shaped his fiction as much as any other influence. The characters in *Vineland* display the paranoid tropes of their predecessors: the fear of psychological, corporate, and state control; the sensitivity to messages and codes; the quasi-religious obsession with worlds that intersect; the struggle against the guilt that freights psyches; the search for "higher order variables" that survive transformations of life and death. Dramatizing paranoia on the global scale of *Gravity's Rainbow* enabled Pynchon to indict Western culture itself for crimes committed in the name of angelic flight. As he has since announced in occasional bulletins such as "Is It OK to Be a Luddite?" (1984), however, the dangers posed by the Information Age are almost as profound as those of an age we used to call atomic. The threat implicit in *Vineland* is not the destruction of a planet but the Frankensteinian transformation of a whole culture. Behind the references to game shows and sitcoms, behind the malls filled with "New Age mindbarf," behind Ronald Reagan's "snoozy fantasy" (354) of America, lies a renascent fascist state.

Vineland is set in the United States and Japan, the world's two most advanced information economies. The "silicon wars" of the seventies offer few revelations so sinister as the patent exchanges between General Electric and I. G. Farben in the thirties; and the "faceless predators" who haunt the novel, their connections with South Africa notwithstanding, have little of the historically documented menace of ITT. History is nevertheless at issue here. For *Gravity's Rainbow*, Pynchon chose a metaphorical cusp of history, when the chaos of world war not only loosened the hold of rationalized control but also fostered the advent of a marvelous new technology, then traced the routinization of that technology by rapidly restructured commercial and political forces. For *Vineland*, he chooses a similar moment. This time the "second chance" for America is the "sex, drugs, and rock and roll" revolution of the sixties and seventies led by students appalled at American materialism in general and the Vietnamese war in particular. Those events, in turn, coincide with the technological shift from movies to television, which came into its own when John F. Kennedy attributed his presidential victory to the new "gadget" (Barnouw, 277).

What happened to the rocket happens to television; an instrument for change becomes an instrument of the status quo. The inventors of the rocket in Pynchon's third novel were guided by dreams of escaping gravity, of breaking down national borders, of achieving new knowledge—abstractions easily perverted by the Nazis and the supranational corporations and political bureaucracies who inherited the missile, wedded it to the atomic bomb, and transformed it into a permanent threat hung over the planet. Similarly, idealistic young Americans were enthusiastic over the power of television to expose political or economic malfeasance ("The whole world is watching!") and to reset social agendas (on civil rights, poverty, and peace). The medium seemed endowed with a democratic potential not unlike the promise associated with space flight. These hopes are cherished by the documentary filmmakers of *Vineland*, who believe in cinema verité, "the 24-frame-per-second truth" (241), an abstraction just as easily thwarted by a corporate state impatient with "too much math, too many abstract ideas" (240).

A historian of American broadcasting working along similar lines might point to the crucial years between 1963 and 1971. Before 1963, networks fielded their own crews to gather news. In that year, however, ABC aired David Wolper's *The Making of the President*, a documentary on the presidential election of 1960. The other networks followed suit by broadcasting various documentaries of increasing liberality, made by independent filmmakers—as opposed to videographers, whose cameras were still nowhere near as good—with an almost euphoric passion for capturing the shortcomings of the Great Society. This experiment in diversity was abruptly halted when an enraged Congress reacted by holding hearings in 1971 on *The Selling of the Pentagon*, with various subcommittees demanding outtakes and records (Sterling and Kittross, 412-13). Thereafter the industry refused to air material from independents, and it limited documentary work to network crews closely monitored to ensure bland programming. But Pynchon starts farther back in the history of visual media, with patterns that began in the forties when East Coast banks gained control of the Hollywood studios, a parallel to tracing corporate control of the rocket to the chemical cartels of the thirties in *Gravity's Rainbow*. That Ronald Reagan was an important figure in the labor racketeering and corporate machinations that suppressed diversity in the movie industry allows Pynchon to suggest the dimensions of establishment power. This train of events shapes the persona of *Vineland's* Frenesi Gates, a guerrilla filmmaker who is also the daughter of industry radicals who struggled against corporate efforts to gut the Hollywood unions.

As *Vineland* depicts events, the government represses the unrest at the College of the Surf with surveillance, provocateurs, and concentration camps. Over time, however, electronic media defuse outrage by distorting revolutionary messages that were none too well coded to begin with. As Isaiah tells Zoyd, the "minute the Tube got hold of you folks that was it, the whole alternative America, el deado meato" (373). Video supersedes film, recycles the older medium, and extends its grasp over the culture by means of the cable systems whose tentacles reach even into rural areas (319). Diverse, novel, or radical ideas become lost in the enormous traffic of programs whose content is "a timeless, defectively imagined future of zero-tolerance drug-free Americans all pulling their weight and all locked in the official economy, inoffensive music, endless family specials on the Tube, church all week long, and, on special days, for extra-good behavior, maybe a cookie" (222). At the beginning of *Vineland*, federal agencies keep tabs on troublemakers by sending them government checks. By the novel's end, television has rendered that expense unnecessary. Bureaucrats in Washington refuse to continue funding detention centers for flower children, says Hector Zuñiga, because "they did a study, found out since about '81 kids were comín in all on their own askín about careers, no need for no separate facility anymore" (347).

Communication shapes culture, which, like all functioning systems, is structured by hierarchies of information channels. Hierarchies govern a system by organizing, programming, distributing, and monitoring the flow of information within and without; that is what *control* means. Communication ordinarily helps maintain a healthy balance between order and change, so that the system remains stable but also flexible, or, in the case of a culture, tolerant of diversity. Put another way, culture is a processor of messages in many different codes: in processing, it determines meaning, again on a hierarchical basis, assigning greater value to some messages than to others. The highest value should be assigned to messages that are not wholly redundant, because only those messages can provide useful information about the system. That is the principal premise of information theory, a discipline that grew out of the thermodynamics that has fascinated Pynchon for so long. In a highly rationalized culture such as Protestant America, however, hierarchies—the political and economic equivalents are bureaucracies—select messages for redundancy. Given the sheer volume of messages in our television culture, "the ever-dwindling attention span of an ever more infantilized population" (52) may not be up to the task of sorting information from redundancy.

According to information theorists, we "know" the world of matter and energy only through information about them. Knowing is dependent on symbolic representation, and representations are our most primal technologies, whether coded as language or as image. Although many of Pynchon's characters hope that there is a ("direct" and "epileptic") reality apart from representation, it is rare, perhaps impossible, to apprehend it in its unmediated state. If there is a Nature that persists beneath or beyond representation, then it must be apprehended in some other way, when "message[s] from beyond" (124) intrude "accidentally." For Pynchon's paranoids, of course, such messages might not be accidental at all, might just as well be programmed by someone or something seeking to control them. Deciding which messages contain "real" information, deciding how to interpret them, and deciding how to act on them are for Pynchon the most pressing of human issues; and they surface again and again in *Vineland.*

The problem, as deconstructionists are fond of insisting, is that all ways of knowing—scientific, artistic, technological—are inherently vulnerable to distortion. Language and image are both self-reflexive, that is, they constitute environments in which the medium is message. These environments enculturate—or program—those who live in them. Although *Gravity's Rainbow* dealt with both language and movies, it gave priority to the former. Blicero strove to penetrate a reality shrouded by the rationalized structures of language, just as other characters searched for a Word that cosmically antedates, metaphysically precedes, and epistemologically stands apart from mere words. In *Vineland,* the most important characters lust for the reality beyond images. Like Blicero, Brock Vond tries to penetrate representation to quotidian levels of life and death. In both cases the goal is legitimate, but in both the means are perverted because they lead to the deaths of human beings. The most committed deconstructionists in both novels are fascists, a syndrome that reflects the modern origins of that philosophical method in the work of the Nazi sympathizers Martin Heidegger and Paul de Man. Vond's obsession corrupts Frenesi, mistress of film technology, just as surely as the same desire corrupted Blicero, master of the rocket.

In some ways, visual imagery is more insidious than language, because it seems more "real." Individual words can be decoupled from the reality they represent (there need be no chair for the word to signify it) and can be combined and recombined endlessly into abstractions. Images are more limited in terms of the distance between the object and the picture of it; images are direct representations of things and cannot be entirely decoupled or divorced from them. For that reason, it is not true that a picture is worth a thousand words. Images carry less *meaningful* information than words because they cannot be combined to the same levels of complexity. Despite their supposed fidelity of reproduction, they are bloodless surrogates. Television, our dominant visual medium, is also our most redundant. The criticism most often leveled at television genres is that they shape human relationship and aspirations and glamorize their value as entertainment. Pynchon works variations on that charge by having his characters identify, more or less harmlessly, with Mr. Spock or the detectives of *Hawaii Five-O;* even the son of a Mafia don in *Vineland* wants to be in show business. But the real threat, as Pynchon sees it, is more serious.

Like Marshall McLuhan's *Understanding Media*, one of Pynchon's major influences, *Vineland* deals with the difficulties of establishing and maintaining genuine human relationships in a culture in which the electronic medium mimics community. At the same time, he reminds his readers that there *are* other channels that *do* offer authentic communication.

Generally speaking, the more physical the channel, the more Pynchon prizes it. Basketball is one of these because the game combines playful expertise and bouncing balls, a favorite Pynchonian device—also manifest in the pachinko balls associated with DL. By training her body and senses according to Ninja precepts, Darryl Louise Chastain achieves the kind of individual control that can counter the state control of minds appropriate to a state in the year 1984. Mind and muscles communicate so well that she can slip, virtually invisible, through official barriers. Forced to try to assassinate Vond by the Mafia, whose only virtue is its sense of rivalry with other arms of the Establishment ("we're a wholly-owned subsidiary" [93], the Mob boss

Ralph Wayvone tells his son), DL misuses her power in the episode of the Vibrating Palm. She does penance by apprenticing herself to her victim, Takeshi Fumimota—presumably the kamikaze of *Gravity's Rainbow*, now a Der Springer-type fixer with some immunity from corporate control—and by serving as mentor to Prairie Wheeler, the "teenage charismatic" (111) whose name unites the twin symbols of Earth and Fortuna (Fortune's Wheel, or chance) that are constants in Pynchon's fiction.

DL can also sing, a form of communication that, like dance, is touched with a "grace" almost magical. When Frenesi Gates is reunited with her mother Sasha, they are said to jitterbug together (352), and even Hector Zuñiga, in some respects Frenesi's alter ego (as Hecate is another aspect of Proserpine), insists on mamboing and cha-chaing with Frenesi in Las Vegas to persuade her of his sincerity (350). Music embodies human longing. World War II turns Sasha Traverse (the name suggests angles at variance to officialdom), the young revolutionary, into a torch singer, and in singing she learns to see injustices "more directly, not as world history, or anything too theoretical, but as humans, usually male, living here on the planet, often well within reach, committing these crimes, major and petty, one by one against other living humans" (80). Obsessed with his ex-wife, the rock musician Zoyd Wheeler dreams of reestablishing contact with Frenesi through a TV commercial for an album of torch songs called *Not Too Mean to Cry* that might reach her late at night (36). Rock and roll unites music and dance in what for Pynchon is the sovereign form of communication for radicals, its rhythms those of love and rebelliousness; the Thanatoids (themselves reduced, virtually, to television images) do not care for it (225). The People's Republic of Rock and Roll created by the radicals of the College of the Surf does not last long, of course, and the paranoid Mucho Maas (who, since his first appearance in *The Crying of Lot 49*, has come to head Indolent Records, a firm known for its bad taste) fears that the genre will go the way of all miraculous forms of communication, its charisma routinized in a flood of data that overwhelms and secularizes. The volume of messages deadens not just the senses but also spiritual hopes for immortality:

They just let us forget. Give us too much to process, fill up every minute, keep us distracted, it's what the Tube is for, and though it kills me to say it, it's what rock and roll is becoming—just another way to claim our attention, so that beautiful certainty we had starts to fade, and after a while they have us convinced all over again that we really are going to die. (314)

Sexual intercourse, the most physical and affectionate of all forms of communication—and terrific for DL and Takeshi, once their abstinence ends—is also susceptible to distortion, especially when used as an instrument by someone like Brock Vond, who fears it. Linked on the one hand with birth, on the other with death (*la petite mort*), sex is a quasi-divine channel. The problem is that its stimuli can be so easily programmed. Frenesi responds, as does her mother, to images of official control; they both find uniforms exciting, like those on the cop shows Frenesi enjoys masturbating to. Brock himself makes Frenesi into a sadomasochistic fetish, but his most outrageous perversion calls for repressive official intimacy:

Brock Vond's genius was to have seen in the activities of the sixties left not threats to order but unacknowledged desires for it. While the Tube was proclaiming youth revolution against parents of all kinds and most viewers were accepting this story, Brock saw the deep—if he'd allowed himself to feel it, the sometimes touching—need to stay children forever, safe inside some extended national Family. The hunch he was betting on was that these kid rebels, being halfway there already, would be easy to turn and cheap to develop. They'd only been listening to the wrong music, breathing the wrong smoke, admiring the wrong personalities. They needed some reconditioning. (269).

The numerous references to a paternalistic state are contrasted to actual families, some pretty good, like Zoyd Wheeler (the classic Pynchon schlemiel, also associated with the unpredictability of Fortune's turning wheel), his daughter, and their dog Desmond, or the generations of Becker–Traverses, a loose and quarreling federation that cherishes its own chaos, the only kind of community, Pynchon implies, that is worthy of the name. The book's most lyrical passages describe their annual gathering in Vineland to honor the persistence of love, "the bond between Eula Becker and Jess Traverse, that lay beneath, defined, and made sense of them all" (369). The Becker–Traverses watch television, which is so ubiquitous as to be unavoidable, but they also forage on the land, horse around a lot, and play Crazy Eights—a game of chance. The Becker–Traverses have kept their faith, however attenuated by time and television, in Emerson's version of karmic retribution and in the moral obligation to oppose corporate control. The residue of that faith, rather than forgiveness of sin, "redeems" Frenesi when she refuses to cross a picket line. "You a good child" (352), says a picket coordinator to a Proserpine thus partly "saved" by her parents.

The images of ersatz domesticity broadcast by television nevertheless usually subvert authentic relationships. This is most apparent among the Thanatoids, who spend their time watching the redundancies of the Tube. Trying to form a community in Shade Creek, they can only imitate television models, like *Celebrity Roast*. Television programs recode human behavior into predictable patterns that audiences accept as desirable because they promise intimacy without pain or trouble, a syndrome particularly destructive of family bonds. Hector Zuñiga never stops talking of the family he wanted to create in the image of *I Love Lucy* with his former wife Debbi; Debbi named their television set as correspondent in the divorce. Ché tells Prairie that even the kids in prison play at being a family: "One's the Mommy, one's the Daddy, and one's the little child—hard, soft, and helpless. I figure, what's the difference, bein' in a family out here, or bein' in the joint?" (330), but she returns again and again to her worthless mother and predatory stepfather anyway. Were it a simple opposition between reality and artifice, choosing between actual and mediated intimacy would be easy. But for the most part, humans know the world only through some form of mediation; strictly speaking, there is no "reality" apart from messages in some code, transmitted by some channel. Only the strongest and bravest, like DL, herself the child of an unhappy family, can accept "entanglement in the world [. . .] with the past as well, and the crimes behind the world, the thousand bloody arroyos in the hinterlands of time that stretched somberly inland from the honky-tonk coast of Now" (180).

The usual effect of television's mediation, then, is alienation. A friend of Frenesi's son Justin says that dealing with parents is easy: "Pretend there's a frame around 'em like the Tube, pretend they're a show you're watching. You can go into it if you want, or you can just watch, and *not* go into it" (351). Even where characters can still care for each other, they are confused as to how to express feeling, as when Sasha, trying to reunite Prairie with Frenesi, insists that her grandchild sing the theme song from *Gilligan's Island*.

The most extreme example of alienation is Brock Vond, who, like most of Pynchon's sinister figures, wishes to find a "reality" that exists beyond language or image, one that he thinks can be seized through power. For Vond, images, even those that can be manipulated, are "not enough" (239). For him, only death is "real," and his engineering of Weed Atman's killing, first through conditioning by a "reality-dentist" (240), then by setting up his death as a media event, is intimately connected with his *possession* of Frenesi. Ironically, Weed returns as a Thanatoid, for such are information technologies that they can loose upon a culture images of its dead, mockeries perhaps of the spiritual immortality that Pynchon's characters want so desperately to believe in, *or*, simply and poignantly, just data remembered, as rebukes to sin: "What was a Thanatoid, at the end of the long dread day, but memory?" (325). Ironically also, Brock finds that "he loved Frenesi but did not possess her, and was driven to fetishism in faraway countries as his only outlet" (141), obsessed by her image.

But he tries to control that image, to keep it *his*, unmediated by convention. In his Plutonic rage he tells Zoyd he does not want his Dark Queen to be "an average, invisible tract-house mom, anchoring herself to the planet with some innocent hubby, then a baby, to keep from flying back to who she really is, her responsibilities" (300). Besides, he says, happy families are fictions of the Tube, and television will just betray them:

next thing you know, there's the three of you, out at the all-night Burger King, dribbling food, having all that fun, the basic triangle, the holy family, all together, heartwarming, hm? they make a commercial, you're all in it, you get famous, and finally that's when it comes to my attention, you see? (301)

Nor, for a time, does Frenesi want that conventional domesticity. Even after she marries Zoyd and gives birth to Prairie, she is haunted by hallucinations of Brock, who tells her that the family is a scam foisted on her by the Tube, just another example of paternalistic control: "This is how they want you, an animal, a bitch with swollen udders lying in the dirt, surrendered," a form of captivity galling to a romantic rebel once "privileged to live outside of Time, to enter and leave at will, looting and manipulating, weightless, invisible" (287). Neither Brock nor Frenesi will endure control passively. Though his class and naked ambition disqualify him (276), Brock wants to rise to the upper levels of bureaucracy, to the real thrones of power. Frenesi, says DL, never "deliberately chose anything" (266) in her desire to escape responsibilities; she just wants to be an objective filmmaker, an uninvolved observer, content with the power that comes from detached documentation of events, which for Pynchon is an untenable moral position.

Brock is not alone in his search for a reality that transcends images. Most of the characters, spiritually hungry and frequently paranoid, try to read signs, faces, and patterns as evidence of "alternative worlds" whose configurations either confirm their fears or—and it sometimes comes to the same thing—promise meaning. If their mysticism seems more demented than traditional, it is probably well to remember that Pynchon is writing about a present in which sizable numbers of Americans really do engage in "channeling" with dead ancestors. Some of the scenes, like the story of the children meeting in dreams (223), are touched by the magic realism doubtless borrowed from favorite Latin American authors, while others, like the astral projections with which Zoyd tries to visit Frenesi, are rendered more straightforwardly. All of them exhibit the sympathy that Pynchon brings to the human need to find comfort and revelation where one can.

At first, drugs, like mystic visions, seem an obvious alternative to official communication channels. At his daughter's birth, Zoyd Wheeler drops acid "on the chance of glimpsing something cosmic that might tell him he wouldn't die" (285). Zoyd is vulnerable to government control because he is a known doper, but as much as anyone else in the novel he retains his integrity, though he has to pay for it with the buffoonery that institutionalizes his role of schlemiel, a posture of survival in a rationalized world. Besides, his essential worth has nothing to do with narcotics, and everything to do with his capacity to love. When, looking at his sick daughter, Zoyd realizes that he "would, would have to, do anything to keep this dear small life from harm," he experiences "his belated moment of welcome to the planet Earth" (321). Because there are few drug revelations, narcotics function in the novel mostly as the symbolic baggage of the outlaw, badges of difference in an establishment dominated by yuppies, non-smokers, Republicans, and other control fetishists. Marijuana growers chant Tibetan tunes that "operationally" join northern California and "other U. S. pot-growing areas [. . . with] the third world" (49), that world—in Pynchonian parlance—being still less subject to corporate control. These and other references to drugs serve one other purpose: they set up two jokes.

The first is that the corporate establishment, attracted by the enormous profits of an underground drug economy, has not only become involved in the traffic but actually controls it, a notion that exfoliates into a vision of George Bush as drug kingpin (353-54). The second joke is that the real narcotic in *Vineland* is television. The principal addict is federal drug agent Hector Zuñiga, who commits himself to a Tubal detoxification facility, where he subverts therapy by bribing attendants to smuggle in sets or by periodically escaping. His manic efforts to shoot what he calls a movie—but which Frenesi dismisses as a television cop show (345)—full of antidrug messages are the funniest sequences in the novel.

Frenesi's involvement with film is more complex than Hector's dependence on television because her illusions are compounded of mysticism and artistic ambition. Pynchon grants the older medium greater creative power, probably because its mechanical and chemical aspects make film more physical and because its artifacts are more discrete than electronic datastreams. Throughout the narrative, he points to actual films with production dates, implicitly contrasting them with the fanciful, formulaic made-for-television movies. Besides, the frames shot by Frenesi *do* convey some truth, enough to provide Prairie with insight into her mother and enough to convince the government that the footage must be destroyed. But in Pynchon's world, no technology remains pure.

Having listened to her mother's description of history as a "movie script," Frenesi crafts her own metaphor linking film and life:

> Frenesi had absorbed politics all through her childhood, but later, seeing older movies on the Tube with her parents, making for the first time a connection between the far-off images and her real life, it seemed she had misunderstood everything, paying too much attention to the raw emotions, the easy conflicts, when something else, some finer Drama the Movies had never considered ennobling, had been unfolding all the time. (81-82)

That drama is humanity's, which she construes as something transcendent, "saintly" (118), a romantic revolutionary idea

> of a mysterious people's oneness, drawing together toward the best chances of light, achieved once or twice that she's seen in the street, in short, timeless bursts, all paths, human and projective, true, the people in a single presence, the police likewise simple as a moving blade—and individuals who in meetings might only bore or be pains in the ass here suddenly being seen to transcend, almost beyond will to move smoothly between baton and victim to take the blow instead, to lie down on the tracks as the iron rolled in or look into the gun muzzle and retain the power of speech— (117-18)

Because it is a conception of a mass that denies individuality, her vision of the People is as flawed as a fascist's vision of the State; neither provides for the diversity that makes for healthy community. Worse, in contributing to her stance as detached artist, romanticism separates her from her fellows, even from the little family that is 24fps. Frenesi's "dangerous vice" is to pretend "that she was on her own, with no legal history, no politics, only an average California chick, invisible, poised at life's city limits, for whom anything was still possible" (236). After she has betrayed Weed Atman, Frenesi retreats into a film metaphor as a way of dealing with guilt, as if "she was walking around next to herself, haunting herself, attending a movie of it all. If the step was irreversible, then she ought to be all right now, safe in a world-next-to-the-world that not many would know how to get to, where she could kick back and watch the unfolding drama" (237).

Film metaphors also preoccupy others. The ongoing debate among the members of the 24fps ensemble "was over the claims of film against those of 'real life.' Would it be necessary someday for one of them to die for a piece of film? One that might never even get used?" (202). Bolder yet are the members of the Death to the Pig Nihilist Film Kollective, which attempts to live out "the metaphor of movie camera as weapon" (197). For the Nihilists, "A camera is a gun. An image taken is a death performed. Images put together are the substructure of an afterlife and a Judgment. We will be architects of a just Hell for the fascist pig. Death to everything that oinks!" (197).

Architecture seems a strange ambition for Nihilists, though the group is no odder than the Harleyite Order of male motorcycle nuns, who also have a version of hell. In fact, lots of characters lay claim to hell, a conceit that Pynchon first began playing with in *Gravity's Rainbow;* in a fully rationalized world, the impulse to control seeks new colonies to imperialize. The Tube, by recoding everything into a bland datastream, extends the meaning of "death-in-life," the condition that overtook so many characters in *Gravity's Rainbow;* in mediating events, the communication channels that shape a culture suck the life from them. "Mediating death" is a way of controlling history, because to interpret images of the dead, to recast them as characters in a story, is to advance one version of the past over others.

At the same time, to claim that everything, even death, is mediated, is also a cop-out—depending on one's motives—a way of evading responsibility. In parroting the Nihilists, Frenesi avoids confessing her complicity in Weed's death to DL, though she admits that her vision of art has been naive.

Feel like we were running around like little kids with toy weapons, like the camera really was some sort of gun, gave us that kind of power. Shit. How could we lose track like that, about what was real? [. . .] And it wasn't only Weed who got offed, story going around the camp is there were others, and the FBI covered it up? So what difference did we make? Who'd we save? The minute the guns came out, all that art-of-the-cinema handjob was over. (259)

Fortunately, there is more to the novel than these slightly shopworn metaphors. Here, as in all his fiction, Pynchon's originality lies in the juxtaposition of popular culture with science. More important to those filmmakers committed to "tak[ing] their witness" (203) before history are "arguments about light that happened so often they came to seem the essence of 24fps" (201). The debates over available as opposed to artificial light and about the virtues of light as opposed to shadow resonate in the novel. Frenesi's father, "Hub" Gates (the wheel image is indicative of his integrity), admits that he "sold off my only real fortune—my precious anger—for a lot of god-damn shadows" (291), which are what movies really are. Aside from being a decent schlemiel who thus carries Pynchon's blessing, Hub is also a worshiper of light, which is associated with spiritual revelation: "Jesus, all those amps. All that light. Nobody told me about the scale of it. After a while I couldn't see that much else. I needed to work with that light" (291). Rochelle, the Head Ninjette of the Kinoichi Attentives, who has trained herself to memorize "all the shadows and how they changed, the cover, the exact spaces between things," can "impersonate" a room "in its full transparency and emptiness" (111). These and other references to light too numerous to list, from indexes of refraction (192) to "Rayleigh scattering" (282), indicate that Pynchon is alluding to modern theories of perception, particularly those associated with the perceptual psychologist James Gibson, whose students use group therapy to decode the information in light.

Gravity's Rainbow put considerable stock in the Copenhagen Interpretation of reality, the collective name for the Principles of Uncertainty and Complementarity, both of which have to do with the nature of light. According to the first, the act of observation affects the observation; according to the second, it is impossible to measure events with certainty because light, a medium of information, sometimes behaves as a particle, sometimes as a wave. Still another motif of that novel is Gödel's theorem, which maintains that in any mathematical system there must be propositions that are clearly "true" despite the impossibility of proving them by the rules of that system. In a fully rationalized, self-reflexive world, in which language itself is so inextricably a part of what is being described that it is untrustworthy, these principles and that theorem validate the limited possibilities for freedom. If paradox is real, then control—determinism—cannot be total. Metaphorically, at least, paradoxes suggest opportunities both spiritual and perceptual. Because *Vineland* is more concerned with the trustworthiness of vision, however, Pynchon looks for additional confirmation in the mathematics of sight.

The mathematical elements of *Vineland* include not only Pynchon's familiar musings on ones and zeros, either as dimensions in computer matrices or as symbols of human choice (e.g., 90-91), but also more classical references. In different scenes, the sun's rays form a "caustic" (155) (a curve to which all rays are tangent when emitted from one point and reflected or refracted from a curved solid surface); light falls in "fractal halo" (381); the rock band the Holocaust Pixels find an "attractor" (384); and Hector Zuñiga, the federal agent turned movie-maker, insists that his share of the profits from the planned *Drugs—Sacrament of the Sixties, Evil of the Eighties* must include a multiple of 2.71828, a "real natural" (342) number because it is an approximation of the *real* number e, the base for *natural* logarithms.

Among the most important mathematical references, however, are those to the theory of groups, the very foundation of modern physics—an intellectual endeavor about "as deep [. . .] as science is likely to get," as the mathematical historian James R. Newman has observed (3:1534). Group theory evolved over time through the kind of collective endeavor that appeals to Pynchon. Hermann Weyl says that "the origin of the *theory of groups* is lost in a past scarcely accessible to history; the earliest works of art show that the symmetry groups of plane figures were even then already known, though the theory of these was only given definite form in the latter part of the eighteenth and in the nineteenth centuries" (xxi). Tradition, however, assigns the invention of that modern form to Evariste Galois (1811-1832), and in *Vineland* Pynchon models a pivotal character, Weed Atman, on Galois, a radical republican killed during the upheavals that brought Louis-Phillipe to power in France in the early 1830s. Galois's is a famous story of failed rebellion and betrayal, told in versions as conflicting as those peddled by Pynchon's veterans, whose competing accounts of reality are one of *Vineland'* s major themes. When DL tries to avoid telling Prairie Wheeler about her mother's role in Atman's death by saying that the years since Prairie's birth have been "full of playin' make-believe, acting on faiths in things that sound crazy now, lying, turning each other in, too much time passed, everybody remembering a different story" (101), she could just as easily have been describing the aftermath of events in Galois's time.

Pynchon probably read about Galois first in Eric Temple Bell's *Men of Mathematics* (1937). Remembering the book himself, the physicist Freeman Dyson says that "the most memorable chapter is called 'Genius and Stupidity' and describes the life and death of the French mathematician Galois, who was killed in a duel at the age of twenty" (14). Bell's account is based in part of Paul Dupuy's "La Vie d'Evariste Galois" (1896),[1] and partly, says Tony Rothman, on Bell's own imagination. According to Rothman, the two other major accounts in English are just as romantic. These are Leopold Infeld's *Whom the Gods Love: The Story of Evariste Galois* (1948), and Fred Hoyle's chapter on Galois in *Ten Faces of the Universe* (1977). Rothman's own article, "Genius and Biographers: The Fictionalization of Evariste Galois" (1982), points out that Bell, Infeld, and Hoyle "invoke a political cause for the duel, with a mysterious coquette just off center" (84). Rothman identifies the woman, Stéphanie-Félicie Poterin Dumotel, though he knows almost nothing of her personality, thus leaving Pynchon room to create one for Frenesi Gates. If Pynchon read Rothman's account, he would doubtless have been stuck by the author's observation that the mysterious Dumotel "is an anonymous casualty of history" (100).

Bell wrote that "Galois was no 'ineffectual angel,' but even his magnificent powers were shattered before the massed stupidity aligned against him" (362). According to Bell, the young fire-eater was victimized by an originality so enormous that not even the great S. D. Poisson (whose theory of random distribution is important to *Gravity's Rainbow*) could at first understand his papers on group theory. Pynchon does not emphasize Atman's brilliance, though he does suggest that he is not good at explaining math. As Frenesi tells Atman's wife Jinx, "He tried once, but after a while he must've forgot I was there, just kept on writing equations and stuff" (211). Pynchon does stress the political naïveté that leads Brock Vond to set up Atman's death as a way of destroying the People's Republic of Rock and Roll at the College of the Surf: "Weed was the only one innocent enough, without hidden plans, with no ambitions beyond surmounting what the day brought each time around" (216).

From the various versions of Galois's life Pynchon would have learned that the mathematician was a sucker for women with blue eyes (like Frenesi's); that he was emotionally immature (as Frenesi discovers Atman is); that he was a leader of the Society for Friends of the People (as Atman is of PR³); that he was shot by a fellow revolutionary (as is Atman) as the consequence of an obscure argument in which he defended the honor of a woman who may have been carrying on simultaneous affairs with Galois and a member of the government (as Frenesi has been with Atman and Vond); that he was accused of being a government agent himself (as Atman is so charged); and, however incidentally, that cucumbers (like those in *Vineland*'s Cucumber Lounge and cucumber brandy) crop up in Infeld's biography (208). Pynchon connects Atman with Galois mostly by association, however. When Weed appears in the text, he is "preoccupied

with the darker implications of a paper on group theory he'd just
been reading" (206) and is so unaware of the political turmoil that at
first he serves as a lookout simply because he is the tallest person in
the "vicinity"—vicinity being described in humorous mathematics.
Pynchon may have called Atman ("soul") "Weed" because Galois
sounds like the name of the famous French cigarette, Gauloise, because he liked the "herbs" in the name of Galois's killer, Pescheux
d'Herbinville, or because he wanted to link the character with marijuana, though Atman is not particularly identified with the drug. As a
character whose chief function is to be betrayed, however, Atman is
subordinate to Frenesi Gates, whose parents, like Galois's, are also
revolutionaries. In other words, Pynchon altered the already confused story of Galois for his own purposes.

John S. Lew, of the Mathematical Sciences Department at IBM's
Thomas Watson Research Center, who pointed out to me the connection between Atman and Galois, notes that Pynchon might have been
attracted to the fictional possibilities of group theory in 1980, if he
saw (1) the film *It's My Turn,* which concerns a female group theorist
at the University of Chicago who falls in love with a retired baseball
superstar, or (2) newspaper accounts that same year of the well-publi-
cized collaborative effort by mathematicians to find all the finite
"simple" groups. Of the "sporadic" groups discovered by the team,
the largest is called "the monster," though Lew thinks that the footprint of the monster that stomped the Chipco lab in *Vineland* has less
to do with mathematics than with the Godzilla movies with which
Pynchon has long been rumored to be fascinated.[2] Although that is
probably the case, one should not entirely discount the humorously
recounted method by which researchers at Wawazume Life & Non-
Life apply the principles of group theory in a Standardized Reflex-
ology Analysis—in which "the 3-D body is projected onto the 2-D sole,
a map of itself" (169)—to discover that the footprint is "consistent
with the foot impression of a saurian creature on the order of—one
hundred meters high!" Group theory permits information about the
larger wholes to be "generated" by a part of that whole; presumably
that is why Pynchon alludes to group theory.

In its explication of patterns and relationships, group theory—as
perceptual psychologists like James J. Gibson use it—reveals invariants beneath surfaces in much the same way, says Jeremy Campbell,
as Chomsky's deep structures reveal the underlying properties or
rules of language (206).[3] Where a mathematician speaks abstractly of
the relationships between elements of a set, a class, or a group,[4]

students of perception talk of the relationship between aspects of perceived objects or events, like features in a frame of vision. As time and motion transform a scene, the mind searches for those invariants that preserve meaning and intelligibility. The persistence of vision that stabilizes the images "moved" by the rapid reframing of a motion picture projector or cathode ray tube can be understood as an exercise in group theory. In these examples, certain elements change while others—sometimes called "identity elements"—remain invariant. When objects are rotated, for instance, their appearance changes, so that a coin seen from the side will look much different from a coin viewed from above, but will still be recognizable so long as enough reference points remain to reestablish the relationships that define it. These invariants permit translation between transformations.

Viewed at dawn, Vineland's landscape shifts appearance in terms explicitly borrowed from group theory:

"It's a trick—of the morning light!" Had they continued to watch from here as the sun rose, they would have seen the town begin to change, the corners of things to rotate slowly, the shadows come in to flip some of the angles inside out as "laws" of perspective were reestablished, so that by 9:00 A.M. or so, the daytime version of what was meant to be seen out the peculiar window would all be in place. (173)

Gibson's theory of perception holds that light reflected from the very real features of the world contains most of the information we need to understand it. What probably attracts Pynchon to group theory, however, is that it can support contradictory schemes of reality.[5] As Cassius Keyser has noted, many of the assumptions of the theory of groups can be found in philosophies of karmic cycles (1554-57). But karmic doctrines, like those espoused by some of Pynchon's mystics, usually characterize the visible world as illusion. According to those doctrines, cycles of transformation recur over cosmic time, following each other in succession like the spokes of the goddess Fortuna's wheel. Individual souls also undergo transformations in which invariant spiritual properties survive the drastic changes of condition occasioned by death. In *Vineland*, Takeshi and DL open a "karmic readjustment" service for the Thanatoids in Shade Creek. (Though Pynchon does not offer any details about this service, it would presumably make use of group theory's notorious "noncommutative" law, which denies that logical operations can be carried out regardless of order, and might involve two successive acts that produced a different outcome in the opposite order—but there is no point in spoiling an amusing idea by examining it too literally.)

In a celebrated passage in *The World of Mathematics*, James R. Newman remarks that

> group theory has to do with the invariants of groups of transformations. One studies the properties of an object, the features of a problem unaffected by changes of condition. The more drastic the changes, the fewer the invariants. What better way to get at the fundamentals of structure than by successive transformations to strip away the secondary properties. It is a method analogous to that used by the archaeologist who clears away hills to get at cities, digs into houses to uncover ornaments, utensils, and potsherds, tunnels into tombs to find sarcophagi, the winding sheets they hold and the mummies within. Thus he reconstructs the features of an unseen society; and so the mathematician and scientist create a theoretical counterpart of the unseen structure of the phenomenal world. (3:1536-37)

Nearly all of Pynchon's characters, karmic devotees and Western logicians alike, are obsessed with "the unseen structure of the phenomenal world," whether that structure be one of control or of some underlying reality beyond normal articulation or representation. In the novel, the latter can be glimpsed across "boundary" regions, like the still-pastoral Vineland (a name redolent of Vinland, the Viking designation for an unspoiled, prerationalized America). Even turn-of-the-century photographs of the landscape offer information, and "the light in these pictures could be seen even today in the light of Vineland, the rainy indifference with which it fell on surfaces, the call to attend to territories of the spirit . . . for what else could the antique emulsions have been revealing?" (317).

The unseen structures Pynchon's characters search for are those that bind them to others in common identity, when "all 'em deeply personal li'l ones and zeros got changed to somebody else's" (352). In marked contrast to Vond, who classifies radical faces according to the racist group theory of criminologist Cesare Lombroso, Zoyd sees himself reflected in other individuals, a sensation also different from Frenesi's vision of the People. In Vineland he spots his friend Van Meter, "a standard-issue Hippie Freak who looked *just like him*. Wooo! An unreal moment for everybody, with the driver staring twice as weirdly *right back at Zoyd!*" (315). Prairie and her friends and relatives constantly search her face for signs of her ancestry. Those signs are tenuous, but enough for affection, continuity, community. Group in its colloquial sense means just that, a group of people, and there are a great many of them: the real families, the parodic versions of family like the Mafia or the characters of *Gilligan's Island*, the various collectives, the rock bands, and so on, all of which satisfy some need for love and intimacy. Or perhaps the Americans in this novel are just looking for whatever invariants remain of an older United States, a "Harbor of Refuge" (316), "Vineland the Good" (322).

Seeing them depends very much on the mix of light and shadows. The elder Becker–Traverses argue "the perennial question of whether the United States still lingered in a prefascist twilight, or whether that darkness had fallen long stupefied years ago, and the light they saw was coming only from millions of Tubes all showing the same bright-colored shadows" (371). It is hard, and will become harder, to see beyond mediation. But even in a world increasingly composed of ersatz images, oppressed by them, even in an age when automatic lenses focus more accurately and consistently than the human eye, it may be possible that we can trust our vision at least part of the time. Every generation has to learn to see on its own, and every generation is at risk. Prairie does have her mother's face; she is associated with daffodils sacred to Proserpine (319), and she may make her mother's mistakes. At the novel's end, she calls into the darkness that once held Brock, "You can come back. [. . .] It's OK, rilly. Come on, come in. I don't care. Take me anyplace you want" (384).

Light at least emboldens humans to ask some hard questions. Zoyd, stoned on the beauty of a natural landscape at his wedding, asks: " 'Frenesi, do you think that love can save anybody? You do, don't you?' At the time he hadn't learned what a stupid question it was. She gazed up at him from just under the brim of the hat. He thought, at least try to remember this, try to keep it someplace secure, just her face now in this light, OK, her eyes quiet like this, her mouth poised to open. . . ." (39).

NOTES

[1] *Annales de l'Ecole Normale* 13 (1896): 197-266.

[2] I am deeply indebted to John Lew for suggesting that Pynchon based Atman on Galois, and for providing information on group theory. John S. Lew to Joseph W. Slade, 16 January, 22 March, and 16 April 1990.

[3] For a lucid introduction to James Gibson's application of group theory to perception in detail, I suggest Campbell's account in "The Strategies of Seeing" in *Grammatical Man*. Gibson's own most engaging work is *The Ecological Approach to Visual Perception* (Boston: Houghton Mifflin, 1979).

[4] The ontology of group theory rests on rules, as outlined by Jeremy Campbell: "one [. . .] is the rule that if the elements A and B are members of the class in question, then combining A and B by some operation, say addition or multiplication, results in an element which is also a member of the class. An-

other is the rule that there must be an 'identity' element in the class, such that, when it is combined with another element A, of the same class, the result is again A, unchanged by the operation. In simple arithmetic, four added to zero is still four, and four multiplied by one is still four. Here the identity elements would be zero and one respectively. A further rule states that there must exist an element, which, when combined with any other element, results in the identity. Only if all these elements are met can the class of elements be called a group. A group may also consist of a class of operations performed on something, one after another in succession. In this case, any two operations must lead to a result which could have been obtained by just a single operation. These operations might be to move certain objects, transforming them into different positions or deforming them into new shapes" (206-7).

[5]Indeed, there is some danger in claiming too much for group theory, which has application to Lie algebras, the theory of equations, differential geometry, number theory, chaos theory, crystallography, atomic and particle physics, theories of symmetry, and a dozen other realms of thought. In a broad sense, of course, almost any work of fiction is subject to analysis by group theory, if only because its methods can be applied to the understanding of any kind of symmetry. *Vineland* has plenty of symmetries, including the parallel relationships between Frenesi and Brock, Sasha and Hub, DL and Takeshi, Frenesi and DL, and Prairie and Ché, with the breakdown in symmetries between Brock's anima and animus, or with cycles of repression: "Communists then, dopers now, tomorrow, who knew, maybe the faggots, so what, it was all the same beef, wasn't it?" (339).

WORKS CITED

Barnouw, Erik. *Tube of Plenty: The Evolution of American Television.* Rev. ed. New York: Oxford University Press, 1982.

Campbell, Jeremy. *Grammatical Man: Information, Entropy, Language, and Life.* New York: Simon and Schuster, 1982.

Dyson, Freeman. *Disturbing the Universe.* New York: Harper and Row, 1979.

Hoyle, Fred. *Ten Faces of the Universe.* San Francisco: W. H. Freeman, 1977.

Infeld, Leopold. *Whom the Gods Love: The Story of Evariste Galois.* 1948; rpt. Reston, VA: National Council of Teachers of Mathematics, 1978.

Keyser, Cassius J. "The Group Concept." *The World of Mathematics,* ed. James R. Newman. 4 vols. New York: Simon and Schuster, 1956, 2:1538-57.

Newman, James R., ed. *The World of Mathematics.* 4 vols. New York: Simon and Schuster, 1956.

Pynchon, Thomas. *Vineland.* Boston: Little, Brown, 1990.

Rothman, Tony. "Genius and Biographers: The Fictionalization of Evariste Galois," *American Mathematical Monthly,* 89 (1982): 84-107.

Sterling, Christopher, and John M. Kittross. *Stay Tuned: A Concise History of American Broadcasting.* 2nd ed. Belmont, CA: Wadsworth, 1990.

Weyl, Hermann. *The Theory of Groups and Quantum Mechanics.* London: Metheun, 1931; rpt. New York: Dover, 1950.

Pynchon's Groundward Art

Joseph Tabbi

A S long as the novel remains a popular medium, it is probably inevitable that readers should regard the artist before the work of art, and tend to celebrate the performing, rather than the creative, personality. An abdication as extreme as Pynchon's only proves the rule. He has given no interviews and made no public appearances, friends keep quiet, and there are only a scattering of photographs from the 1953 Oyster Bay High School yearbook that editors, in an act of pure revenge, have kept reprinting in feature articles and national reviews. For someone of Pynchon's stature, the sheer effort of maintaining anonymity has to be an occupation in itself, and reason enough to avoid publication for seventeen years.

The moment *Vineland* appeared, however, it became clear that the most strenuous public-relations campaign could not have stimulated as much interest. The long wait, the award to the author some years previously of a MacArthur grant, advance articles in *People* magazine and *Smart*, and the secrecy in which Little, Brown cloaked the manuscript—all worked to ensure its being read and reviewed, like any novel of note today in America, as news. Clinching the American reception was Salman Rushdie's front-page review in the *New York Times Book Review*, a message direct from the underground pronouncing the voluntary exile's literary return a "triumph." Dissenting reviews by Frank Kermode and Brad Leithauser registered a cooler international reception, but this has not kept academic critics in the meantime from taking up the novel's explication and getting started on the inevitable revisions of the Pynchon canon.[1]

Throughout his career Pynchon, by avoiding publicity, has created it, and, whatever his intentions, his anonymity has helped to serve the celebrity function of literature. We are used to hearing about media depredations on literary talent, about Norman Mailer's having been ruined, for example, by his wasted efforts either to change or live up to his public image. But reticence, too, can have its price. At its worst, self-promotion in Mailer has been a way at least of making contact with an audience, and of testing its reality. Yet it is hard to know for whom, precisely, *Vineland* was intended, unless it be for the very audience that, through demographic studies and proven interest, the media and the marketplace have themselves created and sustained. With its laid-back style, American matter, and deliberately conventional sixties nostalgia, the novel is all too easily *placeable* in the field of current writing. Its studied superficiality and restricted reference to the ideas and artifacts of mass culture make it the most self-consciously "popular" of Pynchon's books, and this popularity is neither a sellout nor an especially welcome bid for "accessibility" so much as an imaginative shortcut on Pynchon's part, an acceptance of a ready-made audience that frees him from the responsibility of creating the sensibility by which he will be understood.

My dissatisfaction with *Vineland* is not that the book is a falling off—"what wouldn't be?" was a friend's fair response. After *Gravity's Rainbow,* a direct treatment and "return home" to America does make a kind of sense. But for the reader who has been moved by complexities of form and language beyond the alienation depicted in *Gravity's Rainbow,* the return can seem imperfectly achieved, the new optimism arbitrary, settled in advance, and sustainable only by an almost willed holding back from darker forces and paranoia that still come obscurely through. The paranoia of the early novels, so far from being a clinical condition that distorted perception, was a way of making abstract connections, and so presenting real but seldom seen forces that give form to contemporary history. Vast information and computer networks, whole technologies of control, reproduction, and capital formation could at least be suggested through paranoid suspicions of orders beyond the audible and the visible. In *Vineland,* Pynchon retains an aura and a "familiar vocabulary of the mysterious and the invisible," but the paranoia of this novel may be expressive of nothing so much as the writer's increasing distance from sources of political power in America.[2]

This is not to say that Pynchon has opted out of the power structure. As Deborah L. Madsen observed in the English literary journal *Over Here,* the very conditions of commercial publishing in America leave a writer no "outside," unambiguously oppositional standpoint, "except to stop writing."[3] And one might extend this observation to include not only the publishing industry, but the entire mediated culture that is Pynchon's subject. Yet involvement in the operations of the present cultural system does not explain the ease with which *Vineland* rests in its publicity, the slight critical resistance it offers to the cultural climate in which it appears, and a more general failure, in the words of *Gravity's Rainbow*, to "resist the unreal." Instead, Pynchon settles in *Vineland* for exposing the many forms of unreality in America, which he accomplishes despite, or perhaps because of, a new commitment to a debased literary realism.

A first principle of the new aesthetic, "More Is Less," is cited at the very start of the novel, in the guise of "a discount store for larger-size women."[4] There is excess in *Vineland*, to be sure, but it is no longer the linguistic exuberance that comes from relentless psychological probing. A relaxation of tension is apparent in the way that Pynchon allows the language and mannerisms of the time and place—mostly northern California in the sixties and the eighties—to shape his own style; and, where he had often been accused in the earlier novels of creating cold, abstract characters (they are not), now there is an evident and mostly unironic fondness for all but the cops (and even for some of them) that has led many to believe that this, at last, is Pynchon's true face: an old lefty nostalgic for the lost radical history of Pacific northwestern logger unions and Wobbly politics, and who is willing to assert, against all the co-opted radicalism, fallen ideals, and unfulfilled "acid adventures" of the sixties, a positive sense of community with his contemporaries (285).

His loyalties are political and generational rather than literary, as they always have been. But the left-wing politics don't quite sit with the new, right-leaning aesthetic. In two recent semibiographical essays introducing his own and his college friend Richard Fariña's work, he showed signs of dissatisfaction with the flashy technique and experimental difficulty of his writing. After taking pains to criticize the short story "Entropy," an early show-off piece that remains nonetheless a good introduction to Pynchon's abstract imagination, he spoke of preferring fiction that has some "grounding in human reality" and an authenticity "found and taken up, always at a cost, from deeper, more shared levels of the life we all really live."[5] This apparent change in attitude may account for the new attention to scenes of family life and the general suburban ordinariness of the people of Vineland (even when they happen to be undercover agents, ex-anarchist bombers, or a bad-ass woman warrior like DL Chastain). Gone are the abstract epistemological quests that, for many, made the earlier novels such attractive allegories of contemporary reading, whose main characters are acutely aware of themselves as makers and interpreters of signs, and who because not conventionally "full" or "real" have been thought to be only elements in a game. Like Stencil in his first novel, *V.*, Pynchon must surely have seen the likelihood of his work being turned into "merely a scholarly quest after all, an adventure of the mind."[6] The demands made by the earlier work may have selected a more cerebral audience than he ever wanted, and the anti-intellectual rhetoric of the prefaces, like the populist language and mock scholarly references in *Vineland*, seem designed to reach a wider audience, and to defend the work against the allegorizing critics.

In keeping with the new realism, the quest this time is less formally self-conscious, more personal and direct: a young girl, Prairie Gates, after years of separation comes to learn about her mother, Frenesi, and in the process is given a pretty good American political education. Prairie was brought up to believe that her mother, a third-generation daughter of a pro-union family, was a committed revolutionary forced to go into hiding from the government. In reality, Frenesi had betrayed her radical friends to the Drug Enforcement Agency, and later she leaves her family home in Vineland for the security and protective anonymity of a bureaucratic career *in* the government.

To Pynchon's credit, the betrayal is sought not in any simple rejection by Frenesi of her youthful ideals (which are shown to have been vague and naive at best), but in the larger spirit of sixties radicalism—most obviously in the cult of youth, but more subtly in a generation's unthinking embrace of money, entertainment media, and a whole range of technologies that set life at a distance. A political revolution traduced by a revolution in information—at least this is how Frenesi's present husband, Flash, rationalizes his own compromises: "Everybody's a squealer. We're in th' Info Revolution here. Anytime you use a credit card you're tellin' the Man more than you meant to. Don't matter if it's big or small, he can use it all" (74). For Frenesi, the motive for betrayal is a continued insulation, not only from people close to her but from just such quotidian realities as credit cards and checkout lines at the local ShopQuik. Even during her most idealistic years at Berkeley, she had sought exemption in film work, imagining that "as long as she had life inside her Tube-shaped frame, [. . .] nothing out there could harm her." The government offers merely another kind of immunity, one that seems neverending until her budget is cut and she not only loses her job, but—in ironic confirmation of her already lost identity—she has her entire file erased from the Agency's computer.

We could welcome the story as a domestic gloss on the earlier novels, a gloss that reduces, to be sure, but that does serve to correct our overly literary and de-politicized readings of Pynchon. The injunction to "be experimental" can be as much of a trap as any other creative prescription, and he can hardly be blamed for choosing not to push the limits of his art. Perhaps it was only scholarly protocol, and no ambition of Pynchon's, that compelled comparisons of *Gravity's Rainbow* and Joyce's *Ulysses;* should we ever have supposed that Pynchon would labor decades over a postmodern *Finnegans Wake?* He has chosen the route of political directness rather than increased literary complication, topical reference rather than mythic density. Yet, for all *Vineland's* reputed ease and accessibility, he can't resist giving his own, indeterminate twist to his popular and realistic material, and the hybrid fiction that results has neither the emotional charge of realism nor the rich fabulism and science-based clarities of the earlier, more overtly experimental work.

Taking their cue from a review Pynchon wrote of Gabriel García Márquez's *Love in the Time of Cholera,* critics have associated the aesthetic of *Vineland* with a Latin American "magic realism." But for long stretches the novel resembles nothing so much as recent cyberpunk fiction in which the deepest, most "shared levels of the life we all really live" are often hard to separate from the collective reality of brand names, corporations, and network television. If *Gravity's Rainbow* engendered a taste for technological complexities and multiple otherworldly bureaucracies in a younger science-fiction writer such as William Gibson, there is now, in *Vineland,* a hint of Gibson in the ninjette training of the young DL Chastain, and in the subtle alterations, made in bed and on the operating table, to Takeshi Fumimota's nervous system. DL has touched the Japanese businessman with the fatal Vibrating Palm, a hardly noticeable jab to the "dark meridians" along the victim's back that will cause instant death exactly one year later (152). At the time, she was disguised as a prostitute in an upscale Tokyo brothel, wearing false-colored lenses that were taken, she suspects, "from the eyes of a dead person. [. . .] Likely a hooker, [. . .] whose name, even names she'd used professionally, nobody remembered anymore" (152). Later DL comes to believe that she was meant "to witness her own act of murder through the correction to *just this person's* eyesight" (152, Pynchon's italics). Her blurred vision, her excitement, and the concentration demanded by the difficult technique prevent her, even during sex, from noticing that Fumimota is not the man she intends to kill.

Tonally such passages frustrate comprehension, poised as they are between vaudeville and Zen practice, between transcended and mistaken identity. Here is the same mixture, as in Gibson's first novel, *Neuromancer*, of a mock-Oriental mysticism and an equivalent, simulated mysticism in the West. (After DL's mistake is discovered, Fumimota can be cured only by the most advanced procedures, involving repeated use of the most costly medical equipment. In the time it takes for him to recuperate, he is forced to work in partnership with DL in a karmic readjustment clinic.) Ghosts in such a world are no more than technology's "elaborate pretending" (114), a pretense that allows Pynchon to extend the narrative into the world behind the camera lens and the television or computer screen. For a character like Prairie who has never known a world without these things, such pretense offers the best chance of knowing herself and her family history. Watching a street confrontation that her mother had filmed twenty years before, she realizes

that if she kept her mind empty she could absorb, conditionally become, Frenesi, share her eyes, feel, when the frame shook with fatigue or fear or nausea, Frenesi's whole body there, as much as her mind choosing the frame, her will to go out there, load the roll, get the shot. Prairie floated, ghostly light of head, as if Frenesi were dead but in a special way, a minimum-security arrangement, where limited visits, mediated by projector and screen, were possible. As if somehow, next reel or the one after, the girl would find a way, some way, to speak to her . . . . (199)

Another time, after Prairie has shut down the computer that holds a file on her mother, Pynchon's narrator projects the digitalized image of DL and Frenesi into a separate reality: "Back down in the computer library, in storage, quiescent ones and zeros scattered among millions of others, the two women, yet in some definable space, continued on their way across the low-lit campus, persisting, recoverable" (115). The space of this projection, because it is actively constructed and populated with human dreams and passions, can be said to improve on Gibson's cyberspace, that collective semi-consciousness "abstracted from the [data] banks of every computer in the human system."[7] But Pynchon's characters experience the same detachment and feeling of self-watching as do Gibson's, and they all hold on to the same ambiguous promise of technological escape from the confines of the human body.

Pynchon reserves his most powerful writing for such moments of imaginative projection into the past lives of others. More typical of the novel, however, are the purposefully tired descriptions of a society of half-alive "Thanatoids" living on junk food and television reruns, a group that may recall Gibson's "flatliners" and other technological "constructs" of once living personalities. Yet the Thanatoids, too, were already anticipated in the final scattering of Tyrone Slothrop in a passage from *Gravity's Rainbow* that gestures, as Christopher Walker has remarked, toward Pynchon's "own disillusionment with the whole novelistic project":

There is also the story about Tyrone Slothrop [. . .] and there ought to be a punch line to it, but there isn't. The plan went wrong. He is being broken down instead, and scattered. His cards have been laid down, Celtic style, in the order suggested by Mr. A. E. Waite, laid out and read, but they are the cards of a tanker and feeb: they point only to a long and scuffling future, to mediocrity (not only in his life but also, heh, heh, in his chroniclers too, yes yes nothing like getting the 3 of Pentacles upside down covering the significator on the second try to send you to the tube to watch a seventh rerun of the Takeshi and Ichizo Show, light a cigarette and try to forget the whole thing)—to no clear happiness or redeeming cataclysm.[8]

It may be, as Walker suggests, that "*Vineland* is the fruit of this tubal immersion," and that the form of the TV rerun has to an extent replaced "the logic of quest, knowledge and apocalyptic revelation" in the first three novels. Yet this passage also reveals Pynchon in the earlier work as a writer who is capable of questioning his own plots, metaphors, and quests, so as to constantly resist the apocalypse he imagines. The endless replication in *Vineland* of already known forms, like the cyberpunk's retro-future in which the end seems to have already come, can only make any further resistance seem pointless. Pynchon has been criticized for indulging an easy Cold War rhetoric, but the apocalyptic threat could at least make us feel the present urgencies that impel us to act. Slothrop's scattering, described elsewhere in *Gravity's Rainbow* as a mindless collapse into a wholly discontinuous present, was in part a way of showing what can happen when we stop worrying and learn to love the bomb. The Thanatoids, like Frenesi existing "safe in some time-free zone" of their own choosing (90), take this ahistorical mindlessness a step further—into the age of Star Wars and the postmodern eighties.

Whatever the differences between this novel and the last, Pynchon shows no sign of diminishing inventiveness, although the Thanatoid and Chastain/Fumimota subplots, evolving to the complexity of a suburban sprawl, only incidentally touch on the central story of Prairie and Frenesi. In the absence of the deferred apocalyptic moment, that story is even less compelling. A number of readers have expressed disappointment with the anticlimax of the last chapter when, for the first time after some 350 pages of preparation, the mother and daughter finally meet. From the little we are told about it, Prairie seems to have felt more emotion in her sessions of watching Frenesi on film. And if comments on clothes and hairstyle had recently given the exact right emotional coloring to the parting, probably for good, of Prairie and a teenage friend, they don't quite play in this much more important encounter. Despite the betrayals and adult experiences Frenesi has been through, little about her has changed since the sixties, even if the imagery that describes her refers not only to film now, but to the "falsely deathless perimeter" of a video-game screen (293). Her loss of immunity and corporate identity, and a suspect promise of a role in a movie, are all, really, that bring her home to Vineland.

Of course, there is also the presence of DEA agent Brock Vond to bring her back. Vond is the cartoon bad guy who got Frenesi to come over to his side in the first place, which he accomplished mainly through the force of his sex. Now it is true that sex and power have always been connected in Pynchon's work, but never so bluntly, and without entering into a Vond-like fantasy of macho attractiveness, what reader, male or female, would accept Frenesi's plea of helplessness whenever her "pussy's runnin' the show" (260)? At the same time, Frenesi is presented as basically sexless, as unable to experience emotional or even physical connection beyond the sexual act. Like Brock himself, she fears reproduction and resents its demands on her autonomy. When she has Prairie, the newborn child makes her feel as if she were "only an animal with a full set of pain receptors after all" (287). Her desire, no less than Brock's, is to live outside of her body, but, without its grounding in earth and in time, she can only turn, helplessly, "toward images of authority, especially uniformed men" (83).

Her mother Sasha had the same weakness, and its appearance in Prairie is part of the bad-joking arbitrariness with which the book ends. Brock, descending on a helicopter cable to grab the girl out of her sleeping bag, is yanked back at the last second when the Reagan administration suddenly defunds *his* program; then he is carried off to hell. And this is how, in the post-ideological eighties, even the prototypal agent of oppression is made subject to the same economic contingencies as the rest of us. Prairie is rescued, though she is not sure she wanted to *be* rescued: "he had left too suddenly. There should have been more" (384). Safe again in her sleeping bag, she calls on Brock to return, then she drifts, "back and forth for a while between Brock fantasies and the silent darkened silver images all around her, before settling down into sleep" (384-85). To the end, she remains held by the same shadows and simulated passions that govern her mother.

Maybe it is to be expected that Pynchon, working closer than ever to conventional novelistic forms and evoking conventional expectations, would subvert them.[9] But with our expectations Pynchon also raises significant political concerns that are then dropped with the same nonchalance. The novel purports to be about a generation's missed chances, about its addictions and betrayals, and about its replacement, among the educated classes, of an uptight morality and blatant racial prejudice with more subtle forms of mental and economic oppression (there is a running satirical commentary on television, yuppies, and New Age music). Pynchon's refusal to push the narrative to some plausible formal conclusion drains these issues, again, of any felt urgency; and the slapdash, indeterminate ending left me doubting the seriousness of his project in the book.

But then it is not at all clear that he *wants* to be taken seriously, at least not with the kind of seriousness that scholars and admiring critics have brought to the study of his work. Ever since the appearance of *Gravity's Rainbow*, many people have worked very hard to get at Pynchon's accomplishment, and to make its importance more widely felt. It is this critical group, myself included, that *Vineland* is most likely to have disappointed, even if, academic industry being what it is, there will continue to be those among us who will go on tracking *Vineland* arcana and the minutest allusive droppings without asking whether the work this time will bear the scrutiny. The famous assertion in *Gravity's Rainbow* that "*everything is connected*, everything in the Creation," offers a certain justification for the mass of critical explication devoted to *that* novel, if only in nervous and prolific denial of the less frequently cited counter-assertion that "nothing is connected to anything." But is *Vineland* better for our knowing, say, that a minor character named Van Meter might refer to Bob Feller, the great Cleveland Indians pitcher known throughout the nation at the age of seventeen as "the farmboy from Van Meter," Iowa? Or that Frenesi's grandmother, Eula, may have been named after Eula Varner in Faulkner's Snopes novels? Might the appearance on page 97 of an *Italian Wedding Fake Book* by Deleuze and Guattari open up a whole psychic subtext? (More relevant may be the surname of one

Weed Atman, the influence of Hindu religion on *Vineland* having been noted in at least one review.[10])

Pynchon's attitude toward his interpreters might be gathered from his introduction, at the start of the book, of the character Zoyd Wheeler, who must do something certifiably crazy at least once a year if he is to continue to receive his "mental disability" checks from the government. Zoyd's dangerous leaps through the front windows of various establishments in Humboldt County are filmed every year by local television crews and subjected to endless scrutiny by panels of experts, the most recent "including a physics professor, a psychiatrist, and a track-and-field coach [. . .] discussing the evolution over the years of Zoyd's technique" (15). Pynchon is nothing if not self-conscious, and, in the passage describing Zoyd's reluctant leap through a window whose glass turns out to have been replaced by a pane of "clear sheet candy," he could be summing up the effect that intense critical exposure in a culture sustained by media simulations has had on his own style in the book: "[Zoyd] knew the instant he hit that something was funny. There was hardly any impact, and it all felt and sounded different, no spring or resonance, no volume, only a sort of fine, dulled splintering" (11-12).

At the start of *Gravity's Rainbow*, Pynchon taunted us with one of the most brilliant author figures in recent fiction—Pirate Prentice, a kind of fantasist surrogate whose novelistic powers of dreaming other people's dreams are all too readily put into service by the "Firm" and the State. Prentice knows that his talents, his body, and even his private fantasies are subtly implicated in sources of power within the culture; and his eventual initiation into a political "Counterforce" and social "We-system" (as against a decentered and relational "They-system") is a study in power and compromised resistance that rivals and anticipates Foucault's. Now, early in *Vineland*, we have Zoyd, the aging doper who remains uncorrupted in his refusal to collaborate or inform, but who made his peace with the Feds by agreeing to the ineffectual role of a clownish eccentric. These contrasting projections (of the artist, not the person) might mark an increasing marginalization of the creative subject; his feeling of ease proving to be little more than the freedom that comes when one has ceased to resist anymore.

This is why *Vineland* should disappoint more than the scholars: for all Pynchon's evident warmth and generational identity, and for all the new realism, the America he returns to in the book remains a land of simulation—better observed and more fully experienced, surely, than in Jean Baudrillard's *America,* but no more engaging for that. It could be argued, of course, that Pynchon has always been at home in hyperreality, that the lives and even deaths of his characters have always been mediated, and that, in time, the theme-park shopping malls and designer fashions of Vineland, U.S.A., will come to seem as real as the trappings—and inevitable entrapments—of any other culture. But numerous small, seemingly incidental references to earlier times, particularly the period from World War II to the first years of activism in the sixties, provide an illuminating contrast to America in the mid-eighties. In the forties, for example, a navy recruit like DL Chastain's father, Moody, might find himself caught in the industrial spaces of a warship, "surrounded by nothing that did not refer, finally, to steel" (119). A decade later, when DL herself enters the fallout shelter that once housed "the Cold War dream," Pynchon can still have her imagine an "escape to some refuge deep in the earth, one hatchway after another, leading to smaller and smaller volumes" (255).

A desire to occupy an ever-narrowing cultural margin has always been strong in postmodern writing. But if *Vineland* tells us anything, it is that such an "underground" resistance has long since stopped being viable. The repressive operations of earlier decades have been replaced by less visible arrangements instituted during the "Nixonian Reaction" and the Reagan era (239), with the help of media images that only *seem* to give clear and direct presentations of the world. Pynchon cannot be faulted for the accuracy of his own presentation. But neither can his domestic realism nor his playful construction of electronic, virtual realities provide the grounding he wants in "human reality" (*Slow Learner* 18). What is needed, and what has been oddly lacking in recent fiction and theory, is a new style of resistance to the simulation culture that *Vineland* documents. For the moment, the best we can do is to continue to work through the refractoriness and literary complexity of *Gravity's Rainbow,* and hope that *Vineland* turns out to be only an outrider for a harder, more resilient fiction.

NOTES

[1]See Clifford Mead's bibliography at the end of this volume for bibliographic details.

[2]Alan Wilde, "Love and Death in and around Vineland, U.S.A.," *boundary 2* 18:2 (1991): 173. Wilde lists many of the objectless references that help to create a paranoid mood in the novel: " 'another deep nudge from forces un-

seen' (3), 'hidden structures' (61), 'signs and symptoms' (148), 'the realm behind the immediate' (186), 'another order of things' (220), 'a world behind the world she had known all along' (315), 'some invisible boundary' (317) and so forth."

[3] *"Vineland:* An American Saga," *Over Here* 2.1 (Summer 1990): 56.

[4] Thomas Pynchon, *Vineland* (Boston: Little, Brown), 1990, 4; hereafter cited parenthetically.

[5] Thomas Pynchon, *Slow Learner* (Boston: Little, Brown, 1984), 18, 21.

[6] Thomas Pynchon, *V.* (Philadelphia: Lippincott, 1963), 50.

[7] William Gibson, *Neuromancer* (New York: Ace, 1984), 51. Gibson's narrator admits that, although moving through cyberspace feels real, its perceptual matrix is "actually a drastic simplification of the human sensorium" (55).

[8] Passage from *Gravity's Rainbow* (New York: Viking, 1973, 738) quoted by Walker in a letter to the *London Review of Books* (8 March 1990) responding to Kermode's review.

[9] This is the argument of Edward Mendelson's excellent and generally favorable review. While commending Pynchon in this novel for being "less hesitant to speak in the voices of feeling," Mendelson admits that, in Frenesi's case, "Pynchon is less concerned with [. . .] motives or feelings than he is in treating her as an allegory of the willing transformation of the rebellious self-righteous 1960s into the sullen acquisitive decades that followed" (*New Republic,* 9 and 16 July 1990, 42).

[10] John Leonard, *The Nation,* 26 February 1990, 281-86.

Pynchon's *"Elaborate Game of Doubles"* *in* Vineland

Susan Strehle

ORDER and coherence have always been issues for readers of Pynchon's texts. Following the remarkable difficulties of *Gravity's Rainbow*, *Vineland* appears deceptively simple: it has a relatively clear narrative, which develops over three decades among a few central characters. Yet despite the novel's comparative "readability," it has again raised the question of connections, of pattern and meaning. In fact, Pynchon's latest fiction seems to some of its most dissatisfied reviewers to lack design and coherence altogether. One reviewer complains that *Vineland*'s insights "are more like the disembodied flashes of a drug trip or a psychiatric case history than the insights that arise out of a coherent development of character";[1] another argues that *Vineland* "is a loosely packed grab bag of a book," lacking the compression of the "patchy novella, *The Crying of Lot 49.*"[2] Even reviewers who have contributed interesting readings of Pynchon's earlier texts confess to some frustration and bafflement in the face of *Vineland*'s richly diverse, time-whorled surface. The novel "is not nearly as coherent as Pynchon's earlier novels," writes Edward Mendelson,[3] and Frank Kermode finds it "difficult" and "disappointing," partly because of his own "measure of incomprehension."[4]

Vineland may, however, teach us to read Pynchon, whose coherence emerges from loosely pleated variations on a group of related themes and ideas. For Pynchon, the order that makes plot meaningful is not established according to the old-fashioned principles of unity and economy, the full working-out of implications inherent in a single situation. Coherence is especially not expressed through one-way linear time. Rather, the narrative develops its own unique logic of connectedness through permutations, comparisons, inversions, and variations. *Vineland*, in particular, juggles doubles and pairs, configurations of two both alike and dissimilar. As befits a story of double-dealing, the novel is full of images of duplicity: of doubles, twins, partners, and foils, involved in acts of deception, conversion, and disguise. Some of the central characters feel deep, inner divisions; each has a reflected other self or double. The world, too, is zygomorphic; reality itself is not single, any more than Pynchon's narrative is, but rather bifurcated, entwined, duplicitous. Repeated allusions invoke a second or alternative reality beside the one characters seem to inhabit—like that other "mode of meaning behind the obvious" intuited by Oedipa Maas when she understands how reduced the possibilities have become in America.[5]

Beyond forming coherence for the novel through a repeated pattern of specular images, doubling also generates plot events and illuminates Pynchon's concern with choice and responsibility. The narrative develops the intersections of two pairs of characters who resemble each other so closely that they are mistaken for their doubles. The two central women characters, Frenesi Gates and Darryl Louise Chastain, are both similar and very different; their stories run parallel for much of the novel, but diverge markedly over the question of accepting responsibility for choices and making amends for errors. Because she accepts her own agency, DL ends in a partnership with Takeshi that gives way to magic and art. Accomplished through careful attention and hard work, their union anticipates the choice between ideas voiced by Emerson and Sister Rochelle in the last pages of the novel: whether justice is innate, a given, or achieved by struggle and effort. Doubles of various kinds play off against each other throughout *Vineland* to establish, in their bifurcating routes, the gravity of choice.

Duality and Division

Because they're scattered through a densely textured novel, the images of pairs, doubles, and twins are easily overlooked; collecting them begins to make their importance visible. Twins Rick and Chick find Jesus and establish an auto-conversion shop called Born Again, home of the "automotive second chance."[6] Their friends Eusebio ("Vato") Gomez and Cleveland ("Blood") Bonnifoy, mates from Vietnam, partners in a towing business, and foils, sing a company theme song modeling their partnership on that of the chipmunk twins Chip 'n' Dale (180). They tow questionable cars to Rick and Chick for conversion to other, more legal automotive forms. The narrator's comment furnishes my title, as well as a metaphor for Pynchon's playful novel: "It was some elaborate game of doubles they played with the twins every time they came in here" (44). At the Kunoichi Retreat, Prairie takes over an amateur kitchen staff, including twins who speak "in hasty overlap" (190). Gifted editors for the 24fps film collective, sisters Ditzah and Zipi Pisk wear "matching oversize Jewish Afros" and speak in "a strange personal code, kind of idiolalia you find in twins" (194, 263). Zoyd Wheeler has a moment of total disorientation when he sees his car driven past by "a standard-issue Hippie Freak who looked *just like him.* Woo-oo! An unreal moment for everybody, with the driver staring twice as weirdly *right back at Zoyd!*" (315). Other, more significant resemblances—to which I will return—establish paired doublings between Frenesi Gates and Darryl Louise Chastain and between Brock Vond and Takeshi Fumimota.

Minor pairings occur throughout the novel. In addition to Rick and Chick, Vato and Blood, most of the work undertaken in *Vineland* is done by pairs in a partnership. The anti-drug movie of which Hector Zuñiga gains control is produced by the team of Liftoff and Triggerman. Hub Gates employs a team, Dmitri and Ace, to help him with his spotlights. DL goes to rescue Frenesi with Howie and Sledge. Takeshi invokes the legendary TV pair from *I Love Lucy* to describe his "adjustment" service: "Like Lucy and Ethel—if you're ever in a jam!" (67). Hector and Zoyd Wheeler have an extended "romance over the years at least as persistent as Sylvester and Tweety's" (22). Frenesi watches TV cop partners Ponch and Jon on *CHiPs.* Brock's partner Roscoe resembles "the perfect underling, whom he imagined as a sort of less voluble Tonto" (271). Prairie's best friend and double, Ché, plays with her an elaborate "star-and-sidekick routine" (327). Pairs, partners, and running mates abound in the most casual sequences of *Vineland,* suggesting balance and stability in all configurations of two.

Doubling isn't limited to pairs of characters linked by outer physical resemblance; some of the main characters experience inner divisions that leave them containing an internal pair of opposite or misaligned impulses. Split by opposed desires they can't reconcile, they become a pair of running mates—they contain their own estranged doubles. Brock Vond, who seems as single as an "ambulatory erection" to one reviewer,[7] carries with him a vengeful anima against which he constantly struggles. This "watchful, never quite trustworthy companion personality, feminine, underdeveloped," appears to Brock in dreams as "the Madwoman in the Attic." Guarding a mansion not his own, Brock comes on this "uneasy anima" in the twilit attic: "blurry, underlit, except for the glittering eyes, the relentless animal smile," she leaps on him and kills him. Brock's dream reflects his subconscious awareness of the cost he pays in psychic wholeness for ruthlessly clinging to a posture of aggressive masculinity. The angry anima on which he will not focus his daylight mind returns as a repressed and murderous animal (274-75). She appears, too, in his nightmares of women approaching from overhead to procreate, producing children whose birth reflect his death (276-77).[8] Implicit throughout is Brock's deadly model of the relation between the sexes as a pitched battle for control and conquest.

Frenesi Gates, like Brock, contains "another Frenesi, one they were prohibited access to" (237). Her ghostly double reflects Frenesi's own inner division, triggered by the wish to slough off consequences, into one thinking self and one acting self. Her "dangerous vice," the narrator comments, is to "make believe" her actions are not real and binding, that she can choose without choosing (236). When she betrays Weed Atman, Frenesi makes her acting self unreal; she becomes an estranged double:

she had taken at least one irreversible step to the side of her life, and [. . .] she was walking around next to herself, haunting herself, attending a movie of it all. If the step was irreversible, then she ought to be all right now, safe in a world-next-to-the-world that not many would know how to get to, where she could kick back and watch the unfolding drama. [. . .] even sex was mediated for her now—she did not enter in. (237)[9]

Frenesi's experience strips away her own agency: she is being entertained, as if at a show, in a world next door. Frenesi's estrangement from herself leads to her loss of closeness with her mother Sasha, "her once-connected self," with whom she can no longer talk honestly (292). This same self-estrangement leads her to marry twice without love, to abandon her daughter Prairie, to betray commitments in both marriages—to work, in fact, as a government agent who specializes in seduction and betrayal (70).

As suggested in Frenesi's fantasized retreat to an effect-free world-next-to-the-world, the intuition or dream of an alternative reality exerts a powerful appeal for the paired souls of *Vineland*. References to a doubled world beside or beneath the apparent one abound throughout the novel. One group of allusions, like Frenesi's, reflects various characters' fantasies of escape from conditions they abhor; an inverse group charts their fears of annihilation. On the one hand, long after Weed's ghost arrives in Shade Creek and shortly before he is murdered, the narrator traces an alternative future for Rex and Weed, who avert the murder and meet in later years to picnic "on an impossible hillside" (232); on the other hand, Prairie tells Ché, "I go into this alternate-universe idea, and wonder if there isn't a parallel world where [Frenesi] decided to have the abortion, get rid of me, and what's really happening is that I'm looking for her so I can haunt her like a ghost" (334). Brightly colored parrots descend, as if out of a Gabriel García Márquez novel, to tell complicated bedtime stories "to years of children, sending them off to alternate worlds in a relaxed and upbeat set of mind" (223). At the office of the sinister dentist Dr. Elasmo, Weed feels "a borderline, invisible but felt at its crossing, between worlds. [. . .] Inside [. . .] was an entirely different order of things" (228). No wonder the Sisters of the Harleyite Order, a group of male motorcycling nuns, "pursued lives of exceptional, though antinomian, purity" (359).[10]

Beneath these two groups of alternate-world ideas runs a common assumption: that the first or everyday world is material and plausible, while the second world is spiritual and therefore admits magic of both benign and malevolent kinds. The third and most important set of allusions to alternate worlds makes such a configuration explicit: in and around Vineland, at the edge of the continent, on a river navigated by primeval spirits, worlds of matter and spirit meet without provoking either fantasy or nightmare—only a deepening attention to the inner and after life. As they ride north on the bus to Vineland, eighteen-month-old Prairie talks back to the trees: "It seemed now and then as if she were responding to something she was hearing, and in rather a matter-of-fact tone of voice for a baby, too, as if this were a return for her to a world behind the world she had known all along" (315). When they arrive, the narrator records the sense shared among early visitors "of some invisible boundary"; the juncture of worlds appears in "the light of Vineland, the rainy indifference with which it fell on surfaces, the call to attend to territories of the spirit" (317). Vineland's Seventh River is "a river of ghosts"; the surrounding landscape is full of *woge*, spirits who withdrew as the first humans arrived. The land contains trails to the subterranean world of the dead, the river a passageway "through the realm behind the immediate" (186). Shadows suggest "another order of things" and "warp like radio signals at sundown the two worlds, to draw them closer, nearly together" (220). From places as remote as Vietnam, Thanatoids flock to the area near Vineland called Shade Creek.

Vineland appears hospitable to spirit—its status as a small town on the edge of the continent allows it to remain open to spiritual forces that have largely disappeared (or been expelled) from more urban areas. A few other places remain open to intrusions from the beyond: the Kunoichi Retreat, high above the city, has access to other orders of being; Godzilla's footstep from the beyond onto the coast of Japan; faceless forces enter a Kahuna Airlines plane above the Pacific. But Vineland—an invented safe harbor with two spits and two bridges — becomes the central locus of Pynchon's double-sighted novel because its history, setting, agriculture, architecture, and citizenry represent variations on the conjoining of alternate realities. It appears as a place where matter and spirit coexist, together with harvests of craw-fish and marijuana, loggers in "three-figure-price-tag jeans by Mme. Gris" and punk-rock-violence enthusiasts in Mohawk cuts "colored a vibrant acid green" (6, 18), Victorian wood houses and a jagged black federal building (317), the Vineland Palace Hotel and the Bodhi Dharma Pizza restaurant, irascible sheriff Willis Chunko and theatri-cal lawn-care contractor the Marquis de Sod. Even the geography of the place, with open meadows and tall forests of redwoods, high coastal mountains close to the ocean, conjoins differences. In such a place, partnership is possible.

Frenesi Gates and Darryl Louise Chastain

The complicated movement from the sixties to the eighties in *Vineland* arises from the intersection of two pairs of doubles, each provid-ing one central strand of the novel's twinned plot. Takeshi Fumimota stumbles upon Brock Vond, "and thought for a terrified second or two it was himself and something radical, like death, had just hap-pened. It was a stressed and malevolent cartoon of his face, of what he shaved and had long looks at" (148); lest this close resemblance between Asian and Caucasian seem a private delusion, DL Chastain confirms the resemblance on the next page. Brock sends his double to take his place in an assignation at a Japanese whorehouse where, it turns out, DL is disguised as her own double, her friend and lover Frenesi Gates: "the minute they brought out the wig she was to wear, dyed and styled precisely, she knew. And when she saw it on, a shiver-ing crept all over her skin, as she looked at her own face on Frenesi's head" (140). Her green eyes tinted Frenesi's bright blue with contact lenses, DL can't see Takeshi well enough to tell him from Brock Vond. These two enact the roles of their passionate doubles, Brock and Frenesi, whose sexual attraction drives much of the plot; but DL is so intent on her assignment to murder Brock that she doesn't register her own passion, any more than she notices Takeshi's non-Brock-like qualities. She reverses her partner's chi flow, producing a corrosive energy that will kill him within a year.

Although the Takeshi–DL Chastain subplot has seemed to some reviewers extraneous and irrelevant,[11] it actually doubles and illuminates the novel's central plot, the connection between Brock Vond and Frenesi Gates. Reading the paired stories together highlights Pynchon's concern with choice and responsibility, for they diverge on the crucial question of accepting and dealing honorably with the consequences of one's actions. The doubling and the divergence between the two central women characters, in particular, is so elaborately orchestrated as to signal its clear importance.

The narrator insists that DL is Frenesi's opposite as well as her double: DL is red-haired, green-eyed, educated in Japanese ninjitsu, while Frenesi has intensely blue eyes, light hair, and a background in American labor politics. Frenesi is the social idealist, active behind and in front of the camera, a vocal advocate of social justice. "To see injustices happening and ignore them," she says on Action News, "that's more 'dangerous' in the long run" (195). DL, in contrast, is a defensive and less optimistic force of "cold practicality." She avoids the camera, and "when she talked, it was about tactics and timetables" (195). Frenesi inherits from her father Hub a deep love of light, and argues in the film collective for "pouring in as much light as they could liberate from the local power company" (201); she stands holding the light as Weed Atman is murdered. "If Frenesi's realm was light," Pynchon writes in explicit comparison, "DL's was the dark" (250). DL uses darkness to gain invisibility; she wears black and moves, like the Tristero, under cover of night.

More important to the opposition that reflects on these central women characters and their role in the primary plot events of the sixties, DL appears to possess an integrity that Frenesi lacks. DL has a "fine clean self-command they'd all taken for granted," even a "saintlike control," while Frenesi acknowledges that she is neither pure nor in command of her body's passions. Her ninjitsu training has taught DL self-possession; she thinks "of her time with Inoshiro Sensei as returning to herself, reclaiming her body" (128). Frenesi, in contrast, responds to the image of Brock, the masculine other, taking possession of her by force: in their first meeting, Brock touches a deep chord in Frenesi with his comment, "a man in a uniform, with a big pistol, would have to make you come" (201). In Frenesi's perception, DL is "the steady-beating heart of the collective, who could never have made the deal with Brock that Frenesi had" (260). After the murder of Weed Atman, DL rescues Frenesi from Brock's camp and poses the questions, as partner and friend, that Frenesi must answer. DL is the judge before whom Frenesi pleads guilty, though she summons a range of excuses and appeals for mercy.

A more intricate reading of the doubling between DL and Frenesi suggests, however, that DL *could* have made the same deal with Brock —and thus helps to place both women's failings more clearly. Frenesi agrees to serve Brock's will, to betray Weed Atman and to set up his murder, in a hotel room in Oklahoma City. A lightning storm approaches like a giant beast, lighting the clouds with "electric blue and now and then, all creviced in black, a terrible final red," sounding a "booming death-drone" (215). The storm confronts Frenesi with her own mortality and need for comfort; in its face, she sees that she isn't in control, that she is a small pawn in a large game of time and death. Pages earlier and years later, DL has a strikingly similar experience in a hotel room in Tokyo. Ralph Wayvone offers DL an equally odious proposition: she should kill Brock Vond, using her command of the martial arts in a way that violates their defensive intention. Meanwhile, "a lightning storm had appeared far out at sea and now, behind them out the window, was advancing on the city, taking brightly crazed shots all along the horizon" (138). DL drinks champagne as the storm approaches, while Frenesi in her hotel room drinks "a promotional magnum of Grand Cru de Muskogee Demi-Sec" (214). And DL makes the same decision Frenesi has made—"after a night and a day of jackhammer sex, amphetamines, champagne, and Chaliapin Steaks ordered up from Les Saisons" (140), she agrees to betray her own "fine clean self-command" and to commit murder.

Having precipitated a slow death for the wrong man, DL regresses into the same self-pitying childishness that Frenesi displayed in their last encounter in Mexico. Still dressed and disguised as Frenesi, she flees from the damage she has done to Takeshi and returns to the Kunoichi Retreat; Frenesi finds a similar escape in Brock's reeducation camp, which she does not want to leave. DL, a non-smoker, stays up all night and smokes, recalling Frenesi's behavior in Mexico (153, 259). Her confession to Sister Rochelle resembles Frenesi's to her. Frenesi in Mexico is "reduced to playing helpless, blaming external drug molecules for each of her failures, complicities, and surrenders," speaking in a "nasalized little-girl croak" (260). DL claims she was coerced by Wayvone—"I was taken!"—and begs to stay at the Retreat, with a flirtatious little-girl appeal: "Oh, child. Thirty-year-old, hardcase, cold and beautiful child," says Sister Rochelle (154-55).

In Pynchon's carefully doubled plot, both Frenesi and DL blind themselves to consequences. Understanding her own relative power-lessness, each of them shuns her own relative responsibility; both subscribe to the faulty logic that makes a small human force no force at all.[12] Each of them commits a peculiarly mediated murder—DL's, by her own hand, but delayed in time, and Frenesi's immediate in time, but through Rex's agency. Both women initially deny the gravity of what they've done, and both seek to avoid making amends or restitution.[13] Both women are precipitated out of the special exemp-tions from death and consequences that mark all the young in Vineland's sixties and dropped instead into a tragically real world of time and death. Both mourn the loss of their own special privilege far more than their victim's life. Instinctively, both seek escape, retreat, and comfort.

The divergence between the two stories begins at the point when their central women characters face the damage they've done. Though it costs her plenty, DL turns the rest of her life to acts of reparation, to taking adult responsibility for the wrongs, social and cosmic, that fill Pynchon's world. DL yearns to stay in the Retreat, the dark-walled fortress high above the complicated world, and she re-treats there in memory during rough times (180). She longs also for the escape into transcendent clarity that she's experienced with meditation, but "down here, she hadn't been able to sit and get into even the dustless-mirror phase before some other bullshit crisis would have her paged back once again out of the anterooms of clar-ity" (176). Since "the spilled, the broken world" is "malodorous, cheaply lit, nowhere-up-to-code," who wouldn't yearn to rise above it (267, 176)? But DL can't refuse the page, which calls her back down in to fix what's broken: Sister Rochelle orders her to atone, to be-come Takeshi's partner, "and to try and balance your karmic account by working off the great wrong you have done him" (163). Though it is the Senior Attentive's command, it is finally DL's own decision to atone, redress, make restitution in the cluttered temporal world.

She joins a partner whose business is redress for spiritual wrongs, or "karmic adjustment." As they become joint counselors for the Thanatoids, DL's whole vocation turns to diving into the "waste-pit of time," giving solace to unrestful semidead victims "of karmic imbal-ances—unanswered blows, unredeemed suffering, escapes by the guilty" (173). Though they can't repair the wound, redeem injustice, or restore lost youth, they listen to the stories and run traces on the elusive perpetrators of increasingly distant crimes. For DL, the awareness of time, death, and consequences becomes acute. Inoshiro Sensei has, she thinks, prepared her "to inherit his own entanglement in the world, and now, [. . .] with the past as well, and the crimes behind the world, the thousand bloody arroyos in the hinterlands of time that stretched somberly inland from the honky-tonk coast of Now" (180). While the unconnected present can be a scene of gaiety, drink, music, and forgetfulness, behind it stands a somber and bloody past in which DL and Takeshi grow entangled. Their immersion in these layers of consequential time enforces their close acquaintance with hard and complex truths, and challenges each of them to grow beyond the sixties' wish "to stay children forever" (269).

Frenesi's later story differs: it comprises one capitulation after another to the longing for escape. Left at the side of the road by DL, Frenesi finds cover and forgetfulness with the first man she meets, who happens to be Zoyd but who "could've been anybody" (282). She marries Zoyd because she is pregnant and tempted by the escape of being "just another mom in the nation of moms" (292). But motherhood comes to her not as an escape from consequences but as a yet deeper immersion in them: "She had been privileged to live outside of Time, to enter and leave at will, looting and manipulating, weightless, invisible. Now Time had claimed her again, put her under house arrest, taken her passport away. Only an animal with a full set of pain receptors after all" (287). She seeks a better escape, spending time at her mother's house so Brock can find her; when he does, Frenesi once again denies that she has any choice: Brock reappears, "forcing her over [. . .] ordering her up against her car [. . .] and before she knew it there they were in another motel room" (292). Frenesi thus renews her passport to a transcendent land outside time: "his erect penis had become the joystick with which, hurtling into the future, she would keep trying to steer among the hazards and obstacles [. . .] of each game she would come, year by year, to stand before." In video-land, Frenesi enters "game time, underground time, time that could take her nowhere outside its own tight and falsely deathless perimeter" (293). She stays here for at least a decade, around and through her marriage to Flash and the birth of a second child, Justin.

Working for Brock as seducer, betrayer, and informer, Frenesi finds her own "golden age" of freedom and pleasure:

Come into her own at last, street-legal, full-auto qualified, she understood her particular servitude as the freedom, granted to a few, to act outside warrants and charters, to ignore history and the dead, to imagine no future, no yet-to-be-born, to be able simply to go on defining moments only, purely, by the action that filled them. Here was a world of simplicity and certainty no acidhead, no revolutionary anarchist would ever find, a world based on the one and zero of life and death. (71-72)

As a government agent, Frenesi claims the same freedom Brock does (and Reagan, Nixon, Meese, and others named in the novel) from the laws and charters on which the government is based. Free of both the past and the future, she can ignore the dead and the unborn: in short, the world of spirit. Far from the risk-affirming momentary creed of *Gravity's Rainbow*'s Leni Pökler,[14] Frenesi's moments are precisely risk-free and certain; as in video-land, action has no moral consequence, and because they are rigorously controlled, life and death are as simple as the fates of Mario and Luigi. Only in the 1984 present, as Reaganomics cuts them off and she can't cash the last check she'll be issued, does Frenesi understand that she's "been kept safe in some time-free zone all these years but now [. . .] must reenter the clockwork of cause and effect" (90).

Many characters in *Vineland* share Frenesi's longing to escape from their own mortal liability in time: Zoyd Wheeler and Mucho Maas, among others, gain in the sixties drug experience a blissful certainty that they will never die (285, 313-14). But Pynchon's communal, harmless, spiritually earnest dopers use the momentary lifting of the burden of mortality as an impetus to resist the state, which wants them fearful of death so they can be controlled. However distanced the narrator may be from their sixties rhetoric—"It was the way people used to talk," he comments as Zoyd and Mucho discuss the state's manipulations—he echoes, in his own words, their assumptions about the state: "outside spread the lampless wastes, the unseen paybacks, the heartless power of the scabland garrison state" (314). Their quest for transcendent timelessness makes these men impotent to solve the deeper problems that afflict the state; Zoyd takes risks harvesting the marijuana crop and refuses Hector's repeated invitations to snitch, but these gestures of resistance won't change the conditions of repression. Still, their evasions of time appear idealistic and innocent in comparison to the drives leading Frenesi to stop the clock. She runs from her own past, from the deliberate betrayal of her own innocence, and therefore "for Frenesi the past was on her case forever, the zombie at her back, the enemy no one wanted to see, a mouth wide and dark as the grave" (71).

When she comes back to consequential time, Frenesi has relatively little to say for herself. Expelled from the computer by Reagan-controlled forces, she envisions God as a computer hacker, indifferent to human motives and aspirations (91). She feels, as she has felt before at major moments of decision, like a small pawn with no free choice in the face of enormous forces—like the storm in Oklahoma City, like Brock the cop. She goes to Las Vegas with Flash and Justin, and she takes a job as a cocktail waitress; if, as his lawyer tells Zoyd, "life is Vegas" (360), Frenesi can be envisioned tuning in to reality in these game rooms where chance and controlled odds intersect. At the same time, she can also be understood finding her way to another protected timeless game-land in rooms where there are no clocks. Hector Zuñiga finds her there and tempts her, with a picture of Prairie and a film to direct, to return to Vineland. She returns, labor idealism intact (she refuses to cross a picket line until given the picketers' permission), to intense but almost wordless reunions with Sasha (361) and Prairie (368). She has virtually nothing to say to either; she articulates no recognition or relief. She makes no evident contact with Zoyd, though Flash does. Small wonder the reviewers find Frenesi's return so anticlimactic: she has no light to bring to the novel's culminating events.[15]

In her last appearance in the novel, Frenesi runs into her father Hub. She recalls a dream of the night before, in which Hub has walked away from her, delivering a clear warning that she must come to terms with the past: "Take care, Young Gaffer. Take care of your dead, or they'll take care of you." She rejects the warning, the blame, and the exhortation to take care; the lost connections are the fault of the indifferent dead: "Yeah, or maybe they're just too busy being dead." Again, at the very end, Frenesi refuses the call to responsibility for her own actions and choices. She is left at the side of the road in her own dream, feeling "the emptiness that came into" her father's face (370).

Frenesi takes her place among a group of Pynchon's characters who attempt to solve the problem of time by reducing their awareness to a tiny fragment of unanchored "now." In particular, she resembles Tyrone Slothrop of *Gravity's Rainbow*: he too neglects the dead and flees the past, shuffling his own free will off onto large forces and faceless persons. On the *Anubis*, where he refuses Bianca's call to transformation, Slothrop "has begun to thin, to scatter. [. . .] the narrower your sense of Now, the more tenuous you are. It may

get to where you're having trouble remembering what you were doing five minutes ago, or even—as Slothrop now—what you're doing
here [. . .]. So here passes for him one more negligence . . . and
likewise groweth his Preterition sure" (*GR* 509). In seizing the freedom "to ignore history and the dead, to imagine no future," Frenesi
accomplishes her own similar erasure from the field of consequential
human time (71). Although, unlike Slothrop, she has her moment of
recognition and her chance to go home, she has likewise sunk far
enough in forgetting and narrowing that she can't, even in Vineland,
achieve a realignment with her past or a reunion with her lost double
—DL remains to the end of the novel ten minutes down the road.

DL and Takeshi achieve a qualitative change near the end of the
novel; they become partners in a broader sense and their work becomes a metaphor for Pynchon's own. Their immersion in time enables their discovery and creation of a complex relationship that
brings fulfillment to both of them. DL learns that Brock has been an
obstacle to finding her real goals or to perceiving Takeshi. After a
decade, they make love for a second time, while the sun sets outside
the window in "otherworld transparencies of yellow and ultraviolet."
The light echoes in DL's hair, weaving "a fractal halo of complica-
tions that might go on forever": a metaphor for intense feelings, both
hers and Takeshi's, of which she hasn't been aware, and for their
ramifying future (381). Takeshi and DL become, in the final pages, a
magic act that resembles the novel itself, "with its imitations of defiance, nightly and matinees, of gravity and death" (384).[16] Fending off
the "unrelenting forces" and defying the "faceless predators" who
follow implacably "ever after the partners into Time's wind" (383),
Takeshi and DL perform daily a resolute resistance to the authority
of all downward gravitational drags. Their defiance is no more victori-
ous, their imitation no less consoling, than Pynchon's own. Without
ceremony or sentimentality, this pair fulfills the promise of partnership developed through the novel.

Emerson and Sister Rochelle

Pynchon's novel concludes with a final and most peculiar pairing—
this time, of myths regarding earth and heaven, as developed by
Emerson and Sister Rochelle. The quotation from Emerson (mediated through James's *Varieties of Religious Experience*) is delivered by
Jess Traverse, the frail elderly patriarch of the Becker–Traverse clan.

As one would expect, the passage proclaims a transcendent order immanent in nature:

"Secret retributions are always restoring the level, when disturbed, of the divine justice. It is impossible to tilt the beam. All the tyrants and proprietors and monopolists of the world in vain set their shoulders to heave the bar. Settles forever more the ponderous equator to its line, and man and mote, and star and sun, must range to it, or be pulverized by the recoil." (369)

This passage calls justice "divine," but characterizes it as a wholly natural force, a gravitational field governing human affairs with the same impersonal power it uses to regulate stars and suns. Those worldly manipulators who profit from injustice (tyrants, proprietors, and monopolists) may indeed disturb the level, tilt the beam, heave the bar. But retribution arises like the action/reaction recoil of Newtonian physics to restore the innate balance of justice and to pulverize the guilty in the process.[17]

Emerson's ringing affirmation appears to some readers to radiate optimism through the end of Pynchon's novel;[18] for others, including David Porush and Elaine Safer, Pynchon traces a falling away through history from "transcendent origins" of the kind voices by Emerson and located in America's past.[19] In my reading, Pynchon is more skeptical: justice is *not* innate but won only through hard work and human struggle; injustice is seldom punished; origins are neither outside time nor above confusion; nostalgic and romantic myths about the past always reveal mistaken history and misplaced energy. He expresses a more plausible and compelling version of the human invention of a myth of retribution through Sister Rochelle. Pynchon sets this doubled but very different narrative of origins and of justice very near Emerson's; he gives Sister Rochelle not only the last word, but also the scope to develop her account in terms clearly relevant to *Vineland:*

"When the Earth was still a paradise, long long ago, two great empires, Hell and Heaven, battled for its possession. Hell won, and Heaven withdrew to an appropriate distance. Soon citizens of the Lower Realm were flocking up to visit Occupied Earth on group excursion fares, [. . .] till the novelty wore off, and the visitors began to realize that Earth was just like home, same traffic conditions, unpleasant food, deteriorating environment [. . .]. And then all the gateways to Hell were finally lost to sight, surviving only in local tales handed down the generations, sad recitals that asked why the visitors never came anymore, and if they would again [. . .]. So, over time, Hell became a storied place of sin and penitence, and we forgot that its original promise was never punishment but reunion, with the true, long-forgotten metropolis of Earth Unredeemed." (382-83)

Heaven and Hell have both left Earth on its own, and stories of transcendent sin and salvation are equally delusive myths. Earth begins both as a paradise in its own right, without Heaven's possession or intervention, and as Hell, with its share of problems and dissatisfactions. It was never defined by its transcendent visitors or their wars for possession, but from within, by itself. When the visitors quit coming, Earthlings build mistaken myths of both empires, denigrating their own earthliness in the story of sin and salvation. Hell was never a place of punishment, but only a divided and lost double whose promise was reunion.

According to Sister Rochelle, justice is created by and on Earth rather than soaring as a transcendent given in Heaven and Hell. It is a human longing, not something established with the order of the universe. Transcendence itself is a figment of the human imagination: though spirit and magic are everywhere in the novel, they are human rather than divine. In another of Sister Rochelle's appearances, she rejects the hope for transcendent illumination: "knowledge won't come down all at once in any big transcendent moment," she tells Prairie; "common sense and hard work's all it is. [. . .] Here it's always out at the margins, using the millimeters and little tenths of a second, you understand, scuffling and scraping for everything we get" (112). The dream of transcendence is illusory and dangerous: Frenesi's wish to be exempt, Zoyd's to be immortal, Brock's to be omnipotent, DL's to be invisible—all these are different faces of a longing to be "saved" from beyond, with no hard work.

Sister Rochelle speaks for the values of immanence rather than transcendence throughout *Vineland:* for effort, for "a serious attention span," for "continuity," "persistence," and a deep and serious attention to the immediate (112, 154-55). In another of her allegories, women are "content to just be" until men invent categories of good and evil and make women the custodians of morality; she urges Takeshi, "Don't commit original sin. Try and let her just be" (166). Paying attention, accepting the Other, working hard for understanding, persisting in one's commitments: these, I believe, are the earthly values Pynchon affirms in *Vineland.*

The novel doubles back to conclude with a second waking on a second summer morning in 1984. Desmond, rather than Brock, has come back for Prairie: "roughened by the miles, face full of blue-jay feathers, smiling out of his eyes, wagging his tail, thinking he must be home" (385). The blue jays have, at the outset, stolen Desmond's dog food on a routine basis; they "stomp" on the roof to wake Zoyd and they chase cars down the road and bite those who protest (3-4). Desmond has clearly caught up and bit back. While the feathers could signal a "secret retribution" restoring the ponderous equator of divine justice, they make better sense in purely natural terms. Prairie feeds Desmond a breakfast of Count Chocula on the first morning, but since then he's had to rely on his own hard work, on scuffling and scraping, just like Prairie. He's found his own breakfast by paying careful attention, and he's selected one better suited to his constitution than chocolate cereal. If the blue jays have their comeuppance, as Brock has his in the accidental crash of his helicopter, it's a victory not for justice but for the "faceless predators" who follow us all "into Time's wind" (383). Desmond isn't home, any more than Frenesi has found reconciliation, or Zoyd his lost love, or Prairie the mother she wanted for years. For Desmond, however, the morning's reunion in the meadow is enough.[20]

Writing itself can be seen as an "elaborate game of doubles," so that Pynchon's play with repetitions and variations makes a double commentary on reality and on art. Neither is single, simple, linear; neither derives its coherence from a given order innate in the universe. Both, therefore, invite participants to play, much as Pynchon does, with plural possibilities that create occasions for consequential choice. Pynchon's elaborate game demands readers attuned to echoes and parallels, to second orders of meaning, and to their own partnership in the play.

NOTES

[1]Carol Iannone, "Pynchon's Progress," review of *Vineland, Commentary* 89 (April 1990): 58.

[2]Brad Leithauser, "Any Place You Want," review of *Vineland, New York Review of Books,* 15 March 1990, 7.

[3]"Levity's Rainbow," review of *Vineland, New Republic,* 9 and 16 July 1990, 44.

[4]"That Was Another Planet," review of *Vineland, London Review of Books,* 8 February 1990, 3.

[5]Thomas Pynchon, *The Crying of Lot 49* (New York: Bantam, 1967), 137.

[6]Thomas Pynchon, *Vineland* (Boston: Little, Brown, 1990), 44; hereafter cited in the text.

[7]Leithauser, 8.

[8]N. Katherine Hayles sees this dream reflecting Brock's plausible fear that, because he represents the "snitch system," the "kinship system is his greatest antagonist [. . .] if he were to slip within it, he would become powerless, wrenched from the role of seducer to seduced." See " 'Who Was Saved?': Families, Snitches, and Recuperation in Pynchon's *Vineland,*" p. 19 above.

[9]David Cowart reads Frenesi's pact with Brock as a "bargain with the devil," in which she helps to murder "a man whose Hindu surname [. . .] denotes the supreme spiritual essence" and whose first name suggests both marijuana and garment, a metaphor for the body. "Frenesi, like the original Eve, has promoted the death of both the body and the soul" ("Continuity and Growth," review of *Vineland, Kenyon Review* 12 [Fall 1990]: 186).

[10]Joseph Slade suggests that Pynchon refers throughout *Vineland* to the theory of groups and that he models Weed Atman on one of its founders, Evariste Galois. "What probably attracts Pynchon to group theory, however," Slade writes, "is that it can support contradictory schemes of reality" ("Communication, Group Theory, and Perception in *Vineland*," above, p. 85).

[11]See Mendelson (44) and Joseph Tabbi, "Pynchon's Groundward Art," above, 95.

[12]N. Katherine Hayles traces Frenesi's encoding in the snitch system to the meeting when Brock tells Frenesi that she is only a set of holes for carrying messages back and forth between himself and Weed. "She exists not as a person with choice, free will, consciousness, but as a message sent back and forth between two male rivals and/or vicarious lovers. It is a small step from here to her full co-optation into the snitch system, complete with monthly stipend check and computer code" (see above, p. 23). I would argue, instead, that Frenesi exercises conscious will in choosing to accept the role Brock constructs—Pynchon emphasizes her repeated choices, as I will show, even while she claims she has no agency. Frenesi's attraction to Brock (a very odd choice, as all her friends agree) reflects her wish to abdicate her own free agency.

[13]David Porush misses DL's reluctance to make amends when he writes: "In a fit of remorse, DL persuades Takeshi to take refuge among the Sisterhood of Kunoichi Attentives" (see above, p. 33). In reality, Sister Rochelle commands her to go find Takeshi, who arrives at the Retreat through the assistance of Ralph Wayvone.

[14]"There is the moment, and its possibilities," she says of her activist life in the streets: Pynchon, *Gravity's Rainbow* (New York: Viking, 1973), 159; hereafter cited in the text.

[15]See, for example, Tabbi, 95-96 above. Mendelson calls her reappearance a "deliberate anticlimax" (46).

[16]See Cowart (*Kenyon Review,* 182) for a reading of Takeshi as the author's surrogate.

[17]The passage appears in an essay titled "The Sovereignty of Ethics," originally published in the *North American Review* in 1878, when Emerson was seventy-five years old. It is reprinted in *Lectures and Biographical Sketches* (Boston: Houghton, Mifflin, 1883), 176-205; the passage appears on 186. James quotes it to illustrate Emerson's faith in the *active* quality of the ordering principle in *The Varieties of Religious Experience* (1902; rpt. Cambridge: Harvard University Press, 1985), 35. Emerson begins the essay by linking the laws of the physical world (he mentions galvanism, electricity, and magnetism) with the laws of the moral and intellectual world, and throughout he uses metaphors of force and gravity to describe the moral order. The "idea of right exists in the human mind," Emerson says, and "lays itself out in the equilib-

rium of Nature, in the equalities and periods of our system, in the level of seas, in the action and reaction of forces." In that context, injustice attempts to violate a planetary order, but cannot succeed. This "is a doctrine," Emerson continues after the passage James and Pynchon quote, "of unspeakable comfort."

[18]See, for example, John Leonard, "The Styxties," review of *Vineland*, *The Nation*, 26 February 1990, 283, and Zachary Leader, "Living on the Invisible Boundary," review of *Vineland*, *Times Literary Supplement*, 2-8 February 1990, 115.

[19]Porush argues that Pynchon reserves his "gestures at transcendence" for the sixties as a way "to romanticize" this era and its politics. The novel's conclusion displays a nostalgic "desire for a return to the transcendent origins to which Pynchon has been pointing" (above, pp. 32-32, 35). Reading *Vineland* as an ironic narrative of the loss of the American dream, Safer likewise finds in "Zoyd's nostalgia for the primordial beauty of his wedding day" a personal parallel to the "desire to celebrate the transcendental meaning inherent in the beginning of a new nation, whose unsullied beauty is evoked by the novel's title" (above, p. 64).

[20]Hence the novel's epigraph, by Johnny Copeland: "Every dog has his day, / and a good dog / just might have two days."

When You're a (Nin)jette, You're a (Nin)jette All the Way—or Are You?: *Female Filmmaking in* Vineland

Stacey Olster

MICHAEL (Head Ninja): This time we must get *rich.*
NINJA CHORUS: Yea!
NINJA #1: What has happened, sir?
MICHAEL: The government said they will give us great re-
wards if we'll work for them.
NINJA #2: But what kind of work do they want us to do?
MICHAEL: Unravel strategic secrets and assassinate people of
high rank.
NINJA #2: That should be easy, sir, we're qualified for the
job.
NINJA #3: Not so fast. Don't you remember? One of the
rules of our ninja organization is *never* to get involved
in politics.

—Ninja Masters of Death (1988)

WHEN the last paragraphs of *Gravity's Rainbow* present the novel as a film, they encapsulate an immersion into movies that has been on display all along, as evidenced by references to actual films (*King Kong, Manhattan Melodrama, Die Frau im Mond*), genres (monster movies, gangster movies, sci-fi flicks), and techniques (Slothrop edited out of existence, the novel as a series of jump cuts). Concurrent with such cinematic rapture, however, is a large degree of revulsion, in that Pynchon remains acutely aware of the voyeuristic (Katje Borgesius tracked by secret cameramen), fetishistic (Greta Erdmann whipped and chained on-screen), and politically repressive ends (Goebbels's private collection) for which the medium can be employed. In this awareness, he anticipates the concerns of much feminist film theory of the 1970s, in which critics like Annette Kuhn, Laura Mulvey, and Mary Ann Doane focused on the ways in which woman has been constituted through processes of cinematic signification in which the spectator plays a central role.

119

To the extent that *Vineland* includes women who make films, women who appear in films, and women who watch films, the novel explores many of the questions that these early feminist critics raised with respect to the medium: what is the role of a feminist text? what are the processes of female spectatorship? what, ultimately, is a feminist intervention in culture? Yet to the extent that Pynchon is unwilling to accede to Mulvey's call to view "the decline of the traditional film form" with little more than "sentimental regret" (18), he deviates from the position his earlier exploration of film would suggest he take. Mulvey called for a cinema of "passionate detachment" that would destroy the satisfaction and pleasure that traditional cinema grants the spectator (18), and "detachment" is certainly key to *Vineland*'s conception of filmmaking. The problem is that the most detached person with respect to film is the one who should be most committed in that she is a woman making movies for a New Left collective, and the person least detached is the ninjette most overdetermined by forms of popular culture in which a man's gotta do what a man's gotta do, which generally means doing it stoically and alone. Both are "independent contractors" in their own ways. Yet the detached conception of independent filmmaking that Frenesi Gates practices ends up killing, while the hired assassinations for which DL Chastain trains end up invigorating. In other words, if confronted with the "Be groovy or B movie" choice contained within the kissoff of Frenesi's old film collective (252), Pynchon still would opt for the formulae of popular movies as a means of delineating what he feels to be politically groovy.

When 24fps, "the old guerrilla movie outfit" to which Frenesi has belonged (194), takes over the Berkeley Death to the Pig Nihilist Kollective, it also takes over much of the earlier group's manifesto and asserts: "A camera is a gun. An image taken is a death performed. Images put together are the substructure of an afterlife and a Judgment. We will be architects of a just Hell for the fascist pig. Death to everything that oinks!" (197). Stirring rhetoric, to be sure, and rhetoric that recalls the words of New Left filmmakers who saw film as "a weapon to counter, to talk back to and to crack the facade of the lying media of capitalism" (Buck and Ross 44), but not rhetoric unique to filmmakers documenting social protest in the late 1960s— the Workers Film and Photo League of the 1930s, for example, incorporated the notion of film as "weapon" into its founding statement, believing as its members did that film was instrumental in "spread-[ing] the message of struggle against unemployment, starvation, and

police clubbings" (Rosenberg 4), and this, in turn, echoed Dziga
Vertov's still earlier pronouncement of film acting "not as a *mirror*
which reflects the historical struggle, but a *weapon* of that struggle"
(Giannetti 243).[1] Yet denoting film a vehicle for transmitting existing
ideology does not necessarily mean dealing with film as an ideological medium itself, and in their failure to understand that property of
the medium with which they were working, the proponents of New
Left cinema seem, in retrospect, somewhat naive in their imaginings.
They described American mass media as producing a society of "spec-
tators" and they dedicated themselves to proving "that people don't
have to be spectator-puppets" (Buck and Ross 44), but their discus-
sions of the ways in which film could open those stupefied minds
"like a good can opener" (Kramer 46) invariably restored the filmmaker as purveyor and the audience as recipient of predigested information. "[W]e shoot what's important to us," Robert Kramer stated,
"what meets our perceptions of our lived reality; we cut according to
our priorities, our ideologies, [. . . and] we present it to them in its
nakedness, in our true understanding of it, not vitiated by analyses
and 'in-depth studies' that we do not accept, but just exactly what
counts from our point of view" (47). They spoke of defining "new
values, forms, new criteria" for individuals joined together as a collective (Buck and Ross 44-45), but operating under constraints in which,
as one member admitted, it was "[e]asier to define than make the
films we want" (Fruchter 44), they relied, particularly in early works
like *Boston Draft Resistance Group, Four Americans,* and *Meat Cooperative,*
on inherited cinéma vérité forms of straight exposition and minimal
interference. "New forms?" Norm Fruchter inquired. "But how much
will time, limited energies, finance, and the wearing pressure of
events, the race to stay responsible, limit us?" (44). Therefore, for all
its talk of making films like "battle footage" that would "explode like
grenades in peoples' faces" (Kramer 47, 46), the most famous of the
1960s collectives produced films that functioned more "as a barom-
eter, not a vanguard, of the New Left," as Bill Nichols has written,
which certainly befit a group that called itself Newsreel.[2]

24fps's method of hit-and-run filmmaking, so much like Newsreel's
trademark of making films "on the hoof" (Fruchter 45), displays a
similar approach. As Pynchon writes, "They went looking for trouble,
they found it, they filmed it, and then quickly got the record of their
witness someplace safe" (195). More to the point, having conceived
of the product of their efforts as a "record," and themselves, by extension, as mere "recorders," they are able to see the process of filmmak-

ing as removed from everyday actualities. Debates that center around "the claims of film against those of 'real life,' " specifically the possibility of one world intruding into the other and someone having to die for a piece of footage, end with invocations of moral certainty: "Long as we have the light, [. . .] we're OK" (202). And so unlike Oedipa Maas, who views the "act of metaphor" as "a thrust at truth and a lie, depending where you were" but can come to no conclusion as to whether she is "inside, safe, or outside, lost" (*Lot 49* 95), the members of 24fps feel few doubts about their own degree of safety: a camera is a gun as long as it remains in the realms of figurative language. Frenesi Gates distances herself even further through film. Defining moments as mise-en-scènes determined "only, purely, by the action that filled them," she imagines the "mysterious people's oneness" for which the Left strives in terms of photographic stills, achieved once or twice "in short, timeless bursts" that are adequately lighted—not even a movie, in which actions may be shown to have consequences, but snapshots in which temporal and causal connections are shattered (72, 117). Conceiving of the Canon that covers her face as her shield, she effaces herself as a person to become an extension of that which she holds in her hands—not the "cine (or 'kino') eye" lens that transmitted for Vertov a subjectively transformed "world the likes of which only I can see" (Feldman 9), but the impersonal machine itself.

For Robert Flaherty, whose camera unselectively recorded everything in front of it and whose stance of "non-preconception" was adopted by the practitioners of direct cinema in America (Mamber 9), such a completely uninvolved position was impossible: "Sometimes you have to lie," he admitted, and so he did, most obviously when filming *Man of Aran*, in which he fashioned a heroic family battling the sea from three people who hardly knew each other (Giannetti 240, 241-42). For feminist film critics who presume from the outset that representation is never a direct rendering of any "real world," such a neutral stance is patently untenable. Not only does the realism that the documentary—and especially the direct cinema or cinéma vérité variety—purports to convey perpetuate what Kuhn calls "illusionism," both in its assumption of a preconstructed single reality that exists beyond the screen and its positioning of the spectator as a passive recipient of that world that is already preconfigured (156-57), it also reinforces codes that permeate both the seemingly "natural" world and the "filmic" world. As Eileen McGarry has argued, physical reality is encoded long before the documentary filmmaker arrives, pro-filmic events photographed are coded further by virtue of the fact that filmmakers and equipment alter the shapes of scenes and the actions of participants, and the activity of filming itself is subject to codes of cinematography, film stock, and editing (50-54). The allegedly "factual" account that emerges as documentary is not the "true cinema" that the phrase "cinéma vérité" suggests but perhaps more a product of existing ideologies than a feature film because what it represents has been filtered through the codes of the worlds both on and off the screen (55-56).[3]

Pynchon indicates his awareness of film's political ramifications early in *Vineland*, with a substitution of linguistic interface for the metaphor of 24fps. "I don't believe this," Zoyd Wheeler tells DEA field agent Hector Zuñiga, "you wantin' to be in the world of entertainment, when all along I had you pegged as a real terrorist workin' for the State? When you said cuttin' and shootin' I didt'n know you were talkin' about film" (52). Yet nowhere is Pynchon's awareness dramatized more forcefully than in the scene in which the real world intrudes into the cinematic world of 24fps and the camera in point of fact becomes a gun: the assassination of Weed Atman. Frenesi's reassurances of "no one is judging you, Weed, the camera's only a machine" notwithstanding (244), the alleged neutrality of metal here ends in more than the mere witnessing of atrocities as happens when, for example, the protagonist of Isherwood's "I Am a Camera," already once removed for being the author's persona, observes Nazis beating Jews in Germany. It is not merely a question of the *Vineland* film being compromised by Frenesi's involvement in bringing the gun that kills Weed into the house and, in effect, staging the entire pro-filmic event. It also is a question of the presence of the camera affecting people's behavior while in front of it. When Frenesi aims the light on Rex after he has just shot Weed, what is photographed is a set piece: "Weed was on his face with his blood all on the cement, the shirt cloth still burning around the blackly erupted exit, pale flames guttering out, and Rex was staring into the camera, posing, pretending to blow smoke away from the muzzle of the .38" (246). The fact that it is Brock Vond who encourages Frenesi to believe that the real world of the gun and the make-believe world of the camera can remain separate and that her worst dilemma will be the necessity to choose between the two someday is comment enough on the repressive ends to which maintaining such a stance of objectivity contributes. And DL is correct in assessing Frenesi as never having deliberately chosen anything in her life (266). The point Pynchon makes in

Vineland, however, is that in a world in which cutting *is* shooting, choosing not to choose is a choice unto itself. It is Frenesi's absolving herself from coming to any decisions that turns her into the "legendary observer-participant" that those in the novel's 1984 present recall (51), but a participant whose legendary acts justify the producers' desire to have her make an anti-drug picture for the government's most recent blacklist campaign in Hollywood.

Moreover, one does not have to wait for Frenesi's deal with Vond to see the consequences of assuming art and life to be separate, for her later actions are prefigured in the filmmaking techniques that she favors all her life. Her parents' World War II courtship she processes as a jitterbugging-boys-just-home-from-the-war "costume drama" (75). Their joined narration she cuts together as shot-reverse shots (81). Even her own interview with a television newscaster she edits in close-ups, "[a]ware at each moment of the lens gathering in her own image" (195). By the time she first meets Vond, whom she tracks like a voyeur with her 16mm Scoopic before he sees her (200), and the time she photographs Weed, whom she fetishizes by zooming in and out to his crotch in time to the rhythms of Led Zeppelin (210), objectifying others in film has become standard operating procedure. She can set up Weed as a snitch, "attending a movie of it all" for remaining safe herself "in a world-next-to-the-world [. . .] where she could kick back and watch the unfolding drama" (237). She can watch Weed being "taken out" with impunity as Weed has already "gone turning into a character in a movie, one who as a bonus happened to fuck like a porno star" (237). She eventually can work for a government that is run by Ronald Reagan by presuming that each new sting operation is merely "another script" for her to learn (72). The irony, as it turns out, is that the moment Frenesi objectifies others is the moment others objectify her: tracking Vond with her camera prevents him from looking at her face, so he, possessed by "uneasy anima" and "scared to death" of sex despite his obsession with it (274, 276), transfers his gaze to her legs and nullifies any threat her body might pose by, in effect, cutting it up into pieces.[4] Having dealt with film as "framable pieces" of time all her life, she ends up "a set of holes, pleasantly framed" herself, as Vond is so eager to remind her, the "medium" that he and Weed use to communicate with each other (258, 214).

These cinematic techniques that Frenesi favors, of course, are precisely those that objectify women in the 1930s and 1940s movies that comprise what feminist critics call "dominant cinema"—it is then logical that Prairie, watching Frenesi's old movies, has difficulty making contact with her mother because the films, already "mediated by projector and screen," afford no room for female spectatorship (199).[5] Yet Pynchon suggests the continued impact such techniques have had through the 1980s by portraying television as the medium in which all the old cinematic techniques now thrive. Thus, Frenesi's tracking of Vond is presented as inscribing in her viewfinder "a TV-screen shape so you could frame a shot for the evening news" (200). Her son Justin frames feuding parents as characters in a television sitcom so that, as his smartest friend in kindergarten tells him, "You can go into it if you want, or you can just watch, and *not* go into it" (351). With the made-for-TV movies that Pynchon invents (*The Frank Gorshin Story, The G. Gordon Liddy Story, The Bryant Gumbel Story*) testifying to the rapidity with which living beings are transformed into figures on a screen (*Magnificent Disaster*, the story of the '83-'84 NBA playoffs, forcing even the unflappable Prairie to note how "they've been getting quicker over the years" [371]), it is no wonder that characters in the book start objectifying themselves to the point of speculating who should play them in the TV movies to be made of their lives, Hector wanting to be the Popeye Doyle of the eighties in both the movie and *Hector II*, the sequel, and finally the network series, with Ricardo Montalban in the title role (338, 348). With Sophia Loren, Theresa Saldana, and Suzanne Sommers having immortalized their own lives on celluloid a TV fact, and Amy Fisher and Joey Buttafuoco providing continuing proof that everyone (and anyone) really *is* entitled to two hours (minimum) and three versions (at least) of network fame, such speculation—if not downright immodest —is fully in keeping with the spirit of things.

Unfortunately, the spirit of things in *Vineland* proves less than spiritual. Television's rise to power occurred during the precise time that Hollywood's blacklist was providing the movie industry with "one of American misoneism's most notable hours," a reactionary backlash Pynchon directly links with Ronald Reagan's term as Screen Actors Guild president (289). By connecting the two in a book that takes place during another Reagan presidency, Pynchon establishes an indirect political connection between the power of the studio heads and the power of the heads of state, a connection reaffirmed by the concurrent campaigns waged by both in the book's northern California borderlands: one by cable TV companies that force a partitioning of the county into zones "which in time became political units in their own right as the Tubal entrepreneurs went extending their webs even where there weren't enough residents per linear mile to pay the rigging cost" (319); the other by federal Campaign Against Marijuana Production troops that act "as if they had invaded some helpless land far away" in order to force the frontier territories to rejoin, "operationally speaking, the third world" (357, 49). Because the damage perpetrated by cable riggers on "virgin redwood grove[s]" is no different in concept from the destruction "a great nation pursu[ing] its war on a botanical species" inflicts upon another kind of foliage (9, 271), the campaigns dovetail—and not only with each other. "Vowing to extinguish the feared herb from the soil of Vineland" through daily "search-and-destroy missions" (373, 334) recalls not just the legacy of Vietnam that *Vineland* explicitly considers, but a whole litany of genocidal campaigns mounted in *Gravity's Rainbow*, beginning with the earliest Slothrops' slaughter of trees, which are paradigmatic of the way that those who possess power deal with those who do not, whether the latter be dodoes, Hereros, or Jews, sustained in their efforts by a business cartel that turns concentration camps into tourist attractions.

Vineland, of course, provides no actual portraits of such genocidal endeavors, but it does offer evidence of the ways in which the media's representation of humans as characters, of *any* kind, on a screen, *any* screen, makes the act of extinction that much easier to effect. "If patterns of ones and zeros were 'like' patterns of human lives and deaths, if everything about an individual could be represented in a computer record by a long string of ones and zeros, then what kind of creature would be represented by a long string of lives and deaths?" Frenesi wonders with respect to what happens on the smallest of the novel's screens that presents to its viewers photographic images (90). More to the point, if all individuals can be represented as characters on a screen, and any operation on them performed by tap-dancing across "alphanumeric keyboards that stood for weightless, invisible chains of electronic presence or absence," how much easier it is to effect a "massacre" in which no blood appears to be spilled (88). God no longer has to throw thunderbolts, just have a hacker flip a switch: "less electricity than you think," as Flash is told by one of his old handlers, "put it across your dick on a good night chances are you wouldn't even feel it" (352).

To counter the tendencies that representation promotes in dominant cinema, and, one can assume, all dominant visual media, Claire Johnston calls for "a revolutionary strategy," to be achieved through films concerned not only with "substituting positive female protagonists" and "focussing on women's problems," but films that provoked "an analysis of how film operates as a medium within a specific cultural system," a cinema she found, ideally, in avant-garde filmmaking (4). Annette Kuhn's discussion of "deconstructive" or "counter-cinema," however, offers an alternative more appropriate to the realistic narrative that Pynchon provides in *Vineland*. Defined by its "articulation of [politically] oppositional forms with oppositional contents," deconstructive cinema self-consciously positions itself "in relation to dominant cinema" and takes its shape, "in an inverse manner," from the changing forms against which it reacts. Unlike avant-garde film, then, which can ignore prevailing trends, "deconstructive cinema is always, so to speak, casting a sideways look at dominant cinema" (160-61).

Vineland, in fact, casts a sideways look at visual images from many sources: Hector's longtime pursuit of Zoyd replays *The Fugitive* with male bonding its major theme; the sitcom *Say, Jim* remans *Star Trek's Enterprise* with an all black crew and one white freckled redhead named Lieutenant O'Hara (370). Significantly, *Vineland's* sideways glances invert gendered characteristics in particular, as is consistent in a work whose tale of daughters seeking mothers and mothers returning to homes besieged by interlopers can be viewed as inverting the *Odyssey*, complete with appropriate flashbacks.[6] Frenesi's riding into Zoyd's life "like a whole gang of outlaws" and making him feel "like a schoolmarm" exchanges both six-gun and feminine mystiques (36). Prairie's questioned paternity revamps the secret of the *Star Wars* saga that Pynchon cites (7), with Vond standing in for Vader. And Ché and Prairie's "Daughters of the Freeway" capers burn rubber an entire history of vehicular buddydom (*Route 66, Easy Rider*) well before Thelma and Louise even leave their front doors (331).

The creation of DL Chastain in particular serves as a magnet that brings together all these deconstructive inversions. "Oh, I need Superman," Frenesi prays, "Tarzan on that vine" (116), at one of the few moments that she looks up from her viewfinder during a riot and realizes that filmmaking has real consequences, and, unlike all those superheroes listed in *Gravity's Rainbow's* "Chase Music," whose faulty programming prevents them from arriving on time, DL cruises in right on cue, dressed in black from head to toe, a veritable wild bunch as wild one. Designating DL a ninjette only ups the superheroic ante, for, as a character in Eric V. Lustbader's ninja books points out, "Next to a professional hit man [a ninja is] Houdini,

Superman and Spider-Man all wrapped up into one" (*Ninja* 222). (Indeed, one of Lustbader's New York City ninjas does change his clothes in an empty phone booth.) Therefore, by working with formulae that graft codes of American Westerns onto customs of a culture in which men and women use different conversational forms when speaking, Pynchon can retrieve women from forms of popular culture that relegate them with respect to Eastern as well as Western models.[7]

Just how repressive those models are can be seen by looking at the Lustbader oeuvre, where titles like *Sirens, French Kiss,* and *The Miko* (which means "sorceress") are rife with suggestion, and where portraits rarely disappoint. Ninja battle always has sexual connotations, with extended swords "the most holy of holy" extensions of men (*Ninja* 491). Sexual activity is always denoted in terms of battle— Nicholas Linnear, Lustbader's hero, gains his *katana* sword as part of a manhood ceremony and keeps it hanging on his bedroom wall, which proves a handy decorating device in novels in which what men do to women in bed (or futon or garden or shower stall, depending upon the book) is "hilt" them (*Miko* 341, 403). And victory is always determined to the degree that the hero gives battles with men higher priority than beddings with women. Linnear's friend Terry ends his "love affair" with kenjutsu as his love affair with a woman begins, and both are killed for his sacrilege (*Ninja* 107). Lew Croaker, a New York City cop, decides, "I'm tired of caring more for my piece than I do for the woman beside me," and gets his left hand chopped off for such heresy (*Miko* 519). Linnear, who thinks at times that "sex is for the animals" (*Ninja* 436), and whose *dai-katana* is longer than the standard *katana* sword (measuring thirty inches according to two counts of Lustbader [*Ninja* 46, *Miko* 283]), forever emerges triumphant. What else should one expect of a man so attached to his instrument that he takes it with him to his Long Island summer home?

Women, in contrast, have only two options open to them. Good women, characterized as scared children in women's bodies or little girls who miss their daddies, look to strong men to take them in hand. As Justine, who fantasizes about getting her name from de Sade, admits, "I wanted to be dominated," to which our hero responds, "Is it so terrible, then, to want to be dominated?" (*Ninja* 53). Bad women seek to challenge the male's right to dominate by virtue of his sexual superiority. Thus, Akiko, the ninjette sorceress of Lustbader's *Miko*, who is born "a squalling, hairless infant with nothing between its legs but a slit" (293), kills men at the moment of their arousal, and, prior to slicing off their bodily parts with her fan, gloats: "where was his maleness, his traditional superiority?" (225). She never gets to slice anything off Linnear, however, for ninja plots demand that creatures such as Akiko be punished for seeking to upset the natural order. Angela Didion, a fashion model who nonetheless has "a lot of the male in her," is murdered in her bedroom (*Miko* 348). Tanya, a Russian spy who dares reassure an American cop that she is not about "to make a grab for [his] clusters," is killed on a Tokyo monorail (*Miko* 381). And, to drive home the proverbial, not to mention phallic, point even more forcefully, women who go so far as to renounce sexuality entirely are made to see how defined by it they really are, proving: first, that woman's sexuality is all they have to begin with, as Yukio, who has swung with Linnear from a shower head, suggests when describing herself as "nothing but a reflection," after she and Linnear have completed one of their less acrobatic couplings (*Ninja* 260); and, second, even that trait they do not really possess until a man decides to grant it to them. Akiko, who has tried to hide her sexual *wa*, or spirit, and concentrate on wreaking vengeance on Linnear, feels "connected to the universe" only after Linnear "hilts" her (*Miko* 341).

It is not only that Pynchon's granting DL a mention in *Black Belt* and an interview in *Soldier of Fortune* inverts gender roles and reclaims women from secondary, not to mention subordinate, roles in popular culture that is worth noting—William Gibson's conceiving his cyberpunk heroine Molly Millions as "every bad-ass hero, [. . .] the whole lineage back to Lee and Eastwood" does much the same thing (213) —but that Pynchon does so with respect to those ninja products that pander the most blatantly *unrealistic* forms of behavior that popular culture purveys. After all, Superman gained his powers from being born on a different planet; ninjas are born on Earth, though one would hardly know it from the feats that they perform; the hero in the movie *Revenge of the Ninja* (1983), for instance, catches blades in each of his hands and a third between his teeth while still grieving over the bodies of his just-slaughtered family; his aged mother (exempt from sexual women's constraints) does handsprings in a kimono to land in attack stance, gets off two blow-darts with a knife still lodged in her shoulder, and disappears in smoke behind a *shoji* screen, through which she then is pierced by the villainous ninja who, one can only suspect, has had a recent refresher course in *Hamlet*. By replacing the ridiculously named techniques that ninjas use to gain their edge—like "Bat in the Rafters," "the Human Eagle," and "Injuring the Corners" (*Miko* 410, 473, 522)—with techniques with even more ridiculous names—like "the Hidden Foot," "the Vibrating Palm," and the dreaded "Nosepicking of Death" (127, 131)—Pynchon indicates how unrelated to actuality all the heroics that popular culture purveys are, and this, in turn, enables him to concentrate on the characteristic of DL that distinguishes her from all those ninja prototypes: her *reality*.

Introduced by Pynchon as a "live solid woman" (99), DL gains much of that reality from the fact that the "athletic, even warriorlike" carriage she displays derives from a body that is all her own, and not an amalgam of surgical modifications like those of the medically enhanced Bionic Woman whom Pynchon cites twice (165-66, 327-28) and Gibson's metallically implanted razorgirls who speak the literal truth when ascribing their violent tempers to the way they're wired (25, 267). Yet as Pynchon's delineating DL's state of biological wholeness as "reclaiming her body" and "belong[ing] to herself" suggests (128), the issues here involve more than biology and reflect more than the mere horror of incorporating the inanimate into the animate that pervades *V*. "The schoolroom line was, You'll never know enough about your body to take responsibility for it," DL remembers, "so better just hand it over to those who are qualified, doctors and lab technicians and by extension coaches, employers, boys with hardons, so forth," a surrendering that this daughter of a wife-beater early recognizes as extending physical domination into psychological areas: "Maybe they think people are easier to control that way" (128). She later sustains her own sense of ownership by adamantly renouncing any and all forms of mediation that would compromise it. In clear contrast to the members of 24fps who record events but hide behind a camera, DL, who serves as "the realist wing of 24fps," stays as far out of camera range as possible (198, 195)—indeed, her worst experience is being trapped in representational imagery, as happens when the Depaato beauticians make her over as Frenesi to satisfy Vond's fetishistic longings (140). And unlike the members of 24fps who rely on metaphor for safety, DL serves her ninjette apprenticeship with a sensei who trains her to see no act having "any meaning beyond itself" (127).

It is a lesson that resonates quite loudly in Pynchon's work, for *The Crying of Lot 49* ends with Oedipa's questioning whether the word *America* denotes "a transcendent meaning, or only the earth. [. . .] Another mode of meaning behind the obvious, or none" (136-37).

With *Vineland*'s measuring the intervening quarter of a century in terms of Republican elections, the kind of transcendence that earlier could be counseled and before was achievable in select moments, succumbs to severe skepticism. Sister Rochelle of the Kunoichi Attentives warns Prairie not to expect knowledge to come down to her "in any big transcendent moment" (112). DL's sensei, aware that "the samurai condition of always being on that perfect edge prepared to die" (29) is already a thing of the past and its code of *bushido* totally anachronistic, tells DL that there exist now only "*sarariman*, incrementalists, who cannot act boldly and feel only contempt for those who can" (127). No alternative remains for "all the rest of us down here," as he puts it, but to adopt strategies that seem unpure and devoid of spirit, to take steps that appear "subverted, made cruel and more worldly," in effect to engage in guerrilla warfare (127). To presume, as the younger DL does, that "everybody's a hero at least once," is to be "crazy," as he tells DL, "seeing too many movies, maybe" (127).

Such guerrilla warfare stands in stark contrast to the kind of opposition practiced by the 24fps aesthetes. Frenesi goes so far as to advise DL to stick to the world of superheroes instead of opting for Clark Kent's world of ordinary citizenship: "Superman never has to get involved with any of that. Why should anybody want to be only mortal? Better to stay an angel, angel" (134). At the same time, DL's warfare also departs radically from that practiced by those ninjas up on the silver screen, whose eyes, if villainous, are likened to cameras, and whose hearts, if heroic, are pledged to uphold the State. The State portrayed in *Vineland* is a masculine enterprise, a "private little boys-only arrangement" (347), characterized by "humans, usually male [. . .] committing these crimes, major and petty, one by one against other living humans" (80), and constituted by "men making arrangements with men about the fates of women" whom they need as cover so that "the boys can go on discreetly porkin' each other" (305, 266).

According to Sister Rochelle, it was this "subdivided and labeled" wreck of man's creation that caused the destruction of the female Garden of Eden "where before women had been content to just be" (166). Yet as the question still discussed at the annual Becker–Traverse gathering testifies, the qualities of that primordial paradise need not be lost forever: whether the United States "still lingered in a prefascist twilight" or gained its illumination from "millions of Tubes all showing the same bright-colored shadows" remains a debatable point (371). Indeed, as Frenesi's gaffer father knows so well, "enough people still responded to the mystery of a powerful beam of light" (370). All they need is a proper source. In *Vineland*, that source comes not from the "lighted doorway out in the Amerikan dark" that the distanced aestheticism of 24fps offers (235): the light Frenesi provides when depicted as "the Statue of Liberty, bringer of light" is a "hard frightening light" that she shines as she stands over the corpse of a man who once loved her (261). It comes instead from an active involvement in the real, and is signified by the "fractal halo" that the "blazing beacon" of DL's "light-bearing hair" emits (381, 251). It is for that kind of engagement that Pynchon himself calls when having those at the yearly Vineland gathering read Emerson's call for "secret retributions" to restore the beam of "divine justice" to its proper balance and individuals who "must range to it, or be pulverized by the recoil" (369).

To be sure, it takes DL a while to feel comfortable with being involved in the assignments she is hired to carry out. "Then you know how personal this is," she reminds Ralph Wayvone in response to his proposal that she kill Brock Vond for him. "If you want real ninja product, that could get in the way" (131). Maybe for her, but not for Pynchon, for whom the personal here clearly *is* political. She may botch her attempt, she may lapse into "transpersonal mode" when putting the sting on Takeshi Fumimota (151), but being forced to balance her "karmic account" and being brought, repeatedly, "down again into the corrupted world" (163, 154), she forgoes the path that is taken by all those others, like Frenesi and Flash, who seek a compromised safety in "a government-defined history without consequences" (354). In *Vineland's* world in which Jasonic axes can fall at any minute and every day is a potential *Friday the 13th*, no one can remain safe in any "time-free zone" and, as the end of the book proves, all are forced to "reenter the clockwork of cause and effect" (90). DL just realizes this earlier than most. Granting her this awareness may not make the invisible visible, as feminist film critics would wish, but it sure does make the reel real.

NOTES

[1]For an extensive discussion of 1930s leftist films, see Alexander.

[2]William James Nichols, "Newsreel, Film and Revolution," Master's thesis (1972): University of California, Los Angeles, 51, quoted in Rosenberg 106. For a discussion of Newsreel's aesthetics, particularly the problems resulting

from its later attempts at greater stylistic experimentation, see Braudy 48-51.

[3]Joseph W. Slade makes an analogous argument when comparing the claims to fidelity of representation that visual imagery and language make (73).

[4]The classic cinematic example of such nullification is the shower scene in *Psycho*. For a more detailed discussion, see Bergstrom 53.

[5]For a contrasting reading that views Prairie's spectatorship as recuperative, see Hayles 26.

[6]I am indebted to my Stony Brook colleague Thomas E. Maresca for this insight regarding Pynchon's inversion of Homer's *Odyssey*.

[7]Obviously, conceiving of popular culture as having a history of its own to be inverted differs from the view of it taken by David Cowart, who sees "the virtual absence of historical depth" in the innumerable popular artifacts to which *Vineland* refers and the book's almost complete lack of allusions to high culture making "a devastating statement about the shortness of the American cultural memory" (8).

WORKS CITED

Alexander, William. *Film on the Left: American Documentary Film from 1931 to 1942*. Princeton: Princeton University Press, 1981.

Bergstrom, Janet. "Enunciation and Sexual Difference." *Camera Obscura* 3-4 (1979): 33-69.

Braudy, Leo. "Newsreel: A Report." *Film Quarterly* 21.2 (1968-69): 48-51.

Buck, Marilyn, and Karen Ross. "Newsreel." *Film Quarterly* 21.2 (1968-69): 44-47.

Cowart, David. "Attenuated Postmodernism: Pynchon's *Vineland*." Above, 3-13.

Feldman, Seth. " 'Cinema Weekly' and 'Cinema Truth': Dziga Vertov and the Leninist Proportion." *"Show Us Life": Toward a History and Aesthetics of the Committed Documentary*. Ed. Thomas Waugh. Metuchen, NJ: Scarecrow, 1984, 3-20.

Fruchter, Norm. "Newsreel." *Film Quarterly* 21.2 (1968-69): 43-45.

Giannetti, Louis D. *Understanding Movies*. 2d ed. Englewood Cliffs, NJ: Prentice-Hall, 1976.

Gibson, William. *Neuromancer*. New York: Ace, 1984.

Hayles, N. Katherine. " 'Who Was Saved?': Families, Snitches, and Recuperation in Pynchon's *Vineland*." Above, 14-30.

Johnston, Claire, ed. "Introduction." *Notes on Women's Cinema*. London: Society for Education in Film and Television, 1973, 2-4.

Kramer, Robert. "Newsreel." *Film Quarterly* 21.2 (1968-69): 45-48.

Kuhn, Annette. *Women's Pictures: Feminism and Cinema*. London: Routledge, 1982.

Lustbader, Eric V. *The Miko*. 1984. New York: Fawcett Crest, 1985.

———. *The Ninja*. 1980. New York: Fawcett Crest, 1981.

Mamber, Stephen. *Cinema Vérité in America: Studies in Uncontrolled Documentary*. Cambridge: MIT Press, 1974.

McGarry, Eileen. "Documentary, Realism and Women's Cinema." *Women &
Film* 2.7 (1975): 50-59.
Mulvey, Laura. "Visual Pleasure and Narrative Cinema." *Screen* 16.3 (1975): 6-
18.
Ninja Masters of Death. Dir. Bruce Lambert. Prod. Tomas Tang. Imperial En-
tertainment, 1988.
Pynchon, Thomas. *The Crying of Lot 49*. 1966. New York: Bantam, 1967.
———. *Gravity's Rainbow*. 1973. New York: Bantam, 1974.
———. *V*. 1963. New York: Bantam, 1964.
———. *Vineland*. Boston: Little, Brown, 1990.
Revenge of the Ninja. Dir. Sam Firstenberg. Prod. Menahem Golan and Yoram
Globus. Cannon Group-MGM, 1983.
Rosenberg, Jan. *Women's Reflections: The Feminist Film Movement*. Studies in
Cinema 22. Ann Arbor, MI: UMI Research Press, 1983.
Slade, Joseph W. "Communication, Group Theory, and Perception in
Vineland." Above, 68-88.

Feminist Theory and the Politics of Vineland

Molly Hite

T
HE crucial plot turn of *Vineland* comes with the clunk of heavy machinery stamping a monster footprint in the sands of literary history: "Suddenly, some white male far away must have wakened from a dream, and just like that, the clambake was over."[1]

This abrupt resolution to the central blocking action is of course a classic, nose-thumbing deus ex machina, all the more creaking because it undoes an initial, parodic deus ex machina, Brock Vond's descent on a cable from a Huey helicopter for the purpose of grabbing Prairie and winching her "back up and out" into his own predatory realm of "rapture" (376).[2] The redemptive turn has all the vagueness and arbitrariness of a Reagan budget cut, and the vagueness and arbitrariness emphasize how local, and indeed familial, any redemptive tendency has to be in this novel. If the notion of some white male somewhere waking from a dream echoes other and more celebratory awakenings in the concluding part of the novel—the whole Thanatoid village emerging out of *Bardo Thödol* limbo to to the strains of "one of the best tunes ever to come out of Europe," Bach's "Wachet Auf" (325);[3] and Sasha's dream *of* awakening her enthralled daughter with a "long, passionate kiss of freedom" (362)—it also lays stress on the existence of agonistic corporate and national structures whose "planetwide struggle" eludes these characters' agency and even their apprehension (146).[4] The hypothesized "some white male far away" is thus a synecdoche for a They-system that is largely beyond the reach of the major characters in *Vineland.*

What I want to note, however, is the kind of specificity that Pynchon has given to this particular They-system in making the hypothesized agent of this turn unequivocally white and male. The adjectives "white" and "male," precisely because they are unremarkable and even redundant, insist that power is a function of privilege and that privilege has racial and gender parameters. This insistence makes the oppositional Other of the fictional universe less abstract than in any of the previous novels. Brian McHale calls *Vineland* a sixties novel, perhaps even the definitive sixties novel,[5] but in important respects it is a novel that could only have been written looking back, from a certain perspective on the sixties. I want to suggest that this perspective is what makes *Vineland* Pynchon's most irreducibly political novel and that the major new component of his retrospective analysis is the element of political theory that was conspicuously absent from most sixties speculation and practice. I mean of course feminist theory. Unlike *V.*, in which "the feminine" was a force aligned with deathward-tending natural and historical processes—and against human agency; unlike *The Crying of Lot 49*, in which an allegorically feminine (i.e., open, passive) figure of the reader traversed an equally allegorical landscape of America's disinherited; unlike even *Gravity's Rainbow*, in which, after all, the preterite condition could be glossed by a technologized figure of castration, "the penis he thought was his own," *Vineland* is informed by a meditation on power and gender.

This meditation suggests some of the things Pynchon was reading in the seventeen years between novels. There is, of course, the by-now notorious reference to the "indispensable *Italian Wedding Fake Book*, by Deleuze and Guattari" (97)—and it may in fact be relevant that Pynchon here invokes the French writers whose *Anti-Oedipus* is a sustained diatribe against the psychoanalytic event propelling the subject out of the polymorphous garden of the imaginary and into the phallocentric wasteland of the symbolic.[6] But the allusions especially pertinent to the focus on gender are to two feminist classics, Eve Sedgwick's *Between Men* and Sandra Gilbert and Susan Gubar's *The Madwoman in the Attic*. In *Vineland*, these allusions are woven into a reflection on the social and political construction of masculinity, a reflection that grounds both the universe and the action of the novel.

The phrase "between men" occurs when DL speculates to Prairie about Brock Vond's motives in coming after Frenesi. "I'll admit, this is a lovelorn cop, OK, the worst kind of adversary," she begins, "[. . .] but this is something else between men, it's about whoever's runnin' Brock thinking, What can I get him to do for me, what are his limits, and Brock thinking, I did this deed for him, it wasn't so bad, but what'll he ask me to do next? Maybe your mom's only in there to make it look normal and human so the boys can go on discreetly porkin' each other" (265-66).[7]

The central triangle of what Sedgwick terms "male homosocial

desire" is summed up here in the hierarchical relation between Brock
and his unknown handlers, on one hand, and between Brock and
Frenesi, on the other. DL's point is that Frenesi functions for Brock
as an intermediary; she is not an end in herself. She is there "to make
it look normal and human, so the boys can go on discreetly porkin'
each other"—and it is significant that the word *porkin'*, like most
verbs in the English language signifying sexual penetration, may not
literally denote sexual intimacy. Sedgewick's study notes that the
homo*social* bond maintained by men through the mediation, usually
sexual, of a woman is not necessarily a displacement of a taboo homo-
sexual bond. It may just as well, given historical contingencies, be a
hierarchical bond, in which "porkin' " the woman is a means of serving or propitiating the other man, or an adversarial bond, in which
"porkin' " the woman is a means of gaining clandestine access to or
humiliating the other man.[8] Brock Vond himself articulates a version
of this last possibility when he tells Frenesi, at the point where she is
both his lover and Weed Atman's, "You're the medium Weed and I
use to communicate, that's all, this set of holes, pleasantly framed,
this little femme scampering back and forth with scented messages
tucked in her little secret places" (214).

Frenesi interprets this account of homosocial desire as an admission of homosexual desire when she ventures, "It's why you kill each
other, isn't it? [. . .] Men. Because you can't love each other" (214).
But Vond dismisses this interpretation as "hippie shit"; his own version, as the narrator observes, is that "he was offering her [. . .] a
secret about power in the world. That's what he thought it was. Brock
was young then too" (214). The narratorial tone intimates that both
accounts are still reductive and for that reason naive. In this novel,
neither Frenesi's thesis that sexual relations conceal underlying
sexual drives nor Brock's thesis that power relations hide underlying
power manipulations can be the whole story. In the masculinist upper
echelon where relations between men structure ideologies and institutions, sexuality and power are so interwoven that neither can be
isolated as the "real" ground of motivation—consider the implications of the computer game that includes "elements of sex and deto-
nation" and is called, catchily, "Nukey" (160). And this entanglement
of sexuality and power in turn defines masculinity within the dominant, and dominating, culture.

We see this entanglement in Brock's fantasy of putting a pistol to
Frenesi's head and forcing her to go down on him in front of all the
other countercultural detainees in the PREP camp. The narrator

notes, "Each time he daydreamed about this, the pistol would reappear, as an essential term" (273). But one implication of this entanglement, with its refusal to assign literal and figurative levels—to make the gun a figure for the penis, for instance—is that the operations of oppression become synonymous with the operations of masculinity. The masculine becomes by definition that which oppresses, that which creates its own subject class, thereby constructing the feminine. This account of the construction of masculinity in turn indicates how relations between men, and ultimately masculinity itself, are thereby dependent on the woman, and ultimately on femininity. Just as the woman is necessary to enable relations between men, the feminine here is necessary to the constructed masculine identity, which is threatened and may even disintegrate when the feminine eludes or exceeds its control.

One index that masculinity is a social construction in the world of *Vineland* is the way in which various people, not all of them biologically female, come to occupy the subject position of the woman. Brock's Lombrosian typology feminizes in the process of infantilizing its criminally deviant categories, affirming a right-wing sixties stereotype about counterculturalists as biologically regressive: "the long-haired bodies, men who had grown feminine, women who had become small children [. . .] the sort of mild herd creatures who belonged, who'd feel, let's face it, much more comfortable behind fences" (269). Zoyd Wheeler can choose only between female roles when Hector sets his virginity as a snitch against his maternal responsibility for his child's well-being (295).[9] Brock Vond himself is subject to the same sort of slippage. After Frenesi's escape from the PREP center, he has what the narrator describes as "this out-of-control mind-hardon," a paroxysm of psychic rigidity that translates him, paradoxically, out of the masculine domain of conscious manipulation: evocatively, he is "seized by gravity" (277). By the laws of the relational gender structure of this novel, masculinity out of control is no longer masculinity, as Brock's dream life has already revealed. His dreams are cued by the repressed recognition that as "the careful product of older men" (275), he plays the part of the woman in his dealings with the white males of the larger power structure, "that level where everybody knew everybody else, where however political fortunes below might bloom and die, the same people, the Real Ones, remained year in and year out, keeping what was desirable flowing their way" (276). These dreams are the context for the allusion to the second classic feminist text mentioned in *Vineland*.

For Gilbert and Gubar, the Madwoman in the Attic is the repressed Other of the heroine, and by extension of the author, in nineteenth-century fictions by women.[10] In *Vineland*, she is the repressed Other of the hero of Brock Vond's dreams, and by extension of Vond himself. The narrator defines her as one guise of Vond's "uneasy anima" (274), but in dreams this erstwhile feminine persona debauches Vond's masculinity through rape. As a Mr. Rochester-turned-security guard in the haunted house of his own embattled psyche, Vond repeatedly dreams that "it was his job to make sure that all doors and windows, dozens of them everywhere, were secure, and that no one, nothing, had penetrated." But the fortress proves permeable from inside: "He climbed the attic stairs in the dusk, paused in front of the door. [. . .] helplessly he opened, entered, as she advanced on him, blurry, underlit, except for the glittering eyes, the relentless animal smile, and accelerating leapt at him, on him, and underneath her assault he died" (275). Brock's identity, which in this dream is conflated with the national state he serves, guards, and represents, proves vulnerable precisely to the thing it oppresses—and represses. Because oppression—and, correlatively, repression—are the *determinants* of gender in his world, gender categories prove disconcertingly transposable. Underlying Vond's cocksure posturing is a secret terror of female sexuality as predatory and violating. Recalling the situation in *Gravity's Rainbow*, where death came out of the sky, and in anticipation of his later designation as "Death From Slightly Above" (375), he has nightmares in which he is "forced to procreate with women who approached never from floor or ground level but from steep overhead angles." The culmination of this rape is again and again a reproduction experienced as a drastic diminution: "each child he thus produced, each birth, would only be another death for him" (276-77). The unconscious fantasy underscores his fear of biological processes as a forced descent into a time-bound, mortal world.[11] The social construction of masculinity in which he participates embodies such processes in the constructed Other—in femininity—but the repressed feminine returns to claim his own body night after night. The narrator suggests that such visitations ultimately condition his decision to separate Frenesi from her own baby and that this decision "could only be crippled judgment" (294). Vond's psychic battle to maintain his masculinity by expelling contingency from his own life finally makes him unpredictable, and thus useless to the white men, the Real Ones, that run him.

The unnerving complement to this oppressive and repressive masculinity is the submission to the point of self-abasement that appears to define feminine sexuality in the character of Frenesi Gates.[12] At the heart of *Vineland* is a theme, familiar in many permutations and combinations from *Gravity's Rainbow*, of co-optation and collusion, here given concreteness and immediacy by being located within the vividly evoked history of the indigenous American Left, at a time when the phrase "American Left" sounds dangerously like an oxymoron. Pynchon inscribed the copy of the novel that he sent to his undergraduate mentor Walter Slatoff as follows: "Dear Walt, this is what you get for asking, a third of a century ago in class, 'How about a story where the parents are progressive and the kids are fascists?' See? You never know when somebody might be listening."[13] If the story of progressive parents who have fascist kids is not altogether new (Doris Lessing has been writing versions of it for years), it achieves particular poignancy in this account of the fifth columnist career of a near-red diaper baby, especially given the deep background of West Coast progressive politics in the first five decades of the twentieth century. In making Frenesi both a pivotal and a highly developed character, Pynchon is continuing the kind of psychic exploration found in *V.* in the account of Firelily's rider and in *Gravity's Rainbow* in the development of Blicero: he is forcing understanding of and even empathy for conventionally inconceivable acts. In *Vineland*, the inconceivable act is not genocide or filicide but snitching, a violation defined in terms of susceptibility to the Other rather than in terms of imposition on the Other. It is clearly consonant with the dominant social construction of femininity, and here, just as clearly, it exposes femininity as a limit. Frenesi shares qualities of female characters in the earlier novels, particularly *Gravity's Rainbow*. She has Leni Pökler's political idealism based on a direct and inexplicable apprehension: for both characters, "the street" of the political demonstration is a site of revelation (117). She has Katje Borghesius's odds-weighing turncoat mentality, along with Katje's acute awareness of the ambiguities and responsibilities of moral choice. And most obviously, she has Greta Erdmann's association of submission and abasement with transcendence. She is thus the most fully feminine character that Pynchon has created to date, and the character who most fully exposes the feminine as a necessary construction of the neo-fascist They-system.

In *Vineland*, it is not entirely true that, to quote Sylvia Plath's famous line, "Every woman adores a Fascist,"[14] but the germ of the fatal attraction seems in certain respects genetic if not universal, inhering in the maternal line that runs from Sasha through Frenesi to Prairie as a "wetness of attention and perhaps ancestral curse" (83). Prairie's weakly compliant whisper to the departed Brock Vond, "It's OK, rilly. Come on, come in. I don't care. Take me anyplace you want" (384), seems in ways to go further, striking a deeply problematic concluding note that suggests complicity may be as ingrained and inherent as mortality. But Prairie's particular vulnerability to this particular man is also a matter of family resemblance.[15] It is foreshadowed by the early and in many ways defining description of Frenesi settling down to masturbate while watching a *CHiPS* rerun, a description that establishes her "fatality, a helpless turn toward images of authority, especially uniformed men" that seems inherited from her own mother, "as if some Cosmic Fascist had spliced in a DNA sequence requiring this form of seduction and initiation into the dark joys of social control" (83). This "seduction and initiation into the dark joys of social control" was what allowed an apparent child of the sixties to find, as she sees it, her own Woodstock, her golden age of rock and roll, her acid adventures, her Revolution in the regressive seventies, where she "understood her particular servitude as the freedom, granted to a few, to act outside warrants and charters, to ignore history and the dead, to imagine no future, no yet-to-be-born, to be able simply to go on defining moments only, purely, by the action that filled them" (71-72). Servitude for Frenesi is both sexual and ideological: her specialty is that she is "willing to betray someone she'd been to bed with" (70). As in the social construction of masculinity, issues of sexuality are inseparable from issues of power—in the complementary feminine experience, sexuality is inseparable from powerlessness. But as with Greta Erdmann in *Gravity's Rainbow*, extreme submission provides a paradoxical route away from the merely temporal, the deathward-tending. Only when erased from the computer does Frenesi have to "reenter the clockwork of cause and effect" (90).[16]

And as in *Gravity's Rainbow*, the power structure claiming to transcend this ticking, deathward world is identified with fascism, most explicitly during Frenesi's postpartum depression, when she dreams of Brock as "leaning darkly in above her like any of the sleek raptors that decorate fascist architecture. Whispering, 'This is just how they want you, an animal, a bitch with swollen udders lying in the dirt' " (287). Brock's repeated use of the word *rapture* as code for the fate of disappeared political activists here acquires its crucial association with "raptor," bird of prey, agent of disappearance. Yet for Frenesi, as later for Prairie, to be seized and carried off is also to fly like an eagle. Sexual pleasure becomes for her the illusion of transcending physical process. In a mode of living significantly compared to a computer game, Brock's "erect penis had become the joystick" sending her through the world under the auspices of "game time, underground time, time that could take her nowhere outside its own tight and falsely deathless perimeter" (292-93). The notion of a perimeter that excludes death is a falsity, but it is deeply ingrained in even Frenesi's pre-snitch assumptions. She has a history of believing in frames that purport to exclude undesired aspects of the outside world.

Indeed, Frenesi's vulnerability to co-optation appears to have a second source in a widely accepted tenet of sixties countercultural ideology. If Frenesi seems dangerously unaware of her personal peril when she films violent confrontations between protestors and police —the narrator inquires rhetorically, "did she really believe that as long as she had it inside [the] Tubeshaped frame [of her camera lens . . .] nothing out there could harm her?" (202)[17]—her faith is congruent with the ground assumption of the 24fps collective that the real can be wholly contained within the frame, and kept there, uncontaminated by the ideology of the dominant culture. The collective's belief in "the ability of close-ups to reveal and devastate" (195), the camera eye as the unmediated gaze that sees into the heart of things, is a Romantic notion, central to a major sixties aesthetic and deadly to it, inasmuch as it is the frame that controls the gaze and encodes the presuppositions that will inform the image.[18] The close-up of Weed Atman is a stark illustration of the fallacy. The "frame" of the rhetoric setting him up contains a full set of assumptions: " 'Tell him!' Rex was almost in tears. 'Tell this asshole we know everything' " (245). By the time of the close-up, the fact that Weed is *in* the frame is constructed as proof of his guilt. Photographic evisceration of the image anticipates and guarantees betrayal and death.[19] Frenesi's Scoopic records "the way that what he was slowly understanding spread to his body, a long, stunned cringe, a loss of spirit that could almost be seen on the film [. . .] some silvery effluent, vacating his image, the real moment of his passing" (246). In the most ordinary slang sense of the term, Weed is framed.

Frenesi's naïveté grows increasingly studied as she moves into Brock Vond's orbit. Initially basing actions on the premise that she has unmediated access to a truth uncontaminated by the dominant culture—as she tells DL, "I have to trust the way this makes me feel. Feels right, DL. Like we're really going to change the world this time" (118)—she goes on to use this appeal to direct experience as an excuse and cover: "you know what happens when my pussy's runnin' the show" (260). This idea that sexual response is something like a natural ground for judgment is exploded when she articulates the choice "between worlds" that Brock offers her when he offers her the gun: "So either I pussy out or become a courier of death" (241). In choosing the gun over "pussying out," she incorporates herself fully into a system that not only exploits but also maligns her sexuality. The epitaph for her particular romanticizing and theorizing of the natural and the immediate seems to mourn the end of a whole realm of possibility: "These people had known their children, after all, perfectly" (239). By the time Brock realizes his sexual fantasy, with Zoyd as audience, the gun is no longer the essential term. The phallic guarantor of obedience has been internalized as masochism: "her neck was bent, [. . .] as if willingly, for some high-fashion leather collar" (304).

That *Vineland* does not entirely exclude the possibility of resistance is in a great part due to the fact that Frenesi is not allowed to stand as the sole emblem of female being. Nor is her heterosexual romantic thralldom[20] her only sexual possibility. For the first time in Pynchon's work, homosexualities are not by definition affairs between men. In fact, the only homosexual relationship in this book is between Frenesi and DL, and the bisexuality of these two female characters deepens and complicates the investigation into the links between eroticism and power. DL's response to Frenesi's betrayal—"she might've expected it from a lover, but hell, they'd been *partners*" (237)—laments an egalitarian working relationship that was also an erotic relationship but that was too far gone to elicit, in the scene of recrimination that followed DL's second "rescue" of Frenesi, even the memory of an alternative model of sexuality: "Frenesi wanted to cry, [. . .] 'you saw me do stuff he'll *never* see,' and DL, not as angry by then, might've answered, 'I *made* you do stuff, bitch,' and Frenesi would have felt a bodylong twinge of clear desire for her already ex-partner" (260). Yet insofar as Frenesi is reclaimed on the level of plot at the conclusion, she is reclaimed through the agency of DL, who is the main link between Frenesi and Prairie and who presents the possibility of alternative constructions—both of female being and of heterosexual partnership.

DL's martial arts background offers a parodic version of female adolescence. Ralph Wayvone cites her career in the ring in terms reminiscent of beauty contests: "Darryl Louise, think of who you are—mentioned in *Black Belt* before you were ten, the *Soldier of For-*

tune interview, that centerfold in *Aggro World*, almost made runner-up
in the Dangerous Teen Miss pageant in '63" (138-39). The implication is that these accomplishments are as erotically attractive, and
make her as useful, to the masculinist power structure as success in
the more conventional pageants and centerfolds. But there is a difference. In an important passage about the social construction of femininity, the narrator synopsizes the official ideology about the female
body: "The schoolroom line was, You'll never know enough about
your body to take responsibility for it, so better just hand it over to
those who are qualified, doctors and lab technicians and by extension
coaches, employers, boys with hardons, so forth" (128). Because of
her background, her observation of her abusive father and passive
mother, her "advanced ruthlessness of spirit" that leads her to the
sensei and his own compromises and excesses (122), and other
largely accidental conditions, DL is no host for this spore of masochism: "alarmed, not to mention pissed off, DL reached the radical
conclusion that her body belonged to herself" (128). DL thus stands
in dramatic contrast to Frenesi, who for a large portion of her life
and the novel seems to be, like Wayvone Enterprises, a wholly owned
subsidiary of a major power structure. DL's example also serves to
undermine the hegemony of ownership. Even in *Vineland*'s universe
of multinational capitalism, possession is relative, partial, as ultimately compromised as any tenet of the countercultural ideology.
Most important, it too is subject to unpredictable kinds of slippage.

  Thus in a crucial plot development, Ralph Wayvone *buys* DL to do
in Brock Vond, thwarting DL's own inclination to steer away from the
seductions of ersatz transcendence and to metamorphose back into
Clark Kent, "merely mortal" (134).[21] But the plan backfires for a number of reasons, perhaps most fundamentally because of the lapse in
DL's own powers that Sister Rochelle sums up as "no continuity, no
persistence, no . . . fucking . . . attention" (155, Pynchon's ellipses).
That the lapse is intrinsic is something DL already knows on one
level. Her sensei had already admitted her training "is for all the rest
of us down here with the insects, the ones who don't quite get to
make warrior, who with two tenths of a second to decide fail to get it
right and live with it the rest of our lives" (127). This explanation
echoes the great elegy for the preterite in *Gravity's Rainbow* that begins "The rest of us, not chosen for enlightenment, left on the outside of Earth, at the mercy of a Gravity we have only begun to learn
how to detect and measure, must go blundering inside our front-
brained faith in Kute Korrespondences."[22] In *Vineland*, however, the

emphasis falls not on failure of comprehension but on failure of will, a deficiency that, Sister Rochelle's diatribe suggests, could be remedied. Moreover, there is a quotidian *felix culpa* here. DL's mortal failing forces her into a linkage with former Komikal Kamikaze[23] and current "Jap Robert Redford" (381) Takeshi Fumamota, in the Tube-inspired role of his "big sidekick" (163). As their business dealings take them into the eschatological realm of "karmic adjustment," their relationship evolves to an increasingly egalitarian and finally erotic partnership, of a sort as yet underrepresented inside the Tubal frame.[24]

As cosmic resolutions go, this one is fragile, precarious, and deeply contaminated. It is unclear, for instance, "whether the Baby Eros, that tricky little pud-puller, would give or take away an edge regarding the unrelenting forces that leaned ever after the partners into Time's wind [. . . who] had simply persisted, stone-humorless, beyond cause and effect" (383). But despite a certain similarity in the matter of unrelenting forces, this is not the same order of conclusion as the one in *Gravity's Rainbow* that leaves the apocalyptic Rocket poised above "us." One reason is the complexity that Pynchon has given in the later work to the interconnections between sex and death. The sexuality that the forces of contemporary nationalism, corporatism, and technology have shaped to the point where the subject "might be in love, in sexual love, with his, and his race's, death" (*GR* 738) is by definition masculine sexuality—which is to say, not the only culturally constructed sexuality, even if the cultural construction of this sexuality is presumed to be 100 percent successful. Adversarial characters like DL, the Pisk sisters, Sister Rochelle, and Sasha Gates are, like all Pynchon characters, derivative, emblematic, and parodic,[25] but they indicate that any Other against which masculine sexuality is defined necessarily encodes possibilities of resistance.

Some of these possibilities are realized in the form of developed, resisting characters. The protagonists of this novel's quest—for identity, for origins, for the missing and potentially defining parent—are female, and the centrality of female figures sets up a collective "we" that can instructively be compared to the elegiac, universalizing "we" of *Gravity's Rainbow*. Sister Rochelle's version of the myth of the Fall is a case in point because it reinscribes one of the key narratorial meditations in *Gravity's Rainbow*, where the Fall is a *Totem and Taboo* turn from the world of the Titans, "an overpeaking of life so clangorous and mad, such a green corona about Earth's body that some spoiler *had* to be brought in before it blew the Creation apart," to the

Olympian or Apollonian realm of "Us," "God's spoilers": *"It is our
mission to promote death"* (*GR* 720, Pynchon's italics). The first-person
plural pronoun of such passages includes the reader, who is presumed to have a certain direct stake in the structures favoring death:
as the narrator observes in an important passage a few pages earlier,
"The Man has a branch office in each of our brains, his corporate
emblem is a white albatross, each local rep has a cover known as the
Ego, and their mission in this world is Bad Shit" (*GR* 712-13). In the
global vision of Pynchon's great epic and threnodic novel, "we" are
both victims and oppressors, both adversaries and, inevitably, collaborators in "our" fall from innocence into technologized, deathward-
tending experience.[26] The purportedly all-embracing scope of this
narratorial "we" has much to do with the nearly immediate high-
culture status of *Gravity's Rainbow:* the novel is, in the last analysis, a
treatment of that very literary topic the human condition—which is
to say that for all its historical documentation and political acuteness,
it tends ultimately to subsume historical specificity under comprehensive statements about the Mortal State, the one we all indubitably
inhabit. The Rocket of the culminating Descent passage hangs above
the heads of an "us" explicitly equated with the entirety of the potential readership: "Now everybody—" (*GR* 760).

   In Sister Rochelle's version in *Vineland,* however, the original
Edenic inhabitants were women, and the phallic spoilers who were
the cosmic latecomers "dragged us all down into this wreck they'd
made of the Creation, all subdivided and labeled, handed us the keys
to the church, and headed off toward the dance halls and the honky-
tonk saloons" (166).[27] The "us" here is explicitly adversarial (the story
is intended as an object lesson for Takeshi), a construction of opposition to the dominant, usurping culture that murders to dissect. Unlike the "us" of the *Gravity's Rainbow* passage about the Titans, an "us"
identified with "human consciousness, that poor cripple, that de-
formed and doomed thing" (*GR* 720), it is not universal, precisely
because it is oppositional. It denotes the female half of fallen humanity, disempowered and driven to the margins of the process of subdi-
viding and labeling (the same Original Sin that in *Gravity's Rainbow*
was identified as Modern Analysis [*GR* 722]) and installed in the
demoted subdivisions.

   This account of the Fall occurs in quotation marks and is clearly
ascribed to Sister Rochelle and thus to a particular kind of feminism,
espoused tactically and perhaps only provisionally. But the "us" in
this passage is also cognate with two striking instances in which the

narrator uses the first-person plural pronoun, and uses it intrusively precisely because the group that it designates cannot be coextensive with the whole potential readership of *Vineland*. The "us" and "we" of the two passages are partial, in two senses. First, they group the narrator with a part—here, clearly a minority—of the whole population. Second, they align the narrator with beliefs and experiences that mainstream representations—the interpretations purveyed by what the novel elsewhere terms official reality (205)—perceive as non-normative and biased.

The first of these passages occurs within a discussion of Frenesi's long decline from countercultural idealism, illustrated by her trivialization of the word *love*, a word in turn central to "all that rock and roll, the simple resource we once thought would save us" (217). In the second, the narrator describes Zoyd's first stunned recognition of the newborn Prairie as a legacy of "these acid adventures, they came in those days and they went, some we gave away and forgot [. . .] but with luck one or two would get saved to go back to at certain moments in life" (285). The "we" and "us" of the first passage identify the narrator with an earlier belief in the salvific powers of rock and roll. The "we" of the second passage identifies this narrator as somebody who has taken LSD and who still attributes therapeutic, if not revelatory, properties to his "acid adventures."[28] The plural form of the pronouns enjoins reader participation, not in the innocence of the late-sixties beliefs reported (and, at least in the first case, repudiated) but in recollection of that innocence. This is a novel about how innocence was betrayed—but it is also a novel in which rueful recollection does not necessarily entail complicity, a Man securely lodged in "our" brains.

In *Vineland*, complicity is a fact of life, but it is not inevitable any more than it is always advertent. The exorbitantly self-justifying Flash makes the point when he comments, "We're in th' Info Revolution here. Anytime you use a credit card you're tellin' the Man more than you meant to" (74). Technology has brought government and corporate surveillance to such a pitch that snitching has become outmoded, if not redundant. On the other hand, in *Vineland* complicity is not by definition total and does not by definition rule out resistance. In contrast to *Gravity's Rainbow*, where the only possibility for opposition seemed rooted in a prehistoric, or pre-Western historic, purity, associated with primal Nature and emblematized by such figures as "the Great Serpent holding its own tail in its mouth" (*GR* 412) or the pre-Olympian Titans, *Vineland* suggests that originary purity was always a delusion. The real always did come framed by expectations and preconceptions: in the sixties, by the ideologies of a pop and drug culture driven by the quest for new and bigger markets, as the career of Mucho Maas illustrates. The ubiquitous television allusions in this novel suggest how the Tube has reinforced the hegemony of official reality; in Isaiah Two Four's words, "Minute the Tube got hold of you folks that was it, that whole alternative America, el deado meato, just like th' Indians, sold it all to your real enemies, and even in 1970 dollars—it was way too cheap" (373).[29] But the dominant society of the novel, like the pervasive and coercive universe of the Tube, is also fissured by internal contradictions, suggested by the rival Cable Zones in Vineland, which "in time became political units in their own right" (319). The They-system that aims to infantilize an entire nation into unquestioning obedience—to produce "a timeless, defectively imagined future of zero-tolerance drug-free Americans all pulling their weight and all locked in to the official economy, inoffensive music, endless family specials on the Tube, church all week long, and, on special days, for extra-good behavior, maybe a cookie" (221-22)—still somehow engenders children who repudiate the official father, if in commodified Tubal language. Prairie's initial response to Brock Vond, as he hovers wraithily over her, is "But you can't be my father, [. . .] my blood is type A. Yours is Preparation H" (376).

In the universe of *Vineland*, corrupted and even co-opted innocence can still turn against the Man, and this Man is clearly identified with current political figures—and clearly identified as not-"us."[30] The significantly gendered case in point is the prodigal daughter Frenesi Gates, who returns to the Traverse–Becker reunion and its version of a maimed but still potent alternative. This return is not a restoration; it does not bring back the sixties—or the thirties, or the teens. But it does reconstitute a community of resistance in a widened historical context. This last point is important because if *Vineland* is, as McHale has commented, a sixties novel, it is not thereby a novel that, as Joseph Tabbi charges, takes "an imaginative shortcut [. . .] an acceptance of a ready-made audience that frees [Pynchon] from the responsibility of creating the sensibility by which he will be understood."[31] In *Vineland* Pynchon is again working to create a sensibility, but it is a political sensibility, one that tacitly acknowledges the possibility of bad faith in subsuming considerations of exploitation to considerations of mortality.[32] *Vineland* is Pynchon's most irreducibly political novel because of its vision of the sixties, but this vision, ironic and critical as well as celebratory, is less a source of nostalgia than a basis for reference and comparison. Like the computer screen on which Prairie views reconstructed photographs of her mother, the novel offers certain framed takes on a pivotal period in recent history, a period in which a number of alternatives to the dominant culture and society were proposed, tried out, questioned, and often betrayed. Unlike *Gravity's Rainbow*, it does not offer a We-system that will accommodate all possible readers—that will involve "everybody" equally in its acknowledgments of victimization and oppression. What it does offer is an explicit and articulated They-system, a political analysis, an examination of social and historical differences.

NOTES

[1]Thomas Pynchon, *Vineland* (New York: Penguin, 1991), 376. For the unresolved plot turn involving a Godzilla-style footprint signaling, *Gravity's Rainbow*-style, "some imminent unthinkable descent," see 144-45. All further references to *Vineland* will be to this edition; page numbers will appear within parentheses in the body of the text.

[2]In " 'Purring into Transcendence': Pynchon's Puncutron Machine," David Porush notes the "creaking deus ex machina" and its cancellation "through Pynchon's own machinations" (above, p. 37).

[3]David Cowart finds this high-culture musical allusion "comically undercut" because the chorale is played by sound chips on watches, computers, and timers (above, pp. 6-7). But for hundreds of years the piece has been played with great success by music boxes and clock-tower carillons. The narrative comment "And not the usual electronic stuff—this had soul" (325) adds to a more general suggestion that this awakening, "like a class-action lawsuit suddenly resolved after generations in the courts," is to be read as a genuine turn. After all, "Wachet Auf" was written for organ, a proto-synthesizer, and its polyphony, like that of so much of Bach's work, achieves its effects irrespective of instrumentation. In this, as in so many other instances, it seems unwise to hold Pynchon to current high-culture norms.

[4]The conclusion of *Vineland* is no less equivocal than the conclusions of preceding Pynchon novels, and as always, the readings vary widely. For example, Alan Wilde notes the "gallimaufry of conflicts and equivocal messages" in *Vineland* and finds ultimately a "refusal of the existential commitment it ponders only to evade" ("Love and Death in and Around Vineland, U.S.A.," *boundary 2* 18.2 [1991]: 179-80). David Porush, on the other hand, considers "the happy and transcendent ending" in 1984 as having possible autobiographical implications, perhaps for the long-awaited breakup of Pynchon's writer's block (" 'Purring into Transcendence,' " 38). Brian McHale notes "one major plot-line and a couple of subplots, all of manageable complexity, and all converging toward a kind of climax, admittedly muted and oblique, but a far cry from the centrifugal (non)ending of

Gravity's Rainbow" ("Publishing Events and Unfinished Business," *American Book Review* 12.3 [August 1990]: 8).

[5]McHale, 8.

[6]Gilles Deleuze and Felix Guattari, *Anti-Oedipus: Capitalism and Schizophrenia,* trans. Robert Hurley, Mark Seem, and Helen R. Lane (New York: Viking, 1977).

[7]If such male homosocial bonding is the rule in the universe of *Vineland,* it is a rule regularly noted as such by the female characters. When Zoyd agrees to entrust Prairie to the protection of her boyfriend, Isaiah Two Four, Prairie interrupts, "What is this? Typical males, you're handin' me back and forth like a side of beef?" (53). After Hector and Zoyd have made the deal whereby Zoyd agrees to keep Frenesi from the infant Prairie in order to keep Prairie with him, Sasha comments, "Usual thing, men making arrangements with men about the fates of women" (305).

[8]Eve Sedgwick, *Between Men: English Literature and Male Homosocial Desire* (New York: Columbia University Press, 1985), 21-27.

[9]N. Katherine Hayles notes, "the kinship system is mapped onto [the snitch system] through the trope of virginity," which genders Hector and Zoyd as seducer and seduced respectively (" 'Who Was Saved?': Families, Snitches, and Recuperation in Pynchon's *Vineland,*" above, p. 16).

[10]Sandra Gilbert and Susan Gubar, *The Madwoman in the Attic: The Woman Writer and the Nineteenth-Century Literary Imagination* (New Haven and London: Yale University Press, 1979).

[11]Pynchon has been playing with this alignment of femininity and mortality since at least "Entropy"; in *Gravity's Rainbow* he groups masculinity with abstraction, transcendence, and fascism. Klaus Theweleit's monumental study of the proto-Nazi *Freikorps* after World War I, *Male Fantasies, Volume 1: Women, Floods, Bodies, History,* trans. Stephen Conway (Minneapolis: University of Minnesota Press, 1987), suggests how historically accurate such an analysis is; for both sides of Vond's fantasy, see especially pp. 63-84.

[12]Frenesi's name, a homonym for "frenzy" (David Cowart also sees an anagram for "sin free"—see his "Continuity and Growth," *Kenyon Review* 2.4 [1990]: 185), derives from a classic Artie Shaw recording, according to the narrator (75). The pun cuts across agency (Frenesi both incites and embodies frenzy) and historical periods (she is born into the postwar frenzy of Hollywood blacklisting and the last great resistance on the part of the unions; she comes of age during the sixties frenzy of activism and, as a member of 24fps observes, participates in, and betrays this frenzy). In many respects she is the figure in *Vineland* who cuts across oppositional categories, an ambiguously valued Other who functions as the site of both revolution and complicity. For instance, she is an emblem of "the new," the revolutionary spirit that Brock's Lombrosian force "misoneism" counters, but precisely in her heterosexual desire she is also the chief agent of this misoneism (272-73). As electronically recollected role model for Prairie, she is the paradigmatic progressive parent in this generational saga; as the red-diaper snitch she is the paradigmatic fascist kid.

[13]Title page, copy of *Vineland* sent by Pynchon to the late Walter Slatoff, now in the possession of Jimmy Slatoff.

[14]"Daddy," in her *Collected Poems,* ed. Ted Hughes (London: Faber and Faber, 1981).

[15]There is some suggestion that it is also an attempt at female homosocial bonding, part of Prairie's quest for reunion with her mother.

[16]Such phrases also recall the "clock time" and "mirror time" opposition in *V.*

[17]Pynchon picks up the key term from Richard Fariña's *Been Down So Long It Looks Like Up to Me,* introduction by Thomas Pynchon (New York: Penguin, 1983), in extending this faith to the whole 24fps collective and, by implication, to a whole generation: "They were still young, exempt" (203).

[18]As Joseph Slade notes, "Hierarchies govern a system by organizing, programming, distributing, and monitoring the flow of information within and without; that is what *control* means" ("Communication, Group Theory, and Perception in *Vineland,*" above, p. 71).

[19]Some of the most astute Pynchon critics have been curiously reluctant to accept that Weed really dies here or that the Thanatoids whom he joins are also nonliving, although unquiet. The problem is a pervasive one in Pynchon criticism and may reflect some of the genre unease that Susan Strehle notes in proposing the descriptive term "actualism" where neither "realism" nor "anti-realism" seems appropriate (*Fiction in the Quantum Universe* [Chapel Hill, NC: University of North Carolina Press, 1992], especially the chapter on *Gravity's Rainbow,* pp. 27-65). For all its relevance and reference, *Vineland* violates realist and naturalist conventions as thoroughly as the preceding novels do. Yet Elaine Safer treats the Thanatoids as merely satiric, omitting the element of betrayal and revenge and the references to Vietnam and defining them entirely in terms of their television watching ("Pynchon's World and Its Legendary Past: Humor and the Absurd in a Twentieth-Century *Vineland,*" above, pp. 52-53), while N. Katherine Hayles concludes that Weed is "apparently only wounded by the gunshot" inasmuch as he "shows up years later as a Thanatoid convert" (above, p. 26).

Ortho Bob Dulang's definition—" 'Thanatoid' means 'like death, only different' " (170)—anticipates Takeshi's definition of karmic adjustment, "just like insurance—only different!" (173): in neither case does "different" entail negation. DL blurts of the Thanatoids, "Takeshi-san . . . they're ghosts," but Tai cautions, "That word—around here it's a no-no!" (173). Like the word *death,* the word *ghosts* is taboo among Thanatoids not because it is irrelevant but because it is too relevant (174). Pynchon's authority for the metaphysics undergirding the Thanatoids' mode of existence is the *Bardo Thödol,* or *Tibetan Book of the Dead,* a work so popular with the counterculture of the sixties that it inspired a psychedelic how-to manual (Timothy Leary, Ralph Metzner, and Richard Alpert, *The Psychedelic Experience: A Manual Based on the Tibetan Book of the Dead* [New Hyde Park, NY: University Books, 1964]). But precedent for revenge-seeking shades (as in Shade Creek) ranges from Elizabethan and Jacobean revenge tragedies to the Yurok legends that are also woven into the Thanatoid saga in *Vineland.* As in *Gravity's Rainbow,* the boundary between living and dead is permeable, and in both cases made more so by technology: "We are assured by the *Bardo Thödol,* or *Tibetan Book of the Dead,* that the soul newly in transition often doesn't like to admit—in-

deed will deny quite vehemently—that it's really dead, having slipped so ef-
fortlessly into the new dispensation that it finds no difference between the
weirdness of life and the weirdness of death, an enhancing factor in
Takeshi's opinion being television, which with its history of picking away at
the topic with doctor shows, war shows, cop shows, murder shows, had trivialized the Big D itself" (218).

Most of the Thanatoids seem to have died in Vietnam, a key moment for
this book's continued preoccupation with the theme of American history as
betrayal. But there are less pressing and more sordid sources of restlessness
in the "waste-pit of time" they inhabit (173), including "land titles and water
rights, goon squads and vigilantes, landlords, lawyers, and developers always
described in images of thick fluids in flexible containers" (172): the circum-
locution here carving out a space around the word *scumbags*.

[20]The phrase comes from Rachel Blau DuPlessis's *Writing beyond the Ending:
Narrative Strategies of Twentieth-Century Women Writers* (Bloomington: Indiana
University Press, 1985); see especially "Romantic Thralldom and 'Subtle Ge-
nealogies' in H.D.," 66-83.

[21]Frenesi disagrees, an index of the extent to which she is already invested
in Vond's illusion of transcendence.

[22]Thomas Pynchon, *Gravity's Rainbow* (New York: Viking, 1973), 590. Further citations to this edition will appear within parentheses in the body of the
text.

[23]Referring to what Takeshi calls his " 'interesting work with airplanes'
during World War II," DL remarks, "I can't imagine you in anybody's air
force, let alone the kamikaze, who, I understand from the history books, were
fairly picky about who flew for 'em" (175). Pynchon picks up and develops
Takeshi from the Komikal Kamikaze passages in the last section of *Gravity's
Rainbow;* in my *Ideas of Order in the Novels of Thomas Pynchon* (Columbus: Ohio
State University Press, 1983), I suggest that they are among the figures for the
potentially salvific failure of control in a deathward-tending universe (130-31).

[24]Terrence Rafferty observes: "Like everything else that seems random and
eccentric in 'Vineland,' this pulp-fiction romance has a point: the macabre
coupling of DL and Takeshi is an alternate take, salvaged from the cutting-
room floor, of the grim union of Frenesi and Brock, a vision preserved of the
absurd comedy that this relationship, in a better world (or movie), would
have remained" ("Long Lost," *New Yorker,* 19 February 1990, 109).

[25]Stacey Olster shows, for instance, how DL has antecedents in Japanese
ninja movies and the science-fiction novels of William Gibson as well as in
such Tubal reverse-gender spinoffs as Wonder Woman and the Bionic
Woman (Takeshi watches a Bionic Woman rerun on pp. 165-66). See Olster's
essay in this volume. Other characters have names that allude to pop culture
derivatives: Zipi Pisk, for instance, has something to do with comic-strip character Zippy ("Are we having fun yet?") the Pinhead. But Richard Powers
makes the important point that although the "book is a riot of genres and
genre parodies—California gunshoe, comic book, Japanese sci-fi, kung fu,
prime-time sitcoms," it is ultimately "a character-driven commentary, without
sardonic deflation, about what we can know of *this* world" ("State and Vine,"
Yale Review 79.4 [1990]: 694).

[26]Two parallel maxims from the late sixties illustrate how vulnerable political dissent can be to co-optation by precisely this sort of "literary" gesture. The first comes from the cartoon strip *Pogo* and was widely cited as relevant folk wisdom by mainstream commentators on Left activism: "We have met the enemy and he is us." The second is a peculiarly American reading of Daniel Cohn-Bendit's chant for dissident French students: "We are all German Jews." American television and magazines took the "we" and "all" as universal: we are all German Jews, including Richard Nixon, including Rudolph Hess, how profound to acknowledge that we all suffer. Of course, if the enemy *were* (in this simplistic and globalizing way) "us" or if we were *all* (as humans) German Jews, there would be no oppression and certainly no gas chambers. Unfortunately, some of us, even given all sorts of psychic dimensions to collusion, are still not the ones in power (power is a great differentiator); unfortunately, some of "us" are capos and a great number of "us" are members of the SS. I am inclined to see *Vineland* as an index of Pynchon's political discomfort with some of the evacuating tendencies of the (admittedly brilliant) narratorial "we" in *Gravity's Rainbow*.

[27]Terrence Rafferty sees the myth of the Fall as the structural metaphor for the entire novel: "It's an anatomy of betrayal; a frame-by-frame analysis of the moment when everything turned, when the long troubled sleep, the death in the soul, really began; and a new version of the oldest story in the world—the original sin and exile from Paradise" (109).

[28]I use "he" inasmuch as this narrator seems—and especially at such points —to speak for the author.

[29]But they also suggest the diversity and weirdness of Tubal culture: Pynchon has a great deal of fun mixing real and imagined titles, especially of made-for-TV movies. As I suggested at the 1991 MLA panel on *Vineland,* it would be a serious underreading of the novel to give Isaiah Two Four (as spokesperson for the generation following that of Zoyd, Frenesi, and DL) unqualified authorial sanction. If Pynchon has been reading literary theory, he has also, clearly, been saturating himself in Tubal rays. As always, he takes pop culture seriously—even current pop culture.

[30]He is identified with the administrations of Richard Nixon, Ronald Reagan, and, most suggestively, George Bush: on p. 354 Bush is aligned with CIA drug-smuggling; on p. 366 Weed Atman reports going up a stairway toward increasing responsibility for his own murder, but above Brock Vond "that's when it begins to go dark, and that door at the top I thought I saw isn't there anymore, because the light behind it just went off too." *Vineland* is Pynchon's first novel to name current political names.

[31]See above, 90.

[32]Teaching this novel to Prairie's near-peers amounts to introducing a whole worldview—and entails widely different degrees of acceptance or rejection. The senior seminar that I taught in the spring of 1991 concluded with *Vineland* and split, bitterly, on political and gender grounds, with the young men feeling that the novel described an outmoded perception of reality ("This corresponds to nothing in my experience," one reported soberly) and the young women arguing that it represented the political world that they themselves inhabited.

"Good-bye, Columbus":
Postmodernist Satire in Vineland

William E. Grim

T HOMAS Pynchon's most recent novel received mixed reviews, with most critics registering a sense of disappointment, especially in comparison with *Gravity's Rainbow* (1973). It seems the seventeen-year gap in Pynchon's literary production has induced most critics to concur with Saint Thomas Aquinas that "anticipation is the greater joy."

There is an aspect of *Vineland,* however, that has yet to receive scholarly attention and which, I believe, represents a remarkable evolution in Pynchon's literary virtuosity, namely, the author's use of satire. The satirical element of *Vineland* is vastly different from that of *Gravity's Rainbow.* There, an actual historical occurrence (World War II from the V-2 raids through the early days of the Allied occupation of Europe) was the point of departure for Pynchon's satirical fantasies; in *Vineland,* on the other hand, a historical situation (the United States in 1984) has itself become self-satirizing. The distinction between truth and satire has now been obviated; in other words, truth has actually become stranger than fiction, or we might even go so far as to state that truth and satire have exchanged identities (or perhaps are even indistinguishable). Pynchon's new approach to satire in *Vineland* I would like to categorize as postmodernist.

The postmodernist approach to satire I feel results from the desire of some contemporary authors to come out from under the influence of their modernist predecessors without necessarily abandoning the rich legacy of literary modernism. A useful model for distinguishing between modernism and postmodernism is Friedrich Schiller's dichotomy between the sentimental and the naive: the former being art that is conscious of its antecedents, the latter being art that is unaware of its past. In this sense, the literary modernists were the most sentimental artists of all time. Every page written by Pound, Eliot, Zukofsky, Bunting, Joyce, and others of their predisposition is saturated with an awareness of literary history, forms, and techniques. This awareness becomes manifest in literary works of incredible allusive complexity and intertextual density. The almost unending quotation, reworking, and transformation of earlier artworks by the modernists caused their own works to be highly parodic in nature. Perhaps the modernist condition is best summarized by Thomas Mann in *Doctor Faustus* (1947) when he has his protagonist, Adrian Leverkühn, state: "Why must I think that almost all, no, all the methods and conventions of art today *are good for parody only?*" (134, author's italics). Modernist art, therefore, is sentimental art par excellence: art so aware of itself and its antecedents that its tendency is to become parody.

Postmodernist authors like Pynchon have been confronted with the success of the modernist program; indeed, it is doubtful that it is possible to be more sentimental than the modernists even if one wanted to be. On the other hand, by its very nature Schillerian naïveté cannot be willed into existence. Given this background, many of the techniques of what is termed postmodernism—the seeming abandonment of high art, the willful neglect of plot and purpose, and the almost total denial of authorial control and intention—appear to be attempts to recapture the spirit of naïveté while holding on to the technical advances made by the modernists. Postmodernist satire concentrates on a calculating reuse of the past that appears on the surface to be innocent, but is in actuality the quintessence of sophistication. Additionally, postmodernist satire is an exaggeration of modernist techniques to the extreme. For example, the postmodern satirists give as much emphasis to the moment that has just passed as the modernist did in their efforts to make new the distant past. In many ways postmodern satire is a reflection on the technological advances made in communications, where all world events appear to be happening at once, the term "real time" has entered the lexicon of popular discourse, and cable channels give their program times in Greenwich Mean Time. Time appears to be passing so rapidly that the thing being satirized and the satirical moment are no longer necessarily aligned in a strict chronological progression. An earlier writer, then, could have created "naive" art simply by being unaware of previous artworks. The postmodern author no longer may claim a lack of knowledge of the past as an apology for naïveté. The successes of modern philology and the communications revolution, however, have brought about the unique situation whereby naïveté of a sort is possible since there is simply too much information available for a single person to digest. It is in the satirical program of *Vineland*, then, that Pynchon's ersatz naïveté becomes most obvious.

How does this postmodernist satire work? As an example I would like to examine chapter 9 of *Vineland* (130-91), particularly the section (133-35) dealing with the flight of the character DL Chastain to Columbus, Ohio, and her subsequent kidnapping and return to Tokyo, Japan. The reason that I have selected this passage is that I am a native of Columbus and am very familiar with the city. When I first read *Vineland* I was quite taken with this section because I realized that Pynchon was discussing actual locations and situations in Columbus that would appear to the non-native as being satirical in nature.

Escaping mafioso chief Ralph Wayvone, DL flees across the country in a '66 Plymouth Fury. The choice of automobile is most fortunate. DL is literally, as well as figuratively, "driven" by a Fury, in this case a mechanical rather than anthropomorphic Fury. This, however, is not the only connection between *Vineland* and Aeschylus' *Eumenides*. In the *Eumenides*, Athena dispenses justice, absolving Orestes of guilt and resolving the many conflicts of the House of Atreus. In *Vineland*, DL's disappearance and later kidnapping bring into play forces that will finally mete out justice to the evil federal prosecutor Brock Vond.

DL arrives in Columbus, Ohio, fleeing from the "New World" (Vineland = Vinland) to a city named after one of the discoverers of the New World. Pynchon describes the scene as follows:

> On inertial navigation, knowing she'd know what she was looking for when she found it, DL didn't stop till the outskirts of Columbus, Ohio, which she first beheld around midday in a stunning onslaught of smog and traffic. [. . .] She took a little apartment and found a job at a vacuum cleaner parts distributor's, typing and filing. (133)

The above passage is remarkable for a number of reasons. First of all, Columbus is described in terms reminiscent of the Promised Land or El Dorado, a place where one will realize its transcendent meaning when one arrives there. This seems satirical in that Columbus has the reputation of a solid, unexciting, respectable Midwestern city. Secondly, DL's arrival in Columbus coincides with "a stunning onslaught of smog and traffic," a description redolent of Los Angeles but hardly the stuff of the healthy environment of the Midwest. We will soon discover that the real Columbus is far different from its perception in the minds of the general public. Thirdly, DL takes a job in a company that distributes vacuum cleaner parts, the specificity of which gives the impression of satire whereby one desirous of a cleansing in the spiritual sense takes a position in a firm that sells equipment that cleans the physical environment.

My contention is that Pynchon's selection of Columbus as the goal of DL's flight is a very deliberate act and that the satirical implications of his selection are rooted in a large quantity of verifiable and circumstantial evidence. I further contend that the events described of DL's sojourn in Columbus take place in a relatively small geographical portion of the city and can be identified without too much difficulty, not unlike the way in which the various locales of Dublin are described in Joyce's *Ulysses*. (We must also not forget that one of Columbus's most prosperous suburbs is named Dublin.)

To begin with, Pynchon states that DL rents a small apartment and takes a job as a file clerk in the aforementioned vacuum cleaner parts distribution company. The most logical location for DL's apartment would be in the vicinity of the Ohio State University campus, where many apartments are available, and where the constant ebb and flow of the student population would provide the suitable anonymity for a person in DL's position. Additionally, Columbus has one of the fastest-growing populations in the United States with an extremely mobile work force. Therefore, jobs would be extremely easy for DL to find. The unemployment rate is so low in Columbus and the surrounding Franklin County that proprietors of fast-food establishments at times have to bus in workers from outlying communities as far as thirty miles away.

The 1988 Columbus Yellow Pages lists seven distributors of vacuum cleaner parts, the most likely model I believe to be the Faust Service Company of 696 East Hudson Avenue. The Faust legend has long intrigued Pynchon, and is featured prominently in *V.* (especially chapter 11, "Confessions of Fausto Maijstral") and *Gravity's Rainbow*, and I do not believe that Pynchon could pass up such a fortunate coincidence. Also, the location of the Faust Service Company puts it in close proximity to the Ohio State University campus.

We might ask at this juncture whether it is possible for Pynchon to have such detailed knowledge of Columbus. Given Pynchon's consistent penchant for thoroughly researching abstruse data, it is entirely likely that he did the same for the city of Columbus. Also, Pynchon may have some family ties to Columbus. There is a Pynchon listed in the Columbus White Pages who lives on Walhalla (pronounced Wallhalla) Avenue, which is very close to the Ohio State University campus, being immediately north of it just off High Street. Given the extremely rare occurrence of the Pynchon family name (one of the least frequently encountered names in the United States) and the potentially satirical name of Walhalla (whose Wagnerian implications would seem to the non-Columbusite to be very satirical, I believe), it is perfectly logical to surmise that Pynchon might be intimately acquainted with the city of Columbus.

Pynchon has DL go on to describe Columbus as a city in which Superman could relax as Clark Kent. In fact, DL imagines herself as Clark Kent: "Lois Lane might not give her the time of day anymore, but that'd be OK, she'd be dating somebody from the secretarial pool. They'd go out for dinner sometimes to this cozy Neapolitan joint down by some lakefront, where the Mussels Posillipo couldn't be beat" (134). There is a very likely model for the restaurant Pynchon describes, namely, the trendy Baby Doe's Matchless Mine, which is located at 2399 West Fifth Avenue amidst a host of condominiums on the shore of a lake which is a former limestone quarry. The restaurant is located to the west of the Ohio State University campus, not far from the banks of the Scioto River.

The trendy nature of Columbus is further supported by Pynchon's admission that DL spent most of her spare time either exercising or shopping, the two preeminent yuppie pastimes. Columbus's image as a "cow town" is belied by the fact that its population statistically includes the highest percentage of yuppies of any urban area in the United States. Columbus also has one of the highest concentrations of shopping malls in the United States, so DL's infatuation with shopping is entirely logical and would make her fit in with her surroundings. Strangest of all, though, is the little-known fact that, in one sense, Columbus is the fashion capital of the world. The Limited Corporation, the giant fashion retailing company owned by the billionaire Leslie Wexner, is headquartered in Columbus and its warehousing and distribution facilities are so large that more units of women's fashion clothing go through Columbus than any other city in the world, including New York City and Milan, Italy. Again, the idea of trendy shopping centers in Columbus appears to be satirical, but this is belied by the actuality of the facts.

DL is kidnapped in the parking lot of a Pizza Hut (two such exist in the area of the Ohio State University campus, one at 3416 North High Street, the other at 5152 North High Street) and is taken back to Tokyo where she will ostensibly be sold into white slavery. But how were her abductors able to find her so easily when the highly trained ninja had gone to such elaborate lengths to conceal her identity and blend into the Columbus environment? The answer is that DL made an unfortunate choice of Columbus as her city of refuge. Pynchon repeatedly informs us that the entire details of the lives of DL and Prairie and Frenesi Gates (and by extension all human beings) are contained in files on a computer network, computer connectivity being the quintessential form of Pynchonian paranoia. For example, Pynchon describes as follows the information included in Frenesi Gates's computer file, which is accessed by her daughter Prairie in the Ninjette Terminal Center of the Kunoichi Retreat:

> The file on Frenesi Gates, whose entries had been accumulating over the years, often haphazardly, from far and wide, reminded Prairie of scrapbooks kept by somebody's eccentric hippie uncle. Some was governmental, legal history with the DMV, letterhead memoranda from the FBI enhanced by Magic Marker, but there were also clippings from "underground" newspapers that had closed down long ago, transcripts of Frenesi's radio interviews on KPFK, and a lot of cross-references to something called 24fps, which Prairie recalled as the name of the film collective DL said she and Frenesi had been in together for a while. (113-14)

Another little-known fact is that Columbus has the highest concentration of computer capacity of any city in the world with the two exceptions of Washington, DC, and Moscow. (Compuserve, OCLC, and the Cray Supercomputer at Ohio State University are but three examples of Columbus's monumental computer capacity. Additionally, Columbus has one of the few police forces in the world with a squad devoted solely to solving computer-related crimes.) Therefore, by being in Columbus, DL is in the one geographical location where information about her whereabouts would be most accessible. Additionally, Central Ohio has a very high concentration of Japanese-owned factories and resident Japanese corporate executives, especially in the suburbs of Muirfield Village and Dublin, the latter town being the location of the vast OCLC computer network. The potential exists, therefore, for a large number of Japanese underworld figures to be looking freely for DL in Columbus without arousing any suspicion.

But for all of DL's ninja intelligence, her attempt to hide out in Columbus is further compromised in that she is still attended by her "Fury," the 1966 Plymouth in which she made her escape from California. Although DL has changed her own appearance, she still drives this same eighteen-year-old car (in 1984), which is conspicuous to say the least. Further, DL has taken to emphasizing her relationship with her "Fury" by washing it three times a week, installing in it a new stereo system, and naming it Felicia (a corruption of *Felicitas*, the Roman personification of good luck). The incessant car washing, like DL's choice of employment at a vacuum cleaner parts distribution company, is another form of spiritual "cleansing," which is prefigured earlier in the novel when DL and Prairie seek refuge at the retreat of the Sisterhood of Kunoichi Attentives: "Well you ought to see how many gaga little twits we get up here, 'specially your [Prairie's] age group, nothing personal, looking for secret powers on the cheap. Thinking we'll take 'em through the spiritual car wash, soap away all that road dirt, git 'em all buffed up all cherry again" (112). DL's rituals of obeisance, however, prove to be of no avail. One may embrace one's "Fury," but one cannot change one's fate as DL is soon to discover when she is forcibly taken back to Tokyo.

Although much of what I have presented here is conjecture, and though it is unlikely that the extraordinarily reticent Thomas Pynchon will ever confirm or deny the accuracy of my observations, I believe that his approach to satire is unique and can be characterized as postmodernist. Pynchon utilizes actual facts that at first glance appear to be so outlandish that we automatically assume a satirical intention. But Pynchon realizes that the era in which we live is self-satirizing, that the actuality of events and circumstances is often beyond belief. Besides, if a latter-day Rip Van Winkle were to awake today from a twenty-year slumber and were told that a former professional violist-turned-lawyer Christian Democrat had recently been elected as the last premier of East Germany, that a musicologist was now the president of Lithuania, that a playwright was twice elected as president of Czechoslovakia, and that former actors had been elected to the presidency of the United States and the papacy, he too might assume a satirical intention on the part of his informants.

Argument by Anachronism:
The Presence of the 1930s in Vineland

Eric Solomon

> "I took this course in sociology. [. . .] The reason you're so
> tight with your money, you got the habit of poverty when
> you were a child, in the Depression. You were traumatized."
> —John Updike, *Rabbit Is Rich*

I N the zones of Thomas Pynchon's projected fictional worlds, linear time gives way to vectors, with time frames collapsed, one decade influencing another. In *V.* Fashoda informs Malta; in *The Crying of Lot 49*, to Oedipa Maas World War II corpses impinge on 1960s confusions; and in *Gravity's Rainbow* the Nazi Germany of the 1930s, an "era in which paranoia was erected as state policy" looms over 1940s rocket warfare. While *Vineland* may seem to be a novel where two time references predominate—the betrayals of the 1960s still resonating in the 1980s—subtextually what Auden in "1939" called the "low, dishonest decade" of the thirties (with its echoes in Pynchon's work of the informing and blacklisting of the forties and fifties) provides the deep temporal grammar for *Vineland's* narrative. Frenesi thinks back on the "forgotten home" of the thirties of her radical parents in terms of "no longer the time the world observed but game time, underground time, time that could take her nowhere outside its own tight and falsely deathless perimeter" (293).

"Think back on us, the martyrs and traitors, / Of cowards even, swept by the same flood / Of passion toward the morning that is yours," pleaded Malcolm Cowley, the essential thirties memoirist. And Thomas Pynchon does think back from the 1980s of Prairie to the 1960s of her mother Frenesi—and to the late 1930s and the 1940s of *her* mother Sasha and even to the 1920s and early 1930s of Sasha's father, Jess Traverse, the Wobbly. *Vineland* is seamed with thirties references, echoes, even set pieces that serve to qualify the later decades. The years of depression, rise of fascism—years of panic, hopelessness, and apprehension—were also times of the New Deal, dreams

161

of recovered farm and factory work, left-wing organizing—years of action, hope, and passion. One survivor stated that the decade called for warm hearts, outraged spirits, and rough tongues, for there were brutalities, outrages, repressions, and, most importantly for *Vineland's* texture, betrayals: "Which side are you on?" goes the old Labor song, and Pynchon's novel luxuriates in betrayals: government agencies betray the people; revolutionaries sell each other out; the New Left, as in Doctorow's *Book of Daniel*, is disgusted with the Old Left because of its penchant for doctrinal strife. Perhaps a model for Pynchon's acceptance of the importance of the 1930s is Clancy Sigal's fine 1961 novel *Going Away*, in which a disillusioned Hollywood writer works his way back east, visiting the places and survivors that marked his radical past. (Indeed, a 1980 reprint of the novel bears a cover blurb calling Sigal the transition between Dos Passos and Pynchon.)

Certainly this use of a previous time to help provide resonance to a text is familiar to literary historians. Renaissance writers carried the idea of classical Rome into their poems; Shakespeare often drew on Ovid without mentioning him; Spenser openly used Arthurian elements but also collected analogues to older myths. Such are literary traditions, luxuriated in by Joyce, Eliot, and other moderns. Pynchon, much given to modernist forms such as parody and references to earlier models, incorporates into *Vineland* events and characteristics of the thirties to allow his present time—the sixties and eighties—to refer back to prior events without strain. Thus, the novel is enriched by its own belatedness, by a nostalgia for the nearly dead conventions of formulaic left-wing protest fiction. Just as *V.* seems to anthologize (and parody) an earlier decade of anti-colonialist fiction, so *Vineland* will not let go of 1930s dreams/nightmares.

The novel, like the film DEA field agent manqué Hector Zuñiga hopes to produce, concentrates on the view of the 1960s from the 1980s. He waits "for the big Nostalgia Wave to move along to the sixties [. . .] to make a Film about all those long-ago political wars, the drugs, the sex, the rock an' roll" (51). To Frenesi, the true film-maker of her times, now part of the snitch community of informers, "the past was on her case forever" (71), but even the Nixonian repression becomes ephemeral as darker, more autumnal moods appear under Reagan.

But preceding Frenesi were her parents, victims in the 1950s of their earlier decades' political actions. "Not exactly a red-diaper baby," still, "her childhood and adolescence had been full enough of taps on the phone, cars across the street. [. . .] Her mother then had worked as a script reader and her father, Hub Gates, as a gaffer, always under the dreamlike turns of blacklist, graylist, secrets kept and betrayed" (74). This world of false names and ugly sellouts sustains yet an earlier world. Pynchon moves a layer deeper—back another decade—to the days immediately after World War II when Frenesi is born, named for "the record by Artie Shaw that was all over the jukeboxes and airwaves in the last days of the war [. . .] of being young and alive in perilous times" (75). But the genuine bedrock for this book, the period of commitment and loyalty, emanates from a previous generation, that of Sasha's parents.

Here in Vineland, northern California's logging country, the place where Zoyd can hide in the eighties, where dead hippies—Thanatoids —still exist, where all the characters and themes of the novel will coalesce at the end as surreal forces will combine to sustain family and defeat the government—here started Sasha's father, Jess Traverse, an International Workers of the World organizer of loggers. Sasha's mother, Eula Becker, was a radical from the Montana mining country. And their marriage is one of true radical hearts, to which no disloyalties admit impediment. They meet in the IWW hall in Vineland, the novel's moral center. " 'Jess introduced me to my conscience,' she liked to say in later years" (76), that element of morality starkly lacking in later generations. Their guru is Joe Hill, their venue is the road, "his road, his bindlestiff life, his dangerous indenture to an idea, a dream of One Big Union" (76). Class brother- and sisterhood, jail, fights against Pinkertons, crippling by company goons, the move to San Francisco, "a rip-roaring union town, still riding the waves of euphoria from the General Strike of '34" (77), these are the great moments, the great days, as Dos Passos, who starts *USA* with perhaps his most positive portrait, that of Mac the Wobbly, calls them. Thus, long before Mario Savio is born, before Sproul Plaza is built, a generation of demonstrators fights against the real thing: Tom Mooney's imprisonment or Robert Sproul himself.

The 1930s, then, represent for Pynchon the gloried past of struggle and idealism. Trashed in the 1950s by the Hollywood anti-communist terror, the earlier decade stands to represent a worthy dream. Sellouts and conspiracies of silence lead to the blacklisting period, "with its complex court dances of fuckers and fuckees, thick with betrayal, destructiveness, cowardice, and lying" (81). These are the politics Frenesi absorbs in her childhood, preparing not only for her own embracement of the flimsier 1960s rebellious movements but also for the rejection of her parents' idealism, a shift that turns Frenesi into a double agent who betrays her lover to the FBI. Pynchon's view of the decades is clearly established early in the novel, and they serve as points of interpretive reference throughout the text's discourses. Eighties betray sixties just as fifties betrayed thirties. By revealing how the 1930s generation fell apart, Pynchon prepares for the parodic version in *Vineland*'s 1980s world where destruction of 1960s moods and personas culminates. But by extension, the sixties manage to sustain a sense of radical lyricism—a far cry from Joan Didion's bitter rejections—drawn from the revolutionary spirit of the thirties influence.

Throughout *Vineland*, reminders of this thirties tone and politics appear. DL compares her exile in Columbus, Ohio, to the life a residual self might seek, just as Superman could change back to Clark Kent (133). When Takeshi attempts to recall a lost innocence, he sings of thirties films:

> Well, Lassie's got Roddy McDowell,
> Trigger's got, Dale and Roy,
> Asta's got William Powell, goin'
> "Where th' heck's that, Myrna Loy?" (162)

One of Pynchon's typically awful songs, later stanzas include Tarzan and "Flatfoot Floogie with only one Floy"—which the trivia-minded reader will recognize as an allusion to the thirties song "Flatfoot Floogie with a Floy, Floy" (two Floys). Just as the Thanatoids are Pynchon's construct—ghosts of the 1960s—so Powell and Loy, Tarzan and Cheetah, Lassie and Roddy are, or should be, the properly-educated-in-the-popular-culture reader's ghosts of the thirties and forties.

Nostalgia is not valid in itself; L.A.'s contemporary world of business espionage bears no resemblance to Hammett's or Chandler's "old-movie private-eye's office" (192). Yet in the 1960s Rex Snuvvle is much taken with "the Bolshevik Leninist Group of Vietnam, a section of the Fourth International" (207). Anti-drug agents are led by "the notorious Karl Bopp, former Nazi *Luftwaffe* officer" (221). Typically, Pynchon's mocking humor exaggerates history. Or at times a thirties reference is just that: when Roscoe describes himself as Brock's sidekick, "a less voluble Tonto" (271), there is implied no lost innocence or appeal to the simpler enforcement methods of the Lone Ranger's days of yesteryear.

The decade references help to set characters in place. Frenesi as "third-generation lefty" amuses federal prosecutors; Hub is "never the brave Wobbly [Sasha's] father was" (288) as he sinks into lethargic blacklisted victimhood even though he, in one of Pynchon's rare sympathetic portraits, sticks with the losers till the end. Zoyd, as

mocked anti-hero, tries to be sixties hip, wise-cracking to the drug
agent who has planted dope in Zoyd's apartment: " 'Let me guess—
2001: A Space Odyssey [1968].' 'Try *20,000 Years in Sing Sing* [1933]' "
(294—Pynchon's brackets parody scholarship as well as the relative
innocence of the earlier prison film to highlight Zoyd's absurdity).

As the novel builds towards the ending in Vineland, old IWW
country, the setting for the annual reunion of the "Traverses and
Beckers, my parents and their relatives" (305) where even Frenesi will
ultimately resurface, Sasha realizes that no federal prosecutor in the
eighties can comprehend the nature of an authentic thirties radical;
he thinks she must be his version of "an old push-button lefty, ideology before family" (305). Vineland itself represents the 1930s redux;
it is reached by bridges with spans that are "graceful examples of the
concrete Art Deco bridges built all over the Northwest by the WPA
during the Great Depression" (316). Here is a world of thirties idealism, filled with living redwoods, standing for the New Deal dream.
Here new generations gather to touch the older dream, to discover a
safe harbor in Roosevelt's—not Nixon's, not Reagan's—"Vineland
the Good" (322).

This return to Wobbly territory seems to reawaken Old Left spirits
and rhetoric, even innocence. The hardened informer Frenesi resists
crossing a picket line, and her companion Flash complains about her
return to past virtues: "it's your fuckin' family, tryin' to keep 'at old
union-kid cherry for your daddy" (351). Reunited with her daughter,
Sasha feels younger as they discuss old jitterbug music, the "swing
tunes. 'Polka Dots and Moonbeams,' 'In the Mood,' 'Moonlight Ser-
enade' " (362), and, of course, Frenesi. In a work informed by
Pynchon's constant references to contemporary rock music, the
1930s and 1940s big bands of Glenn Miller and Artie Shaw swing
subtextually through the novel's happy ending. Whiffs of postmodern
parody of parody appear in a new version of the old folk song that is
itself a version of an earlier work; "The Big Rock Candy Mountain" is
a post-Vietnam lyric:

> So we took in, the Mar-ble Mount-ain,
> And the Perfume River too,
> . . . .
> Like the graveyard full of meat loaf,
> And monkeys for your lunch. . . . (363-64)

Vineland draws to a close with all the surviving old lefties, Traverses
and Beckers, holding their picnic to honor a simpler time, to celebrate a bond between two thirties Wobblies. The relatives come

"from Marin to Seattle, Coos Bay to downtown Butte, choker setters
and choppers, dynamiters of fish, shingle weavers and street-corner
spellbinders, old and beaten at, young and brand-new" (369) to listen
to the aging radicals give an annual reading of a passage from
Emerson—that quintessential American idealist—quoted in a jail-
house copy of *The Varieties of Religious Experience* by William James—
that quintessential American pragmatist. As the old-timers argue the
tired 1930s radical questions about whether the United States still
lingers in "a prefascist twilight" (371) or whether darkness has fallen,
past and present, thirties and eighties, Hitler and Roosevelt or
Reagan and Kissinger, commingle.

Prairie's generation, represented by the rock musician Isaiah Two
Four, rejects Frenesi's era: "you believed in your Revolution, put your
lives right out there for it—but you sure didn't understand much
about the Tube" (373). The 1960s made films, the 1980s videos—but
behind all the media events are the Wobbly broadsheets and song-
books, the radical political dreams of 1930s proletarian writers;
dreams of Traverses and Beckers, of Wobblies and longshoremen, of
Sasha and Hub Gates, of Emerson and Joe Hill. Indeed, the novel's
sub-coda may be Joe's last words: "Don't mourn for me, organize."
For Brock Vond, government fascist extraordinaire, his right-wing
"exercise" fails, called off by Reagan. Thus, a right-wing revolution
collapses just as the New Left had. Brock's leader, his god, his president, has failed him, a subtle mockery of the disappointed loss of
belief in communism represented by late thirties defections from the
Party and documented in a collection of essays by betrayed believers
such as Silone, Malraux, Wright, and Orwell, entitled *The God That
Failed*. So Brock's leaders betray him into the hands of the Thanatoids.

The villain is gone; the good folk have their momentary stay from
modern political and social confusion, in the rural safety of a thirties
retreat. The novel ends happily, as the old movies were wont to do.
And Desmond, Prairie's and Zoyd's old dog, frightened away months
ago by federal prosecutor Vond and Drug Enforcement forces, returns: "Prairie woke to a warm and persistent tongue all over her
face. It was Desmond, none other, the spit and image of his grandmother Chloe, roughened by the miles, face full of blue-jay feathers,
smiling out of his eyes, wagging his tail, thinking he must be home"
(385). All 1980s and 1960s political, social, and sexual passions spent,
the survivors of left-wing struggles are safe in 1930s pastures. Lassie
has come home.

Smoking Dope with Thomas Pynchon:
A Sixties Memoir

Andrew Gordon

THIS is a story about the sixties: it's about me and some friends of mine, it's about Berkeley, and it's about Pynchon. It's about a decade in which we were all young together and thought we would stay young forever. Berkeley was our Vineland, a dream of a perfect new world. The time was ripe, America was ours, and we were going to change the world: Paradise Now or Apocalypse Now.

Neither one happened. As the decades pass, is anything left of that refuge, that Vineland, apart from memory and isolated dreams? Where are the sixties now? Where are we? And where is Thomas Pynchon?

Ultimately, I suppose this story is all about me. Everything you write always is, disguise it as you may. I don't know what I can tell you about Thomas Pynchon, but I can tell you something about myself, about the impact that the sixties and Berkeley and Pynchon had on me. *Vineland* looks back on the late sixties, and I'm going to look back on 1964-67, from ages nineteen to twenty-two, when I was first going out into the world on my own and when my life became enmeshed with Pynchon's fictions. I want to trace some of the parallels between life and fiction.

According to his friend Jules Siegel, when Pynchon lived in Mexico in the sixties, "the Mexicans laughed at his mustache and called him Pancho Villa." There's a hoary old joke whose punch line goes, "Did I know Pancho Villa? *Hombre*, we had lunch together!" Mine goes, "Did I know Thomas Pynchon? Man, we smoked dope together!" Except it's no joke; it really happened.

I often feel that way about the 1960s in America: they were no joke, they really happened to us, and they happened to me, although in retrospect they boggle the imagination and seem too incredible to be real. The truth of the sixties is stranger than fiction. As Philip Roth wrote about the period, "is it possible? is it happening?" ("Writing American Fiction" 121). That's why the sixties have so rarely been captured well in American fiction, except by a few authors such as Pynchon: if somebody told you the history of the decade as a story, you wouldn't believe it. You'd wonder: Is this for real? Is this some kind of joke? Is it supposed to be farce or tragedy? You wouldn't know how to feel, to laugh or to cry.

And although I met Thomas Pynchon one evening in Berkeley in June of 1967, I cannot say I really know him. He remains for me a figure as mysterious and ungraspable as Pancho Villa, a dope-smoking guerrilla warrior of the imagination, disappearing into his Mexican desert.

I consider Pynchon a quintessential American novelist of the 1960s because he came of age as an artist during that entropic decade and shows its stamp in all his work: *V.* (1963) covers the century from 1898 to 1956, but most of it was composed during the Kennedy years, and its zany mood reflects the liberatory burst of energy of the Thousand Days, that peculiar mix of Camelot idealism and Cold War paranoia also found in Heller's *Catch-22* (1961) and Kesey's *One Flew over the Cuckoo's Nest* (1962). *The Crying of Lot 49* (1966) is set in the relatively innocent sixties of the early Beatles (when they were still the Adorable Moptops and the Fab Four) and of legal LSD. Nevertheless, all the attraction, danger, and destructive tendencies of the New Left and the counterculture are prophesied in the insidious underground web of the Tristero. *Gravity's Rainbow* (1973), ostensibly about World War II, was written during the Vietnam War and indirectly reflects that topsy-turvy time; Pynchon also sneaks in references to Malcolm X, Kennedy, and Nixon. Slothrop in *Gravity's Rainbow* discovers what many young Americans found out in the late sixties: that our Magical Mystery Tour in the zone of Vietnam was a love affair with death, that the war never ends, and that your own country is your enemy. We weren't in Kansas anymore, the Wicked Witch of the West was after us, but there was no Yellow Brick Road and no kindly Wizard to come to the rescue. Finally, *Vineland* (1990) is the sixties revisited from the perspective of the eighties, about all the unresolved issues, about our sympathy for the Devil and our betrayal of the revolution, and about the long arm of the Nixonian counterrevolution continuing under Reagan. And whether or not his four novels are set in the sixties, they are ultimately all *of* the sixties, and always conjure up the contradictory moods of that decade and evoke the peculiarly mixed response.

I was introduced to Pynchon's fiction in the fall of 1964 at Rutgers by Richard Poirier: *V.* was the last novel assigned that semester in his course on the twentieth-century American novel. I immediately glommed on to Pynchon the way I had to Kerouac in the late fifties. He had an epic, wild, wide-ranging imagination. He was hip, he was funny, alternately farcical and profound. He also had modernist traits: he was learned, complex and allusive, and he liked to write about wastelands (even in the early sixties, in many English departments T. S. Eliot was still God). That Pynchon was camera-shy added to the mystique: he actually lived by the Joycean ethic of "silence, exile, and cunning"!

Unlike Kerouac, Pynchon appealed to two sides of me: the adolescent and the cerebral—the anarchist and the intellectual. Nevertheless, I connected Pynchon to Kerouac because both wrote about restless post-WW II young Americans. Except that Kerouac's heroes were filled with romantic angst and an unfulfilled yearning to burn like Roman candles, whereas Pynchon's were clowns, schlemiels, and human yo-yos, bouncing between farce and paranoia. Kerouac was of the cool fifties; he wrote jazz fiction. But Pynchon was of the apocalyptic sixties; he wrote rock and roll.

Fall 1964 was my last semester at Rutgers. I had enough credits to graduate, and had already been accepted to study English at Berkeley the next fall. I was a New York City boy, but the east couldn't hold me anymore; for years, I had been California dreaming. All I'd ever known of life was school. The summer after high school I had retraced part of Kerouac's route in *On the Road;* now I was ready to live like a Pynchon hero, to start bouncing around the globe like a human yo-yo. Restless and terrifically naive—in other words, a perfect schlemiel—I boarded a boat for Europe in February 1965, just after my twentieth birthday, ostensibly to learn French in Paris but mostly, as it turned out, to bum around. A last fling before graduate school. Fiction imitates life, but life also imitates fiction, in an endless feedback loop: I soon found myself yo-yoing in a Pynchonesque narrative involving historical change, illegal substances, FBI agents, farce, and paranoia.

By June of 1965, I was broke and lonesome and took the Cunard line home from England; I got back just in time to graduate with my class. Despite my insistent letters and packages of French perfume, my girlfriend of the fall had moved on to another guy.

I returned to a different country than the one I had left four months earlier. The first teach-in on the war had been held at

Rutgers that spring. The number-one tune was no longer the Beatles' sweet chant, "I Want to Hold Your Hand"; now people were listening instead to the angry, insistent lament of the Rolling Stones, "(I Can't Get No) Satisfaction." A chemistry major told me about his experiences with a new wonder drug called LSD. He said he had found nirvana and met God. I thought, if it could do that for this schnook, then what could it do for me? I ingested 250 micrograms and wound up in the hospital.

I didn't realize at the time that I had fallen into a Pynchon novel and that the author was about to appear on the scene.

In the fall of 1966 I was writing a seminar paper on *V.* for a graduate course taught by Sheldon Sacks. Sacks was a sweet man and an inspiring teacher, a formalist and neo-Aristotelian of the Chicago school of R. S. Crane; out of place at Berkeley, he soon returned to the University of Chicago, where he edited *Critical Inquiry* and died much too young. Sacks and Frederick Crews—then in his Freudian phase—were my most influential teachers at Berkeley in the late sixties.

Briefly, I argued that *V.* was organized less as a novel than as a moral fable or apologue, and that its message read, "Keep cool but care." Anyway, that's what I believed then; I was a lot more certain about many things in the late sixties than I am now. Maybe that's the message I read because that's the way I was trying to live: cool but caring, a Berkeley hipster.

But I found *V.* so dense that it took my entire paper just to begin to explicate the first chapter. I never went further: I was overawed by Pynchon's complex and daring imagination and intimidated by his learning. Nevertheless, I lived with that novel for a time. And, in a curious way, the novel led me to Pynchon when I wasn't even trying to find him.

I used to carry around a dog-eared paperback of *V.* (I have it still, scotch-taped together. How could I give it up? It has all my notes!) I turned friends on to Pynchon; we became cognoscenti, sharing favorite lines of dialogue: "Oh, man, [. . .] an intellectual. I had to pick an intellectual. They all revert" (111) or "You're turning our marriage into a trampoline act" (113). Later we would similarly appropriate *The Crying of Lot 49*, sending each other letters with the stamps pasted upside down and penciling on the envelopes "W.A.S.T.E." Once again, fiction was infiltrating life.

One friend, a woman graduate student, noticed me carrying *V.*

and said, "Oh, are you reading that? I know the guy who wrote it." I was naturally skeptical about her claim and asked if this mysterious Pynchon really existed and if he was a man or a committee.

She said she had met him in Berkeley in 1965 and that they stayed in touch. She asked if I minded if she sent Pynchon my paper. I gave her a copy, suspecting that it would vanish into a black hole.

Several months later, she mentioned that "Tom" had read my paper and liked it, thought it a lot more perceptive than the reviewers' comments. I thanked her but still wondered what kind of game she was playing.

From time to time, she dropped convincing-sounding details about Pynchon. She said he picked his friends carefully and that they guarded his privacy. She said he had written a second novel in haste and for money and that he was not too proud of it; that would be the just-published *Crying of Lot 49*. She claimed he had people help him with research and that he was working on an endless novel in which all of his friends would appear, including her. Is *Gravity's Rainbow* a roman à clef? If there is ever a biography of Pynchon, someone should investigate that angle. I once combed through *Gravity*, searching for the character who is supposed to be her; there are just too many, and I couldn't be sure.

In fact, she reminded me most of Rachel Owlglass in *V.*: she was a bright, lovely Jewish woman who liked to mother people. I was half in love with her but I was also friends with the guy she was living with. They later married and divorced; she claims he's in *Gravity's Rainbow* too.

One night in June of 1967, my Pynchon connection phoned me at my apartment on Shattuck Avenue. Pynchon was in town, staying with her and her boyfriend. He'd been living in L.A., flown up to Seattle to visit friends from Boeing, and on his way back to L.A. had stopped off for a day in Berkeley. She said, "Tom wants to meet you."

This was like a command audience with the pope. I kick-started my motorcycle and, I think, made it across town to her place near San Pablo Avenue before she had time to put down the phone.

Many years later, I ran into her at a literature conference and she revealed some unexpected details about herself and Pynchon. They weren't just friends; they had been lovers and lived together in Berkeley for a while in 1965. She described him as being then a "prematurely middle-aged" young man with "a lot of hang-ups." She claimed she was the first to turn him on to dope. They broke up because of the "hang-ups," but they remained friends and corresponded. From time to time, he would reappear suddenly and unexpectedly in her life—the last time at her wedding, with a wedding present of a kilo of Michoacán (a superior brand of Mexican weed).

That night in June of 1967 she made it clear on the phone that I was not to ask Pynchon about his work—past, present, or future. Just what did that leave me to talk about with him, I wondered as I drove across town, burning with anticipation. Yet I still had the nagging feeling that, like Oedipa Maas, I might be the victim of an elaborate hoax, that there would be no Pynchon at her apartment, just an imposter—or perhaps a locked door with a mail slot marked with the sign of a muted posthorn.

She had a tiny, one-bedroom house, living room separated from bedroom by a bead curtain. As I entered, the room was flooded with a pungent aroma and enough smoke to induce an immediate contact high; I coughed. A long, lanky young man was methodically rolling joints on the table; his stash box was a One-a-Day Brand Multivitamin pill bottle. He carefully finished rolling and extended the bomber to me, saying, "Hey, man, would you like a joint?" (This was Berkeley, 1967; people really talked that way back then.) I took a toke gladly; it was obvious by the fog in the room that they were way ahead of me.

This man, who was introduced to me as Thomas Pynchon, appeared to be in his late twenties. I'm six foot one, but he was taller than I, about six two or three. He wore a corduroy shirt and corduroy pants, both green, and a pair of those brown, ankle-high suede shoes known as desert boots. He was lean, almost emaciated, and his eyes were wasted. His hair was thick and brown and he had a ragged, reddish brown soup-strainer mustache; I wondered if he had grown it to hide his teeth, which were crooked and slightly protruding.

Pynchon was evidently a man of few words. I wanted very much to talk with him, to sound him out, at least to get him to laugh, but as we sat on the floor and passed around buzz bombers and grew progressively more zonked, he didn't say much, just listened intently as our hostess and host and I talked. The conversation was disjointed, grass talk consisting of little bits and revelations (Leslie Fiedler had just been busted for possession of marijuana) and silly stoned jokes, like the one about the woman who traded in her menstrual cycle for a Yamaha. I thought of Pynchon as a Van der Graaf machine, one of those generators that keeps building static electricity until a lightning bolt zaps between the terminals.

All of a sudden, he pulled out of his pocket a string of firecrackers and asked, "Where can we set these off?"

"Why don't we blow up the statue of Queen Victoria?" I replied.

"O wow, man, have you read that book?" Pynchon said. He'd caught my allusion to Leonard Cohen's novel *Beautiful Losers*, recently released in paperback. Cohen's hero actually does blow up a statue of Victoria, a typically sixties symbolic gesture. I was pleased to finally get a response from Pynchon, yet I still felt like the overeager grad student trying too hard to impress the prof.

There were no Victorian monuments to explode in Berkeley, so we drove instead to the marina and set off the fireworks by the bay. We walked by the water, past junkpiles, setting off cherry bombs and running like hell. A midnight ritual: four heavily stoned people hearing the snap, crackle, and pop, watching the dazzle against the black mud and the midnight waters. At that moment, halfway around the world in Vietnam, equally stoned soldiers were probably admiring in the same way the rocket's red glare.

Suddenly, for some inexplicable reason, everyone had the munchies and I suggested an all-night burger palace on University Avenue, probably the only restaurant open at that hour. It was a huge fluorescent Burgertown. As we sat at formica-topped tables and ate greasy sleazeburgers, Pynchon slouched in the booth, long thin legs in green Levis sprawled out, pensively biting his nails. Then he ripped a styrofoam coffee cup into tiny, meticulous shreds. He had dissipated, tired eyes like Robert Mitchum's.

The place featured a colorful old baroque Wurlitzer jukebox. We fed the machine streams of quarters: the Beatles' "Strawberry Fields" and Country Joe's "Not So Sweet Martha Lorraine." Pynchon chose Procol Harum's "A Whiter Shade of Pale" and the Stones' "Ruby Tuesday," which remain for me associated with that night.

In *Vineland*, after DL rescues Frenesi from the Berkeley street-fighting,

They sat devouring cheeseburgers, fries, and shakes in a waterfront place full of refugees from the fighting up the hill, all their eyes, including ones that had wept, now lighted from the inside—was it only the overhead fluorescents, some trick of sun and water outside? no . . . too many of these fevered lamps not to have origin across the line somewhere, in a world sprung new, not even defined yet, worth the loss of nearly everything in this one. The jukebox played the Doors, Jimi Hendrix, Jefferson Airplane, Country Joe and the Fish. [. . .] Revolution all around them, world-class burgers, jukebox solidarity. (117-18)

DL and Frenesi's "jukebox solidarity" doesn't last. And that night in 1967 I made the mistake of introducing Pynchon to an acquaintance of mine who happened to be in the restaurant, the manager of a local rock band; they became engrossed in a technical conversation about music, and I was lost.

The last thing I recall is sitting with Pynchon in the open back of a red pickup truck, freezing, as we rocketed up into the Berkeley hills. The fog slid in like satin, so thick the water dripped on me. Suddenly, out of a cloud, San Francisco materialized below us. It was dawn.

Later that morning Pynchon caught a plane back to L.A. I never saw him again.

That was twenty-five years ago. Since then, I've met over a dozen novelists of varying degrees of fame. The experience is almost invariably disappointing. You think you know them, but you don't; you only know their works. And they don't know you from Adam, so the conversations are usually the desultory ones of strangers with little in common. Nevertheless, my frustrating encounter with Pynchon continues to haunt my imagination because of the special circumstances: he's the only writer I didn't have to seek out, the only one who ever asked to meet *me*. Perhaps because I was a young student and a friend of a friend, he felt safe. We shared a joint, which creates a bond of sorts; in the sixties, it was a holy ritual, a passing of the peace pipe, one of the generational rites of passage. But now that I'm a certified professor, there is a permanent wall between us. Those times are gone forever.

So what can I say of Thomas Pynchon, except that we once smoked dope together? Does a writer's personality really matter, or only the authorial personality that we read in his works? A science-fiction novelist once told me, "Most science-fiction writers are nerds." He was correct: you meet a novelist whose imagination has sent you to Andromeda, and he dresses like an accountant.

Pynchon is no nerd, but the relative banality of his conversation that evening ("Hey, man, would you like a joint?") and his reticence made it hard to get a focus on the man behind the books. But that's not surprising: Pynchon interposes his fictions between himself and the world. His novels are an elaborate screen he can hide behind, a form of both self-expression and self-effacement. The woman who brought us together once offered to arrange for Pynchon to speak in a university auditorium. She told him she could assure his anonymity by having him speak through a microphone from behind a screen.

He refused: "They would still be able to recognize my voice." Ironically, that is exactly the situation of Pynchon's readers: he speaks to us from behind a screen, but we recognize him by his voice, that unmistakable Pynchon style.

Nevertheless, from my brief encounter with Pynchon I gleaned a few things about the man behind the screen. I know that he follows the reviews and evidently cares what critics say about him. That he probably has help with his research. That he usually works slowly and disparages *Lot 49*—wrongly, I believe—because he wrote it hastily. That he's shy, doesn't talk much, and doesn't open up to strangers. That he's intense and has lots of nervous energy—the nail-biting and cup-shredding. That he picks his friends carefully to guard himself: no wonder *trust* and *betrayal* are central themes in *Vineland*. That he writes his friends into his fiction. That, at least during the late sixties, he was a heavy doper—thus his sympathy with an aging, beleaguered head like Zoyd Wheeler. That he's generous, shares his stash and doesn't bogart his joints. That, like Benny Profane in *V.*, he is "given to sentimental impulses": he writes love letters, remains friends with a former love, and shows up at her wedding. That, despite his reserved, introverted manner, he seems to care deeply: he keeps cool but cares. That he reads a lot, including novels by his contemporaries. That he loves rock music, which is all over *Vineland*. That he's got a zany streak: the sense of play in his fiction is part of his life—he likes to set off firecrackers in the middle of the night. Does that explain the fascination with rockets in *Gravity's Rainbow*? Probably not, but it's nice to think of his fiction as a string of exploding firecrackers.

Most of all, I learned that the sixties profoundly affected Pynchon, or at least I like to believe that they moved him the way they moved me. According to his classmate Jules Siegel, at Cornell in the fifties, "Tom Pynchon was quiet and neat and did his homework faithfully. He went to Mass and confessed, though to what would be a mystery. He got $25 a week spending money and managed it perfectly, did not cut class and always got grades in the high 90s. His only disappointment was not to have been pledged to a fraternity." This well-behaved Pynchon was a member of the Silent Generation that went to college in the fifties, a generation taught to act prematurely middle-aged. In the late 1960s, the critic Theodore Solotaroff looked back on the repressed behavior of his generation in the 1950s:

It was a time when the deferred gratifications [. . .] and the problems of pre-mature adjustment seemed the warranty of "seriousness" and "responsibility": those solemn passwords of a generation that practiced a Freudian/Jamesian concern about motives, pondered E. M. Forster's "only connect" and sub-scribed to Lionel Trilling's "moral realism" and "tragic sense of life." In contrast to today [the 1960s], everyone tried to act as though he were thirty. (314-15)

In the introduction to *Slow Learner*, Pynchon mentions "a general nervousness in the whole college-age subculture. A tendency to self-censorship [. . .] a felt constraint on folks's writing" (6). He didn't enjoy the 1950s: "Youth of course was wasted on me at the time. [. . .] One of the most pernicious effects of the '50's was to convince the people growing up during them that it would last forever. Until John Kennedy [. . .] began to get some attention, there was a lot of aimless-ness going around. While Eisenhower was in, there seemed no reason why it should all not just go on as it was" (9, 14).

In the early sixties, Pynchon felt the "claustrophobia. I wasn't the only one writing then who felt some need to stretch, to step out. It may have gone back to the sense of academic enclosure we felt which had lent such appeal to the American picaresque life the Beat writers seemed to us to be leading" (*Slow Learner* 21-22). All of his novels are picaresque, testifying to his restlessness. Recall Pynchon's zany streak, and the fact that he dropped out of Cornell for two years to join the navy and see the world; this is a writer with wanderlust. After he finished *V.*, he says, "I was on the road at last, getting to visit the places Kerouac had written about" (22).

Nevertheless, when he first got to Berkeley around 1965 he must have felt like a stranger in a strange land, displaced in time and space, as Oedipa did:

It was summer, a weekday, and midafternoon; no time for any campus Oedipa knew of to be jumping, yet this one was. [. . .] posters for undecipherable FSM's, YAF's, VDC's, suds in the fountain, students in nose-to-nose dialogue. She moved through it carrying her fat book, attracted, unsure, a stranger, wanting to feel relevant but knowing how much of a search among alternate universes it would take. For she had undergone her own educating at a time of nerves, blandness and retreat among not only her fellow students but also most of the visible structure around and ahead of them [. . .] this Berkeley was like no somnolent Siwash out of her own past at all, but more akin to those Far Eastern or Latin American universities you read about [. . .] the sort that bring governments down. [. . .] Where were Secretaries James and Foster and Senator Joseph, those dear daft numina who'd mothered over Oedipa's so temperate youth? [. . .] Among them they had managed to turn the young Oedipa into a rare creature indeed, unfit perhaps for marches and sit-ins, but just a whiz at pursuing strange words in Jacobean texts. (*Lot 49* 103-4)

Pynchon arrived in Berkeley in the early sixties a young man with a lot of hang-ups to overcome; that place and that time helped to liberate him, as they did so many of us. Like Oedipa, he had been shaped by the fifties into an uptight, bookish young person. But he couldn't live anymore in his overdeveloped intellect alone. Now he was ready to move beyond the books into experience. In the sixties, Pynchon lived a peripatetic life; as in the Beatles song, he got by and he got high with the help of his friends. Throughout the decade, he was close to the life of the counterculture, absorbing its values and smoking its weed, but always listening and observing intently, storing sensations for later use: "for the first time I was also beginning to shut up and listen to the American voices around me, even to shift my eyes away from printed sources and take a look at American nonverbal reality" (*Slow Learner* 22).

Judging from the evidence of *Vineland*, he has forgotten nothing of that intense, contradictory decade, neither the dewy-eyed revolutionary idealism nor the grim paranoia, neither the comic excesses nor the tragic waste. The era raised issues that are still unresolved in American society and culture. We keep going back to the 1960s, just as we keep going back to the Civil War of the 1860s: these are contested terrains. As in *Gravity's Rainbow*, the war goes on, although at levels more difficult to trace.

The struggle now is to define the meaning of a passage of American history that ripped this country apart, to sift through the shards and determine what remains worth carrying into the future. By creating his Becker–Traverse–Gates–Wheeler clan, Pynchon demonstrates how a certain strain of American rebelliousness is passed down the generations. It is imperfect, but it survives. In the words Jess Traverse quotes from Emerson, "Secret retributions are always restoring the level, when disturbed, of divine justice" (*Vineland* 369). Pynchon has kept faith with all the changes of that decade; they live again in *Vineland*. Even more, he demonstrates that the sixties aren't over yet —no more than Budapest 1956 or Prague 1968 were the end of that particular story.

According to the novelist E. L. Doctorow, "history is a kind of fiction in which we live and hope to survive, and fiction is a kind of speculative history, perhaps a superhistory" ("False Documents" 25).

Vineland is such a superhistory; it provides a countermyth to pose against the official stories, writing our times more truly through the play of imagination. In all his fiction, Pynchon has helped to create and to re-create our history. He has also helped me to write myself.

Do I know Thomas Pynchon? Do I know the 1960s? Both are mysterious and contradictory, but I'm certain they're still hiding out there somewhere in the desert. Their history has not yet been fully written. Pancho Villa lives.

WORKS CITED

Doctorow, E. L. "False Documents." *E. L. Doctorow: Essays and Conversations.* Ed. Richard Trenner. Princeton: Ontario Review Press, 1983.

Pynchon, Thomas. *The Crying of Lot 49.* Philadelphia: Lippincott, 1966.

———. *Slow Learner.* Boston: Little, Brown, 1984.

———. *V.* 1963; rpt. New York: Bantam, 1964.

———. *Vineland.* Boston: Little, Brown, 1990.

Roth, Philip. "Writing American Fiction." *Reading Myself and Others.* New York: Farrar Straus, 1975.

Siegel, Jules. "Who Is Thomas Pynchon . . . And Why Did He Take Off with My Wife?" *Playboy,* March 1977, 97, 122, 168-70, 172, 174.

Solotaroff, Theodore. *The Red Hot Vacuum and Other Pieces on the Writing of the Sixties.* New York: Atheneum, 1970.

A Vineland *Bibliography*

Clifford Mead

L ISTED below are all materials relating to *Vineland* known to me, beginning with pre-publication notices in 1989 of the forthcoming novel, all book reviews (marked with an asterisk), subsequent features and news items, and scholarly essays that have been published through the summer of 1993.

Ames, Sanford S. "Coming Home: Pynchon's Morning in America." *Pynchon Notes* 26-27 (Spring-Fall 1990): 115-23.

*Anderson, Roger. "A Pynchon's Time." *Berkeley Express*, 2 March 1990, 16-17.

Barrett, Jane. " 'Vineland' Is Not Equal to 'Ulysses.' " Letter in response to McManus's review of *Vineland*. *Chicago Tribune*, 28 January 1990, section 13, 24.

Becke, Rosita, and Dirk Vanderbeke. "Chants of dispossession and exile: Anmerkungen zum Motiv der Yuroks in Thomas Pynchons *Vineland*." *Zeitschrift für Anglistik und Amerikanistik* 40.3 (1992): 214-26. English version forthcoming in *Pynchon Notes*.

Begley, Adam. "Thomas Pynchon, Come Out, Come Out, Wherever You Are." *Smart*, January-February 1990, 52-55.

*Begnal, M. H. *Choice* 27 (May 1990): 1504.

Berressem, Hanjo. "*Vineland:* Everything under Control." Chap. 9 of *Pynchon's Poetics: Interfacing Theory and Text*. Champaign: University of Illinois Press, 1993. 201-42.

"Best of Books." *Time*, 31 December 1990, 55, 57.

*Birkerts, Sven. "Pynchon's Strange Trip Through the '80s." *USA Today*, 5 January 1990, 4D.

———. "Mapping the New Reality." *Wilson Quarterly* 16 (1992): 102-10.

*Bishop, Patricia. "Groping Toward a State of Grace." *London* [Ontario] *Free Press*, 24 March 1990, D12.

*Bluestein, Gene. "Tangled Vines." *Progressive* 54 (June 1990): 42-43.

*Bowman, David. "Pynchon's California." *Huntsville News*, 9 March 1990, A4.

*Boyd, Robert. "The Seductive Illusions of a Pynchon Puzzle." *St. Louis Post-Dispatch*, 21 January 1990, 5C.

*Bracewell, Michael. "On Thomas Pynchon's *Vineland*." *Time Out*, 31 January 1990, 31.

*Brady, Martin. *Booklist*, 15 January 1990, 954.

Brett, Laurel. "Pynchon, You're a Part of My Life." *New York Times* [Long Island edition], 15 July 1990, 14.

Brooks, Neil Edward. "The Function of Culture at the Present Time: (Un)mapping Contemporary Culture Studies." *DAI* 53 (1992): 1905A. Notre Dame.

Caesar, Terry. " 'Take Me Anyplace You Want': Pynchon's Literary Career as a Maternal Construct in *Vineland*." *Novel* 25 (1992): 181-99.

Callens, Johan. "Tubed Out and Movie Shot in Pynchon's Vineland." *Pynchon Notes* 28-29 (Spring-Fall 1991): 115-41.

———. "Van buisbaby tot Thanaat in *Vineland*." *Yang* 153 (1992): 91-103.

Carpenter, Humphrey. "Some of Our Authors Are Missing." *Sunday Times* [London], 28 January 1990, Books, 119.

*Casey, Constance. "Pynchon's Latest May Surprise Both Partisans and Detractors." *Yakima Herald-Republic*, 21 January 1990, 7E.

*Chambers, Judith. "There's a New World Just Around the Corner." *Mill Valley Literary Review*, Spring 1990, 1-3.

———. "*Vineland:* Venus at the Mall." Chap. 6 of *Thomas Pynchon*. New York: Twayne, 1992. 184-207.

*Cohen, Robert. "Notes from Underground." *Tikkun* 5.3 (1990): 64-67.

Compton, Michael. Letter in response to McConnell's review of *Vineland. Los Angeles Times Book Review*, 14 January 1990, 7.

Cooper, Ken. " 'Zero Pays the House': The Las Vegas Novel and Atomic Roulette." *Contemporary Literature* 33.3 (1992): 528, 533-34.

Coughlin, Ruth Pollack. "The Puzzle That is Thomas Pynchon." *Detroit News*, 17 September 1989, E2.

*Cowart, David. "Continuity and Growth." *Kenyon Review* 12.4 (Fall 1990): 176-89.

———. "Attenuated Postmodernism: Pynchon's *Vineland*." *Critique* 32.2 (Winter 1990): 67-76. Rpt. above, 3-13.

"Cross Currents." *Publishers Weekly*, 20 April 1990, 22.

*Cryer, Dan. "Gravity's Ashram." *Newsday* [Long Island], 14 January

1990, Back Page, 21.

*D'Evelyn, Thomas. "Life in 11-Minute Segments." *Christian Science Monitor*, 7 March 1990, 12.

Diamond, Jamie. "The Mystery of Thomas Pynchon Leads Fans and Scholars on a Quest as Bizarre as his Plots." *People*, 29 January 1990, 64-66.

"Diary." *Sunday Times* [London], 28 January 1990, H9.

*"A Double Dose of Novelist Thomas Pynchon." *Boston Sunday Globe*, 10 February 1991, A52.

Doxey, William. "The Pinochle-Playing Worms in Pynchon's *Vineland*." *Notes on Contemporary Literature* 21.3 (May 1991): 11-12.

Doyle, Larry. "t.V." *New Yorker*, 2 April 1990, 38-40.

*Dregni, Michael. "After 17 Years, Pynchon's Back With Another Novel." *Minneapolis Star Tribune*, 11 February 1990, 11E.

*Dugdale, John. "Somewhere over Gravity's Rainbow." *Sunday Correspondent Magazine*, 28 January 1990, 34-38.

*———. "Rilly Disappointing." *Listener*, 1 February 1990, 27.

Elkerton, Michael. Letter in response to Begley. *Smart*, March 1990, 12.

Evans, Jeremiah. Letter in response to McConnell's review of *Vineland*. *Los Angeles Times Book Review*, 28 January 1990, 12.

*Feeney, Mark. "Just Like Old Times in the New World." *Boston Sunday Globe*, 7 January 1990, A15-A16.

Feldman, Gayle, ed. "Trade News." *Publishers Weekly*, 30 June 1989, 76.

"Fiction Reprints." *Publishers Weekly*, 11 January 1991, 99.

Fischer, David Marc. "Vineland." *Magill's Literary Annual: 1990*. Ed. Frank N. Magill. Pasadena, CA: Salem Press, 1990. 2: 844-47.

Forbes, John. "Thomas Pynchon's Ad Hoc Nation: Impressions of Vineland." *Scripsi* 6.2 (1990): 177-87.

Friedman, Ellen G. "Where Are the Missing Contents? (Post)Modernism, Gender, and the Canon." *PMLA* 108.2 (1993): 240-52. (240-41)

*Friendly, Jonathan. "Pynched Prose." *Detroit News*, 17 January 1990, C5.

Fry, Donn. "A Genius Among Us—For a While." *Seattle Times/Seattle Post-Intelligencer*, 14 January 1990, L7.

Gale, David. "The Quest for Pynchon." *Tatler*, December 1989-January 1990, 188-92.

Galvin, Kevin. "Enigmatic Thomas Pynchon to Publish New Book—Unless Rumors Prove True." *Journal-World* [Lawrence, KS], 29 October 1989, 6D. Rpt. as "Undercover: Enigmatic Thomas Pynchon

May Have a New Book Out Soon." *Milwaukee Journal*, 12 November 1989, 11E, and as "The Enigma of the Elusive Writer Thomas Pynchon." *Philadelphia Inquirer*, 27 November 1989, 8D.

*Gardner, James. "Thomas Pynchon." *Washington Times*, 8 January 1990, E5.

Geary, Robert F. "From Apocalypse to Nostalgia." *The World & I*, May 1990, 436-41.

Géniès, Bernard. "La fusée Pynchon." Review of the French translation of *Vineland. Nouvelle Observateur*, 5-11 September 1991, 73.

*Gerber, Eric. "Pynchon's Magical Mystery Tour." *Washington Post*, 28 January 1990, E6.

Gilbert, Ruth. "Books." *New York*, 22 January 1990, 30.

Glover, Douglas. "Mytho-delirium." *Books in Canada* 19 (April 1990): 43-44.

*Gottlieb, Alan. "Vineland Satirizes Reagan Era with Slashing Wit." *Denver Post*, 4 February 1990, G1.

Grant, Richard. "Digging Pynchon." *Science Fiction Eye* 8 (1991): 85-89.

*Gray, Paul. "The Spores of Paranoia." *Time*, 15 January 1990, 69-70.

Guttridge, Peter. "And More Anon." *Times* [London], 24 January 1990, 18.

*Hagen, W. M. *World Literature Today* 65.1 (Winter 1991): 115-16.

*Hayles, N. Katherine. " 'Who Was Saved?': Families, Snitches, and Recuperation in Pynchon's Vineland." *Critique* 32.2 (Winter 1990): 77-91. Rpt. above, 14-30.

*Hendin, Josephine. "Pynchon's America." *Dissent* 37 (Spring 1990): 275-77.

Henry, Jacqueline, ed. "Pynchon Apostle." *Long Island Monthly*, April 1990, 12.

Herman, Luc. "Land of the Free." Review of the Dutch translation of *Vineland* (and others). *De Morgan*, 16 August 1991, 19.

*Hiltbrand, David. "Picks & Pans." *People*, 5 February 1990, 21.

Hinds, Elizabeth Jane Wall. "Visible Tracks: Historical Method and Thomas Pynchon's Vineland." *College Literature* 19.1 (February 1992): 91-103.

Hirschorn, Michael. "My Life as a Pop Reference." *Esquire*, November 1990, 90.

Hopkins, Lee. "Who Is Thomas Pynchon?" *West Coast Review of Books* 16.1 (February/March 1991): 62-64.

*Iannone, Carol. "Pynchon's Progress." *Commentary* 89 (April 1990): 58-59.

"In the Margin." *Washington Post Book World*, 14 May 1989, 14.

Iyer, Pico. "History? Education? Zap! Pow! Cut!" *Time*, 14 May 1990, 98.

James, Caryn. "Characters from the Screen Are Invading the Printed Page." *New York Times*, 31 May 1990, C15, C19.

*Janowitz, Anne. "Postmodern Memories." *Socialist Review* 90.4 (1990): 125-33.

*Jones, Malcolm, Jr. "Pynchon's Shaggy-Dog Story." *Newsweek*, 8 January 1990, 66.

*Jubera, Drew. "Legacy of Mystery Envelops 'Vineland.' " *Atlanta Constitution*, 24 January 1990, D1, D4.

Keesey, Douglas. "*Vineland* in the Mainstream Press: A Reception Study." *Pynchon Notes* 26-27 (Spring-Fall 1990): 107-13.

*Kemp, Peter. "A Technicolour Trip Through Tubular Hells." [London] *Sunday Times*, 28 January 1990, H5.

*Kermode, Frank. "That Was Another Planet." *London Review of Books*, 8 February 1990, 3-4.

* *Kirkus Reviews* 58 (15 January 1990): 77.

*Koenig, Rhoda. "Worth Its Wait." *New York*, 29 January 1990, 66-67.

*Koning, Christina. "Vineland the Good." *Guardian* [Manchester, England], 1 February 1990. Rpt. under same title in *Guardian Weekly*, 18 February 1990, 25.

*Lanchester, John. "Talent's Distant Volcanic Rumble." *Sunday Correspondent*, 28 January 1990, sec. 2.

*Leader, Zachary. "Living on the Invisible Boundary." *Times Literary Supplement*, 2-8 February 1990, 115.

*Lehmann-Haupt, Christopher. "Vineland, Pynchon's First Novel in 17 Years." *New York Times*, 26 December 1989, C21.

*Leithauser, Brad. "Any Place You Want." *New York Review of Books*, 15 March 1990, 7-10.

*Leonard, John. "The Styxties." *Nation*, 26 February 1990, 281-86.

"Letters: A Screaming Comes Across the Page." Responses to Begley's review of *Vineland*. *Smart*, May 1990, 10.

*Lhamon, W. T., Jr. " 'Vineland' Is Pynchon's New World of Symbols." *Atlanta Journal & Constitution*, 7 January 1990, N8.

"Lifeline: I'm Pynchon Myself." *USA Today*, 14 March 1989, D1.

"Lit Hits: Our Favorite Books of 1990." *Voice Literary Supplement*, December 1990, 13.

Lloyd, Donald Galen. "The Role of Science and Technology in the Novels of Thomas Pynchon." *DAI* 52 (1992): 4330A. TCU.

Logan, Alexander M. Letter in response to McConnell's review of *Vineland*. *Los Angeles Times Book Review*, 14 January 1990, 7.

*Lukas, J. Anthony. "Vineland by Thomas Pynchon." *Book-of-the-Month Club News*, April 1990, 3.

MacCurtain, Austin, et al. "Paperbacks." *Sunday Times* [London], 24 February 1991, 6, 8.

Mackey, Louis. Review of Chambers's *Thomas Pynchon. Review of Contemporary Fiction* 13.2 (Summer 1993): 268-69.

Madsen, Deborah L. "*Vineland:* An American Saga." *Over Here* 2.1 (1990): 48-56.

⸻. "Postmodernist Allegory and the Postmodern Condition: *Slow Learner* and *Vineland.*" Chap. 5 of *The Postmodernist Allegories of Thomas Pynchon.* New York: St. Martin's, 1991. 114-34.

Maltby, Paul. " 'Vineland the Good.' " In chap. 5 of *Dissident Postmodernists: Barthelme, Coover, Pynchon.* Philadelphia: University of Pennsylvania Press, 1991. 179-84.

*Marcus, Greil. *California*, March 1990, 119-20.

Matuz, Roger, ed. "Thomas Pynchon." *Contemporary Literary Criticism.* Detroit: Gale, 1991. 62:430-55.

McCarron, William E. "Pynchon in *Vineland.*" *Notes on Contemporary Literature*, 20.5 (1990): 10-11.

*McClurg, Jocelyn. "Pynchon's Latest Is Long-Awaited by Cultic Group of Fans." *Hartford Courant*, 24 December 1989, G3.

*McConnell, Frank. "Fabulous, Fabulous California." *Los Angeles Times Book Review*, 31 December 1989, 1, 7. Rpt. as "Pynchon's 'Vineland' Unreels the Plot." *Columbus Dispatch*, 14 January 1990, 8H, and as "Fairy Tale for a Kinder World." *Charlotte Observer*, 14 January 1990, 7F.

McDonald, Philip. Letter in response to Kermode's review of *Vineland. London Review of Books*, 22 March 1990, 5.

McDowell, Edwin. "Book Notes: The Reclusive Pynchon." *New York Times*, 20 December 1989, C26.

*McHale, Brian. "Publishing Events and Unfinished Business." *American Book Review*, July/August 1990, 8-9.

⸻. "Zapping, the Art of Switching Channels: On *Vineland.*" Chap. 5 of *Constructing Postmodernism.* London and New York: Routledge, 1993. 115-41.

McHoul, Alec. "Vineland: Teenage Mutant Ninja Fiction (Or, St. Ruggles' Struggles, Chapter 4)." *Pynchon Notes* 26-27 (Spring-Fall 1990): 97-106.

McManis, Sam. "Pynchon Vivid in Laker–Celtic Description." *Los Angeles Times*, 13 March 1990, C3.

*McManus, James. "Pynchon's Return." *Chicago Tribune*, 14 January

1990, Books, 3.

*McNamara, Eugene. "Pop Culture Bursts in Thomas Pynchon's Vineland." *Detroit News & Free Press*, 28 January 1990, L1.

*Mendelson, Edward. "Levity's Rainbow." *New Republic*, 9 & 16 July 1990, 41-46.

*Mobilio, Albert. "Carnival Knowledge." *Voice Literary Supplement*, February 1990, 22-24.

*Moore, Steven. *Review of Contemporary Fiction* 10.2 (Summer 1990): 264-65.

*Morton, Brian. "Fiction." *Times Educational Supplement*, 2 March 1990, 33.

Murnane, Gerald. Letter in response to Kermode's review of *Vineland*. *London Review of Books*, 22 March 1990, 5.

"New and Noteworthy." *New York Times Book Review*, 3 February 1991, 32.

Nix, Shann. "The Hipper Than Thou Reading List." *San Francisco Chronicle*, 19 April 1991, B3.

*"Notes on Current Books." *Virginia Quarterly Review* 67.1 (Winter 1991): 23.

O'Grady, Karen. Letter in response to McConnell's review of *Vineland*. *Los Angeles Times Book Review*, 14 January 1990, 7.

O'Hearn, Daniel. Letter in response to McConnell's review of *Vineland*. *Los Angeles Times Book Review*, 14 January 1990, 7.

*O'Rourke, William. "Pynchon Checks in at the Hotel California." *South Bend Tribune*, 20 May 1990, C9.

"Out Now." *Books* [London] 5 (May 1991): 16.

*Page, Tim. "The Invisible Author." *Newsday*, 8 January 1990, 4-5.

"Paperbacks." *Observer* [London], 24 May 1992, 61.

Peabody, A. "Novelist Reveals Identity after Twenty Years on the Coast." *Mendocino Beacon*, 29 March 1990, sec. A: 3, 6.

*Pekar, Harvey. *Northwest Extra!* [Olympia, WA], April 1990, 5.

*Perry, R. Christopher. *Perspectives on Political Science* 19.3 (Summer 1990): 188.

Piela, Albert, III. "A Note on Television in *Vineland*." *Pynchon Notes* 26-27 (Spring 1990): 125-27.

Porush, David. " 'Purring into Transcendence': Pynchon's Puncutron Machine." *Critique* 32.2 (Winter 1990): 93-105. Rpt. above, 31-45.

*Powers, John. "The Great American Novel." *Connoisseur*, April 1990, 42.

*———. "A.: Seventeen Years later, Pynchon Remakes a Broken America." *L.A. Weekly*, 26 January-1 February 1990, 37, 39.

*Powers, Richard. "State and Vine." *Yale Review* 79.4 (Summer 1990): 690-98.

*Powis, Tim. "California Dreaming." *Maclean's*, 12 March 1990, 69.

*Pritchard, William H. "Novel Reports." *Hudson Review* 43.3 (1990): 496-97.

*Prose, Francine. "Doubting Thomas." *7 Days*, 17 January 1990, 54-55.

Pütz, Manfred. "The Art of the Acronym in Thomas Pynchon." *Studies in the Novel* 23.3 (1991): 371-82.

"Pynchon Book About to Be Published." *New York Times*, 22 December 1989, B2.

Raddatz, Fritz J. "Der Maschinengott." Rev. of the German trans. of *Vineland. Die Zeit*, 2 April 1993, 11.

*Rafferty, Terrence. "Long Lost." *New Yorker*, 19 February 1990, 108-12.

*Rayner, Richard. "What, in the Name of Satan, Went Wrong?" *Weekend Telegraph* [London], 3 February 1990, xviii.

*Reynolds, Pamela. "Thomas Pynchon: At Long Last, Vineland." *Boston Globe*, 27 December 1989, 23, 27.

*Rieff, David. *Elle*, May 1990, 186.

*Riese, Utz. "Thomas Pynchon: *Vineland*." *Weimarer Beiträge* 36.10 (1990): 1641-48.

*Rifkind, Donna. "The Farsighted Virtuoso." *Wall Street Journal*, 2 January 1990, A9.

*Rogaly, Joe. "Yes, This Is an Everyday Story of Ordinary Tubefolk." *Financial Times*, 3 February 1990, Weekend, xix.

*Romano, Carlin. "Welcome Back Thomas Pynchon!" *Philadelphia Inquirer*, 31 December 1989, 1C, 4C.

Romine, Dannye. "Be Very Quiet: We're Stalking the Wily Pynchon." *Charlotte Observer*, 14 January 1990, 7F.

*Rosenbaum, Jonathan. "Reading: Pynchon's Prayer." *Chicago Reader*, 9 March 1990, 8, 29-31. Rpt. under same title in *City Paper* [Washington, DC], 16 March 1990.

*Ross, John. "Finding Vineland." *San Francisco Review of Books* 16.1 (1991): 35-36.

*Rushdie, Salman. "Still Crazy After All These Years." *New York Times Book Review*, 14 January 1990, 1, 36-37. Rpt. as "Thomas Pynchon" in *Imaginary Homelands*. London: Granta, 1991. 352-57.

*———. "Le retour de l'homme invisible." *Nouvelle Observateur*, 15-21 February 1990, 73-75.

"Rushdie Questions Pynchon's Secrecy." *Yakima Herald-Republic*, 15 January 1990, 4A.

Safer, Elaine B. "Pynchon's World and Its Legendary Past: Humor and the Absurd in a Twentieth-Century *Vineland*." *Critique* 32.2 (Winter 1990): 107-25. Rpt. above, 46-67.

Salusinszky, Imre. Letter in response to Kermode's review of *Vineland. London Review of Books*, 22 March 1990, 5.

Saunders, Kate. "Reading Between the Lines." *Sunday Times* [London], 21 January 1990, G1.

*Schaub, Thomas. "Pynchon Heads North to the 60s." *San Francisco Chronicle*, 21 January 1990, 1, 11.

*Scott, Jay. "Vineland Proves Pynchon a Master." *Chatelaine*, May 1990, 12.

*Shields, David. "Mysterious Mr. Pynchon." *Seattle Times/Seattle Post-Intelligencer*, 14 January 1990, L7.

Slade, Joseph W. "Communication, Group Theory, and Perception in *Vineland*." *Critique* 32.2 (Winter 1990): 126-44. Rpt. above, 68-88.

*Smith, Marcus A. J. "A Visit to 'Vineland' Well Worth the Wait." *New Orleans Times-Picayune*, 21 January 1990, E6-7.

Snider, Burr. "Stalking Pynchon up in Vineland." *San Francisco Examiner*, 25 March 1990, A1, A20.

*St. John, Edward B. *Library Journal* 115 (1 February 1990): 108.

Startle, William. "Review of Reviews." Sunday Telegraph, *11 February 1990, 52.*

*Steiner, Wendy. "Pynchon's Progress: Dopeheads Revisited." *Independent* [London], 3 February 1990, 30.

*Stonum, Gary Lee. "Serious Author Shows a Fun Side." *Cleveland Plain Dealer*, 21 January 1990, 9I.

*Stough, Charles. "Pynchon Yourself." *Dayton Daily News*, 4 February 1990, 6C.

Streitfeld, David. "The Vanishing Act of Thomas Pynchon: After 17 Years, a Novel from the Reclusive Author." *Washington Post*, 6 December 1989, D1, D16-17.

———. " 'Vineland' Ends Thomas Pynchon's Literary Silence, But Not Mystery." *Los Angeles Times*, 10 December 1989, E6-E8.

———. "Over the 'Rainbow.' " *Fame*, December 1989-January 1990, 42-46.

———. "Book Report: Vidal the Tease." *Washington Post Book World*, 9 August 1992, 15.

Sujo, Aly. "Rushdie Defends Recluse in Book Review." *Toronto Globe & Mail*, 11 January 1990, A15.

Swed, Mark. "Peter Sellars at Glyndebourne." *Wall Street Journal*, 18 July 1990, A7.

*Tabbi, Joseph. "Pynchon's Groundward Art." *Michigan Quarterly Review* 30.2 (Spring 1991): 375-82. Rpt. (with additional material) above, 89-100.

Talbot, Stephen. "Territory of the Spirit." *San Francisco Chronicle*, 16 December 1990, Image, 1, 24, 33.

*Tate, J. O. "Sufferin' Succotash." *National Review*, 30 April 1990, 59.

[Thomas, Kenn.] "Pynchon's Vineland." *Steamshovel Press* 2 (1990): 10.

*Tölölyan, Khachig. "In Pynchon's Latest, Optimism Is the Only Problem." *Hartford Courant*, 28 January 1990, G3.

*Tonkin, Boyd. "Forever Young." *New Statesman & Society*, 26 January 1990, 33.

*Vilmure, Daniel. "A Whining Comes Across the Sky." *St. Petersburg Times*, 28 January 1990, 6D.

*Ulin, David L. "The Confounding Return of a Legendary Recluse." *Bloomsbury Review*, March 1990, 1, 18.

Walker, Christopher. "Thomas Pynchon's 'Vineland.' " Letter in response to Kermode's review of *Vineland. London Review of Books*, 8 March 1990, 4-5.

*Weldon, Fay. *Evening Standard*, 1 February 1990.

Whalen-Bridge, John. Letter in response to McConnell's review of *Vineland. Los Angeles Times Book Review*, 28 January 1990, 12.

White, Daniel R. "Literary Ecology and Postmodernity in Thomas Sanchez's *Mile Zero* and Thomas Pynchon's *Vineland." Postmodern Culture* 2.1 (1991): 40 par.

*White, Edmund. "Flower Power-Broking." *Independent* [London], 4 February 1990.

*Whitworth, John. "Not a Novel for Grown-Ups." *Spectator*, 3 February 1990, 28.

Wilcox, Rhonda. "Vineland and Dobie Gillis." *Pynchon Notes* 24-25 (Spring-Fall 1989): 111-12.

Wilde, Alan. "Love and Death in and around Vineland, U.S.A." *boundary 2* 18.2 (Summer 1991): 166-80.

*Wolcott, James. "Boutiques Bloom, the Petals of Flower Power Fall." *Observer* [London], 4 February 1990, 60.

*Wood, James. "Seriously Unfunny, Truly Unreal America." [London] *Times*, 3 February 1990, 38.

*Yardley, Jonathan. "Still Pynchon After All These Years." *Washington Post Book World*, 7 January 1990, 3.

Zand, Nicole. "A la recherche du temps hippy." Review of the French translation of *Vineland. Le Monde*, 20 September 1991, 24.

Contributors

Since taking his doctorate at Rutgers University in 1977, **David Cowart** has taught at the University of South Carolina, where he is now a full professor. He is the author of numerous articles and reviews, as well as three critical books: *Thomas Pynchon: The Art of Allusion*, *Arches and Light: The Fiction of John Gardner*, and *History and the Contemporary Novel*. A fourth book, *Literary Symbiosis: The Reconfigured Text in Twentieth-Century Writing*, has just been published. In 1992-93 he held the Bicentennial Chair of American Studies, a Fulbright Distinguished Professorship, at the University of Helsinki.

Andrew Gordon teaches English at the University of Florida and has been a Fulbright Lecturer in American literature in Spain, Portugal, and Yugoslavia. He is the author of *An American Dreamer: A Psychoanalytic Study of the Fiction of Norman Mailer* and of numerous essays on film and contemporary American fiction. He met Thomas Pynchon in June 1967.

William E. Grim is a musicologist specializing in the relationship between literature and music. He is an assistant professor of music at Worcester State College and the author of *The Faust Legend in Music and Literature*, *Haydn's Sturm und Drang Symphonies: Form and Meaning*, *Max Reger: A Bio-Bibliography*, and articles in *Opera Journal*, *Romance Studies*, *Ars Lyrica*, and other journals. He is also coeditor of the *Yearbook of Interdisciplinary Studies in the Fine Arts*.

N. Katherine Hayles, Professor of English at the University of California-Los Angeles, writes on literature and science in the twentieth century. A chapter on *Gravity's Rainbow* appears in her book *The Cosmic Web: Scientific Models and Literary Strategies in the Twentieth Century*. She is completing a new book entitled *Virtual Bodies: Cybernetics, Literature, Information*.

Molly Hite, Professor of English at Cornell University, is the author of *Ideas of Order in the Novels of Thomas Pynchon, The Other Side of the Story: Structures and Strategies of Contemporary Feminist Narrative,* and two novels.

Clifford Mead is the author of *Thomas Pynchon: A Bibliography of Primary and Secondary Materials.* He is Head of Collection Services and Special Collections at Kerr Library, Oregon State University.

Stacey Olster is Associate Professor of English at the State University of New York at Stony Brook. She is the author of *Reminiscence and Recreation in Contemporary American Literature* and her essays have appeared in such journals as *Modern Fiction Studies, Studies in the Novel, MELUS,* and *Michigan Quarterly Review.* She is presently writing a book entitled *The Trash Phenomenon,* which explores the work of contemporary American authors who chart American history with respect to the artifacts of American popular culture.

David Porush teaches in the Department of Language, Literature and Communication at Rensselaer Polytechnic Institute. He is the author of the critical study *The Soft Machine: Cybernetic Fiction,* the short story collection *Rope Dances,* and of numerous essays in scholarly journals.

Elaine B. Safer is Professor of English at the University of Delaware and divides her critical activities between Milton and the American comic novel. She is the author of *The Contemporary American Comic Epic: The Novels of Barth, Pynchon, Gaddis, and Kesey* and has published articles in a variety of literary journals.

Joseph W. Slade is Director of the School of Telecommunications at Ohio University. He has held NEH, Hegley Museum, and Gannett Institute fellowships, and taught at several institutions, including the University of Helsinki, where he was the Bicentennial Professor of American Studies. His *Thomas Pynchon,* the first book-length study of the novelist, was reissued in 1990. He is the coeditor of *Beyond Two Cultures: Essays on Science, Technology, and Literature* and the author of *Pornography: A Reference Guide.* In addition, he has published several dozen articles on literature, film, technology, broadcasting, and culture.

Eric Solomon is Professor of English at San Francisco State University. He is the author of two books on Stephen Crane and many articles on British and American fiction. He is currently completeing a book on Jewish-American baseball novels.

Susan Strehle is Acting Vice Provost for Graduate Studies and Research and Associate Professor of English at Binghamton University in New York. She is the author of *Fiction in the Quantum Universe* as well as numerous essays on contemporary fiction.

Joseph Tabbi is Assistant Professor of American Literature at Kansas State University and currently a Fulbright Professor at the Universität Hamburg. He has just completed a book entitled *The Technological Sublime* and is coediting a collection of essays on technology and the novel. His essays and reviews have appeared in the *American Book Review, Contemporary Literature, Modern Fiction Studies, PMLA,* and the *Review of Contemporary Fiction.*

The Editors

Geoffrey Green, professor of English at San Francisco State University, is the author of *Freud and Nabokov, Literary Criticism and the Structures of History: Erich Auerbach and Leo Spitzer,* and coeditor of *Novel vs. Fiction: The Contemporary Reformation.* He has published essays and short stories in a wide variety of publications, and he is, with Donald J. Greiner and Larry McCaffery, executive editor of the journal *Critique: Studies in Contemporary Fiction.*

Donald G. Greiner is Carolina Professor of English at the University of South Carolina. He has published books on John Hawkes, John Updike, Robert Frost, Frederick Busch, and on American fiction of the 1980s. His most recent book is *Women without Men: Female Bonding and the American Novel of the 1980s.*

Larry McCaffery, professor of English at San Diego State University, is the author/editor of several anthologies, casebooks, and collections of interviews, most recently *Are These Experiments Really Necessary?: Interviews with Innovative American Fiction Writers, Storming the Reality Studio: A Casebook of Cyberpunk and Postmodern Science Fiction,* and *Avant-Pop: Fiction for a Daydream Nation.* He is currently writing a book on rock music's mythology.